MW01008403

The Walk of the Spirit — The Walk of Power

The Vital Role
Of Praying in Tongues

by

Dave Roberson

The family of Dave Roberson Ministries and The Family Prayer Center wish to state that this book is not for sale. It is given with the hope that the message within will touch hearts, enlarge understanding, and motivate all of its readers to pray more in the Spirit, resulting in changed lives, families, and nations.

Unless otherwise indicated, all Scripture quotations are taken from the *King James Version* of the Bible.

The Walk of the Spirit — The Walk of Power:
The Vital Role of Praying in Tongues

ISBN 10: 1-929339-10-0
ISBN 13: 978-1-929339-10-5

Dave Roberson Ministries
The Family Prayer Center
P. O. Box 725
Tulsa, OK 74101

Contents

Introduction

The past few years have been some of the greatest years of my life. I've been in the ministry more than twenty-five years and had many wonderful encounters with the Lord, but I can truthfully say that the revelation knowledge God has imparted to me in these last few years has completely changed my life, taking me to a place in God I had never before imagined.

However, you can't put up walls where there is no foundation. You can't add a roof where there are no walls. The life-changing truths God has been showing me couldn't have been added to my life had not a strong foundation of the Word been built inside of me line upon line, precept upon precept, through many hours and many years of praying in tongues while meditating on the Scriptures.

I now know more than ever before that praying in tongues is the revelation gift that helped lay a scriptural foundation in my life. God was getting me ready for the awesome, eternal truths He is now pouring into my spirit in preparation for the days to come. He is using the culmination of all those years of praying in tongues to open up to me a whole new realm of understanding in Christ.

The very measure of God's power in a believer's life is dependent on how much of his life is ordered by the Holy Ghost. Therefore, from the very beginning, the primary message of this ministry has been praying in tongues. Over the decades, the Lord has imparted a wealth of revelation knowledge to my spirit on this subject. Step by step, He has taught me how to walk out of a life dominated by the flesh into a new life dominated by the Holy Spirit through the matchless gift of praying in my heavenly prayer language.

Then in 1997, the Lord spoke strongly to my spirit, saying, *"This message on tongues has come to maturity."*

At first, I thought God meant the message had come to maturity in *me.* Later I came to understand that He wasn't talking about me in particular at all. He was saying that the time had come to share in a broader measure the revelation knowledge He had given me over the years regarding praying in tongues. The message had come to maturity for the Body of Christ.

The Lord has commissioned me to teach believers how to live a life of power as they walk in the Spirit, always building on the foundation of the Word and praying in tongues as the Holy Spirit gives utterance. This book is written out of my desire to be faithful to that divine commission.

I have not only taught the truths contained in this book for many years; I have also pursued them with all my heart in my own personal walk with God. So believe me when I tell you this: As you read this book and diligently apply its principles, the day will come when you look back on your life and say in awe and wonder, "I'm not the same person. I have learned to walk in the Spirit, and it has completely changed my life forever!"

Dave Roberson

For in My Spirit is the depth of wisdom
   that by My Spirit you may glean,
   saith the Spirit of Grace.
For these things are hidden in a mystery.

Oh, I have made these mysteries available
   to those who are in the Church of My grace.
Learn how to stay in My Presence.
Learn how to stay on your face.
And I will open up treasures hidden in a field.
And you will see, saith the Spirit of Grace,
   that even the devil will have to give place.

Chapter 1

───────── ⋘✦⋙ ─────────

The Holy Spirit's Work Within

In the eternities of time past, a vast, complex plan for mankind unfolded on the inside of God. In His infinite wisdom, He left nothing out as He looked down through the ages. He passed through generation after generation, planning every intricate detail of every life that would live on the face of the earth. God's desire was to recover as many as possible from Satan's rebellious camp and to gather unto Himself a people He could call His family.

Somewhere in the midst of this divine planning session, long before the eons of time began, God came across *your* name! Then He formulated a perfect plan just for you that is unlike any other plan for any other person who has ever been born. Imagine — God the Father looked out across the great void of space and time and saw the moment in time when you would live on this earth. Then He decided precisely how that moment should be filled!

We Must *Choose* His Plan

God conceived a wonderful plan for every one of us. In His plan, we were predestined to become His sons and daughters at the Cross. But one potential obstacle stands between us and God's perfectly conceived purposes: Using the free will God has given us, we must choose to walk in the plan He has ordained for our lives.

God looks for a way to approach each of us in order to present His personal plan for our lives. He begins with the preaching of the Cross that encourages us to accept Jesus Christ as Savior and Lord. If we accept Jesus, we take our first step into the plan God predestined for us before the foundations of the world. But if we reject Him, then like so many before us, we will live and die without ever taking that first step — salvation — into the divine purpose for our existence.

Once when I was ministering in India, I looked out at the crowd of thousands before me and marveled that God could have a specific plan for every individual in that vast multitude. The truth is, God formulated a perfect plan for every single person born since Adam. He only waits for each person to find out what that plan is and then to choose to walk in it.

Jesus talked about His plan of eternal life for mankind in Matthew 7:13,14:

> **Enter ye in at the strait gate: for wide is the gate, and broad is the way, that leadeth to destruction, and many there be which go in thereat:**

> **Because strait is the gate, and narrow is the way, which leadeth unto life, and few there be that find it.**

Jesus' words indicate that the majority of people end their lives with one final journey into a godless eternity without Him. A person can live and die and go to hell without knowing Jesus or fulfilling God's plan for his life. However, that doesn't change the fact that

10

God had a perfect plan of redemption and purpose for that person; he just never discovered it.

But, praise God, you don't have to be one of that number! If you have found the Cross and made Jesus your personal Savior, nothing can stop you from discovering the rest of God's plan for your life. All you have to do is *choose* to obey Him.

The Holy Spirit Prays for Us

So somewhere, somehow, in God's great and marvelous plan for His creation, your name came up. And God, in His eternal wisdom and counsel, laid out a perfect plan for your personal life.

Then the Holy Spirit did a wonderful thing. He listened intently to every detail of your life as the Father planned your birth, your ministry, your prosperity, and every aspect of your redemption and personal life.

In fact, the Holy Spirit is the One who has been put in charge of overseeing God's plan for your personal life. No one can represent that plan better than He can. He was there. He heard God the Father plan every minute detail.

And that's not all. This third Person of the Godhead stands face to face and absolutely coequal in every way with the other two members of the Godhead, the great Jehovah and the mighty Logos (Jesus). But upon your regeneration as a child of God, the Holy Spirit actually consented to take up residence within your spirit and to offer His services to you! And one of the main reasons He came was to pray for you.

Why did God send the Holy Spirit to live inside of you? So He could change you into the image of His Son. And in order to accomplish that goal, the Holy Spirit brought His own prayer language with Him so He could pray for all that concerns you.

With that prayer language, He gets involved directly with you in a one-on-one relationship that is independent of anyone else, even of your own mind. When the Holy Spirit prays for you, He takes the plan He hears the Father utter and pours it through your spirit. And the language He uses to express that plan as it flows through you is *the supernatural language of tongues.*

Every time you give the Holy Spirit opportunity, He will use that language to pray for your calling, to pray out the plan of God, to edify you, and to charge you with His holy power. He will lend Himself to you as your faith allows Him to be activated within your spirit. He will pull you *out of* everything Jesus set you free from and *into* everything Jesus says that you are in Him.

If you want to, you can go into your room and pray in that supernatural language for two, four, or even twelve hours, and God the Holy Spirit will create every single word that comes out of your mouth. It is your choice to pray or not to pray. But every time you do choose to pray, you will come out of that time of prayer more edified in His plan and purpose for you than if you hadn't done it.

God's plan for you is in the Spirit, and the Holy Spirit is in you. The Holy Spirit is armed with the knowledge of everything He heard about God's redemption plan for you before the foundations of the earth. And every time He searches your heart, He does it with the intention to pray that plan — the mind of God concerning you — into existence in your life.

Natural Law Brought Under Subjection

I have been filled with the Holy Spirit a long time, and I still marvel that the third Person of the Godhead would choose to come and take up His abode with us! To think that, at our invitation, He fills us in baptism and oversees God's plan for our lives is more grace than we could ever hope for. And the supernatural language He brings with Him to help us find that perfect plan is perhaps the greatest phenomenon of all.

The more of God's plan we find, the more the Holy Spirit (who is the Executor of spiritual law) will be able to bring natural law under subjection in our lives. Natural law governs the circumstances that surround us, causing things to go for or against us — making us either rich or poor, sick or healthy, happy or sad.

But God designed natural law to be made subordinate to spiritual law. And since the divine plan for our lives comes from the very heart of God, it is enforced as spiritual law.

When we spend any amount of time at all praying in the Holy Ghost, we are uttering divine secrets, or spiritual laws. The Holy Spirit then employs those laws to see that circumstances — natural laws — line up with the purpose and plan of God for our lives. We cannot pray consistently for very long before the things that don't belong in God's plan for us begin to fall away.

Once I asked the Lord, "Why did You give us such a peculiar language to use in prayer?" This is what He spoke to my spirit:

"Among men a language has never come into existence that carries the vocabulary to express everything I am in you through Christ Jesus. Since there was no language with such a vocabulary, I had to create My own and loan it to you while you are on the earth. I just loan it to you till you come up to Heaven; then it will cease.

"Meanwhile, you know in part, and I know everything — My entire redemption plan for all eternity. Whenever the devil comes against you, don't worry about it. Because of your infirmities, I will start making intercession for you according to that plan. And even though you only know in part, I will pray the part you need."

The Great Exchange: Trading Our Plan for God's Plan

There is a supernatural exchange that takes place as we pray in other tongues. Look at what Romans 8:27,28 says:

And he [the Holy Spirit] **that searcheth the hearts knoweth what is the mind of the Spirit, because he maketh intercession for the saints according to the will of God.**

And we know that all things work together for good to them that love God, to them who are the called according to his purpose.

What does it mean, "he that searcheth the hearts"? It means that the Holy Spirit continually searches your heart with the intention of removing everything that is contrary to the will of God, your Father the Planner. Then the Holy Spirit replaces it with the plan He heard for your personal life before the beginning of time when God formulated His plan for you. He prays the perfect plan of God into your spirit so you not only know *what* you are called to do but *how* to fulfill that call in the perfect timing, will, and power of God.

God trades your natural plans and ideas for His through the supernatural medium of exchange, *tongues for personal edification.* You can *know* beyond a shadow of a doubt that as you yield to that divine exchange, all things will indeed work together for good for you, because you love God and are called according to His purpose.

He Helps Us Find Our Calling

However, you can't discover the purpose God has called you to fulfill just by reading His Word. Now, you *can* find out in the Word everything you need to know pertaining to the inheritance that belongs to every believer. You can learn all about salvation, healing, prosperity, righteousness, Heaven, the blood, and ministry offices. But you cannot find out from the Word alone what God has called you to fulfill as an individual member of the Body of Christ.

There is no "Book of Roberson" that I can turn to for personal instruction. I have to discover my divine calling by revelation through the personal inward work of the Holy Spirit.

No one knows our calling better than the Holy Spirit. He was in the Presence of God when our call was first planned. That's why He brought His supernatural language with Him when He came to live inside us. We're just too ignorant to know how to pray about our call. So His great reservoir of wisdom and counsel resides within our spirits, just waiting to be released through tongues.

First Corinthians 14:14 says that when we speak in an unknown tongue, our human spirit is doing the praying, and our understanding is unfruitful. So, in essence, the Holy Spirit creates that supernatural language on the inside of our spirit man. Then a transfer of language and authority takes place from the Person of the Holy Spirit to our human spirit.

This divine transfer enables us as individual members of the Body of Christ on this earth to pray in tongues with the authority of God, knowing that the other two members of the Godhead will answer our prayer. If the transfer never took place, it would be the Holy Spirit praying, not us. But with the transfer, it is literally our human spirit praying as the Holy Spirit creates the prayer.

God's Way Is Best

We may know how to claim our inheritance. We may be good at declaring, "Healing is mine. Provision is mine!" But how can we get the tremendous power of the Holy Spirit that resides on the inside of us — the power that raised Jesus from the dead — out onto the problems that face us so those blessings can be manifested in our lives? And even more importantly, how can we discover our divine call?

Well, are we so wise that we can find a better way to answer those questions than the way God gave us when He designated the Holy Spirit to come and represent us?

You see, God didn't trust us to any of the many thousands of angels in His service. We're worth more than that to Him. No, He went as high as He could go and entrusted us to the Holy Spirit Himself, who then came to take up residency in us. So how can we fail when the third Person of the Godhead creates the prayer and the other two members of the Godhead see to it that it comes to pass? I'd call that a foolproof plan!

God's Wisdom Against Satan's Strategies

The day you decide to lock yourself in your prayer closet to spend some quality time with the Lord in prayer — that is the day you will enter Heaven's classroom here on earth with the Holy Spirit as your Teacher. You need that "classroom" if you're ever going to fulfill your divine calling.

Remember, God tells us to be as wise as serpents and as harmless as doves (Matt. 10:16). Why would God say something like that? Because Satan has an entire arsenal of weaponry that can only be combatted by the wisdom of God.

For instance, suppose Satan walks in the room with horns and a tail and says, "Pardon me, nice Christian, while I remove the Word of God out of your heart." You would look at him and say, "You're not getting my Word!"

He says, "Why not?"

"Because you're the devil!"

"What gave me away?" he asks.

"Your horns and your tail." (That's the traditional way the devil dresses in Christian folklore.)

At that point, the devil says, "I'll never come dressed this way again. I'll go get a sheepskin and put it on. Then I'll sneak in unawares and steal the Word out of you. You won't even know who's doing it because I'll use religion to seduce you. I'll use circumstances. I'll blame it on the economy. Or I'll blame it on your husband or your wife. But one way or another, I *will* take the Word of God out of you, and you won't even know who's doing it!"

Jesus let us know that Satan only comes for one reason in three parts: to kill, to steal, and to destroy (John 10:10). And you may as well know — the devil is good at it! He doesn't do anything else but those three things. Killing, stealing, and destroying have been his specialties ever since his light went out and he fell from Heaven (Isa. 14:12). And if you misjudge him — if you don't take him seriously — he can destroy *you!*

Now you see why we must be as wise as serpents yet as harmless as doves. Yet some people say they don't need the Holy Ghost's help in prayer. They push His language aside and refuse to allow Him to pray the mind of God for them hour after hour. Who do they think they're operating against — a spiritual wimp?

Satan is not an enemy to take lightly. He's a smart fellow, and he comes for only one reason: to kill. He doesn't do anything else; he doesn't know anything else. And if you don't take care of his strategies by the wisdom of God, he will succeed in killing everything good in your life.

Since this is true, how can a believer consider spending two or three hours in prayer a sacrifice? What is he really saying? "I made a big personal sacrifice last night. I let God pray for me for three hours!"

No, that believer didn't make a big sacrifice. He just enjoyed the priceless privilege of praying in the Spirit. The Holy Spirit created a prayer language on the inside of him that tapped into the mind of Christ and the infinite wisdom of Almighty God for his life!

It's beyond my natural understanding how that supernatural process works. But I guarantee you, I will use what He has given me!

My Heavenly Father has promised me this, and I can pass it on to you: If you will faithfully continue to get to know God by His Spirit — and an important part of that process is praying in other tongues — then five years from now, you will not be the same. You won't look back over the years and lament that every day was the same, one month just like the next, until three and then four years slipped by, and you ended up just as defeated and unchanged as you were at the beginning of that time period.

No, if you will pursue God by the Spirit, then at the end of five years, you will be able to look back and see that you *have* experienced spiritual growth. You *have* changed for the better. You are getting to know Jesus

Himself as the Holy Spirit reveals Him to you. And you are well on your way to fulfilling your divine call as it unfolds before you!

So enter in and know Me by the Spirit,
And I will take you from glory to glory,
    feeding you with an inheritance
    that causes you
    to know how to quench the hunger
    and the burnings inside
    to know Me after My power.

I will show you these things,
But you must enter into My Presence
    and stay there until I have fed you
    with your ministry, saith the Spirit of Grace.

Chapter 2

My Personal Journey To Revelation Knowledge

I didn't tap into God's plan for my own life until I was an adult. There was no one in my life as a child who could teach me how to do it.

The Beginnings

My mother was what I call a "periodic alcoholic." She died in her early fifties with cirrhosis of the liver.

My dad was a preacher's kid, but I didn't find that out until long after I had answered the call to the ministry as an adult. He was a preacher's kid who went wild, spending most of his life in and out of jail. He came and went when I was little. When I was old enough to understand, Mom told me that she finally ran him off when I was almost two years old because he would beat me so badly.

I can remember hiding a toy airplane under my bed. Mom had saved her grocery pennies to buy it for me. When my dad came around, I had to hide it; I knew that much. He was always threatening me, saying things like, "I'm going to shoot you with a shotgun full of salt!" I can't remember much about the beatings. As I grew up, I had many other temporary fathers who came and went. I didn't know much about them either.

Sometimes the neighbors would come over to get me, my brother, and my two sisters. They would scrub our faces, load us in the car, and take us to church. It was obvious that we were neglected.

Our grandpa finally took us in. He made a work-horse out of me through my high school years — and when I say work, I mean work! By the time I entered the United States Navy, I was in top shape. I had never worked out or done one sit-up or push-up in my life, yet I won the arm wrestling championship on my ship! I was also asked to box for the Navy. All my physical strength and training came from Grandpa working me like an animal through my teenage years.

Grandpa was from the old "hard track" school of thought in raising children. I never knew very much about the love of God nor had anything to call my own. Nearly every chance Grandpa had, he told me, "You will never amount to anything, *never*! You are going to grow up to be no good just like your old man Roberson."

When I was sixteen years old, a friend of mine (who was also a preacher's kid) convinced me to go to a Pentecostal church with him every weekend for the sole reason of meeting girls. After church, we would go out drinking.

Well, the pastor's preaching didn't bother my friend at all, but it started to get to me. One night I became so convicted that I went over to the pastor's house after the service had ended.

I knocked on the pastor's door. When he answered it, I told him, "I think there's something wrong with me."

"That's conviction," the pastor replied. "What you need to do is accept Jesus Christ as your personal Savior." So he told me to get down on my knees next to a chair, and then he led me in the sinner's prayer.

I left the pastor's house feeling light and happy, and the next time I was out with my friends, I refused to drink with them. However, no one from the church "went after me" to get me filled with the Holy Spirit or to help me grow in my spiritual walk. So my good intentions only lasted about two weeks, and then I returned to my partying lifestyle.

I quit high school and left home when I was seventeen, never to come back. That's when I joined the Navy. Soon after I finished my term with the Navy, I came back to God at an ultra-Holiness church. It was there that I met my future wife, Rosalie.

These Holiness people told me that my Heavenly Father was doing the same thing my natural father did to me — punishing me for making mistakes. They were teaching me legalism, but I didn't understand that. I thought to myself, *Well, I guess I lost one father like that and picked up another one!*

The Sawmill Preacher

The first year after I got saved, I had trouble staying in church. But soon after marrying Rosalie, I was baptized in the Holy Ghost, and I never went back to my godless life again. I never wanted to go back.

A few years later, we moved to a little town in Oregon called LaPine, where the only church was a little Holiness church that was even more strict than the one we had left. There were no other churches or Christian meetings. I got a job in a sawmill and started preaching on the job!

Everyone around me at the sawmill was living in sin, but God strengthened me to stand in the faith. Hell threw everything it could at me to cause me to turn away from God. But because of the Lord's upholding hand, I stood.

Once in a while a preacher would hold a revival in our area. When that happened, all seven men who pulled the chain with me at the sawmill would come with me to the revival because I had worked on them so hard, trying to persuade them to attend.

The Vision
That Propelled Me Into Ministry

At thirty years of age, I still lived with the image that was built on the inside of me while growing up. I would never amount to anything. I deserved nothing but punishment.

I was born again, and I had such a strong hunger and thirst for God. I knew in my heart I was called to preach the Gospel. But I couldn't see how He could or would ever use me. I was a Holiness boy, lost in legalism.

But I loved God with all my heart, and He had mercy on my soul. He gave me a vision that launched me into the full-time ministry. It wasn't something I experienced because I ate too late at night; it was *real*.

I never will forget it. We had moved a couple of times and were living in a little town called Oakridge, where I had continued to work in the local sawmill. Early one morning I woke up in the Presence of God. I opened my eyes, expecting to see my familiar bedroom. Instead, I saw a big auditorium. There were several wheelchair cases on the platform. I was three rows back on the left.

An associate pastor was conducting the worship service. Something was electrifying about the meeting, and somehow I knew it was *my* meeting.

The associate pastor returned to the pulpit after the praise and worship ended and said, "Now our evangelist..." As he spoke, he looked right at me to respond. I had my Bible open — in fact, I had it open to Jude 20 and 21, the passage that would later launch our ministry!

> **But ye, beloved, building up yourselves on your most holy faith, praying in the Holy Ghost,**
>
> **Keep yourselves in the love of God, looking for the mercy of our Lord Jesus Christ unto eternal life.**
>
> **—Jude 20, 21**

But as I started to stand up, the associate pastor turned and pointed to the stage curtain. A blond-haired woman came out onto the platform. It was obvious that she was full of God's love, and the anointing — the power of the Holy Spirit — flowed out of her like honey. It was so thick and sweet, you could almost cut it! I sank back into my chair in utter disbelief. I knew it was supposed to be my meeting.

The woman took the microphone and ministered the grace of God beautifully. Then God's power fell, and all the people got up out of their wheelchairs. The altar filled with people confessing Jesus as Savior. The whole service was full of power and anointing.

When it was all over, the rest of the crowd disappeared; it was just me and this woman in the auditorium. Then she looked directly at me and said, "I don't know why God has given me this kind of ministry; one of you men must have failed."

I came out of the vision shaking. I woke Rosalie and told her everything I had witnessed in the vision. I decided that I couldn't live the way I had been living anymore — torn between my call to preach and my deep feelings of unworthiness. I was being beaten from the inside out.

I told my wife, "I have to answer the call to the ministry — sink, swim, or drown. If we eat beans, sleep under a tree, or dress the kids in gunny sacks, will you still go with me?"

Rosalie said yes. So together that morning, she and I decided that no matter what it took, we would press in to God. Two weeks later, I resigned my job to go full time into the ministry.

The Prayer Closet

Having quit my job at the lumber mill, I didn't know what to do with my time. Then I thought of the little church Rosalie and I had started just a few months before. (Although I had started the church, I asked a minister from another town to come every week to preach. At that time, I still didn't have the courage to preach myself.)

In the old bowling alley where we were holding services, I had recently partitioned off an eight-by-eight area that had once been a concession stand, making it into a tiny nursery. I decided that I would use that little area as my "prayer closet." I figured somehow that if I prayed the same amount of hours that I normally worked, God would "pay" me by providing for our needs.

I had no idea how hard it would be to carry out my decision to pray eight hours a day. That first morning I went into the closet, closed the door, got down on my knees, and started to pray in English. "Oh, God, now I'm full time in the ministry. Oh, God, keep our cupboards full. Don't let our children starve. Use me, God, please use me!" (I spent a lot of time begging God. I was just a Holiness boy who had learned almost nothing about faith yet.)

I prayed for everything I could think of. I prayed for all the missionaries around the world that I knew about. I even spent some time cursing the cockroaches in that closet, commanding them to die in Jesus' Name! But despite my efforts, I ran out of things to pray about in just fifteen minutes.

So just to survive the long hours that stretched in front of me for which I had committed to pray, I switched to praying in tongues. I didn't start praying in tongues because I knew it was a good thing to do. The truth is, I didn't even know if it was scripturally legal! Some Holiness people had told me that I couldn't pray in tongues anytime I wanted to. Then I had heard from others that it was okay to use tongues as a prayer language.

I wasn't sure which belief was right. All I knew was that I had to stay in that closet because I had resigned my job. So I began to pray in tongues that first day in the closet just to kill the hours.

Finally, the ten o'clock mill whistle blew. It was coffee break time! I hurried down to the coffee shop, ate a few doughnuts, and ran back to my prayer closet. In my mind, I had to be in position for prayer again in fifteen minutes — the same time the mill workers started their work again.

I kept on praying in tongues. I prayed for what seemed to be several hours, but it wasn't even noon yet!

Then the scream of the mill whistle brought me back to the reality of my friends' daily schedule and the radical choice I had made for myself. It was lunch break for the workers at the mill, and the darkness of the closet seemed to close in on me.

My former fellow workers had spent the last four hours in the sunlight, cutting and shaping wood that would be shipped all over the world. At the sound of the whistle, everyone would take their lunch boxes out and sit on benches, ready to eat, relax, and tell jokes. I knew what the men were doing, but I wasn't with them. Did I really believe God? Would this really work? I had to believe it would.

Memories of the Search for Answers

My mind drifted back to that late evening service at the Pentecostal church where I first listened with a mixture of apprehension and excitement to the revelation of the baptism in the Holy Spirit and the gift of tongues that accompanied the experience. Rosalie and I discussed what we had heard all the way home as our three young sons slept huddled together in the back seat of our Volkswagen bug.

Rosalie had received the baptism of the Holy Spirit in her late teens. I began to wonder if this experience could be my answer to a life of frustration and repeated repentance for sins I couldn't seem to shake.

It seemed that for so many Christians, transformation occurred immediately after they were born again. Was this true, and if so, why did it seem so difficult for me to change? Could a prayer language prayed through me by the Holy Spirit be the answer I needed to cross over that invisible line and truly become an overcomer?

Soon afterward, I came home to Rosalie and the boys after a dismal evening of struggle that had resulted in spiritual and personal failure. The look of disappointment on Rosalie's face was enough to drive out the lingering influence of the few drinks I had shared with the guys. A strong sense of conviction rose up on the inside of me. I was on the brink of settling into self-pity and despair.

Rosalie tucked the children into bed as I sat in the kitchen, my head hung in shame and remorse. Then she walked over to me and silently took my hands in hers, as if to say she was with me in this struggle.

From that night on, Rosalie and I began to pray together more often, and my desire to know more about the baptism in the Holy Spirit continued to grow. We talked often about this gift. I was so hungry to really know God, so hungry for the answers to my many questions.

By then I knew about Hebrews 11:6:

But without faith it is impossible to please him: for he that cometh to God must believe that he is, and that he is a rewarder of them that diligently seek him.

Could this praying in the Spirit be a part of diligently seeking God?

Now as I knelt in that closet praying in tongues, the answer to that question seemed all the more important. I returned from my world of memories, thinking, *What am I doing in this little closet, when by all standards I should be putting in my eight hours at the local lumber mill?* Was I crazy, or had I begun a true adventure into the deep waters of God?

'Putting In My Time' With God

The answers to these questions were still in the future as I began this first day in the prayer closet — putting my time in with God. My mind swirled with questions, doubts, and anxiety as I prayed in the Spirit. Could a man really "go deeper into God" on purpose — just because he wanted to?

Let me tell you, those hours in that closet were *long!* I would pray in tongues for what seemed like an hour and then look at my watch. "Oh, no, it's only been five minutes!" So I'd start praying again.

The next few months found me reporting to my closet just as before I would have reported to the lumberyard. When the mill whistle signaled the start of each work day, I was always in position on my knees, ready to pray.

Every day the hours just dragged by, but I stayed with it. I memorized every discoloration on the carpet and the wall. I got to know that prayer closet so well that even today, I could still take a pencil and paper and draw it in minute detail. I felt like I was in prison.

From my closet, I could smell burning wood as the saws split the tall trees. I could picture my friends dipping into lunch pails full to the brim and sipping steaming cups of coffee.

One day I was having a particularly difficult time of it. Why had I quit my job to do this? What did this supposedly supernatural language accomplish anyway?

My spirit man rose up and spoke the Word to my wavering emotions: "God is a rewarder of those who diligently seek Him" (Heb. 11:6). Then through my mind flashed a continuous series of pictures of my seemingly endless failures. I found myself choking on the emotions that those memories brought up. "Oh God," I cried, "let that word be true!" Gradually peace began to calm my troubled mind.

God had not told me to quit my job and pray in the Spirit for eight hours every day. It was a decision I had made from a place of desperation. I wanted more of God but wasn't sure how to find it.

From reading the Word, I had learned that my prayer language was given for my edification and that I could pray out mysteries, but I didn't have a grasp of what those truths really meant. Still, I was determined that if it was possible for me to edify myself by praying in tongues until my mind was able to receive divine mysteries, that was what I was going to do.

A Welcome Break

So I kept on praying, hour after slow hour, day after long day. About two months dragged by. Then a woman whom I had met at a Charismatic Bible study heard about what I was doing. She came over to the church one day and knocked on my closet door.

"Brother Roberson," she called, "I hear you've been praying all these hours and days."

"Yes, Ma'am."

"I want to know," she said, "can you tell any difference?"

"Do you mean a difference in my walk with God or what?" I asked.

"No, I just want to know, can you tell any difference?"

"As a matter of fact, I can," I answered.

"Would you mind sharing it?"

"Not at all," I said. "My tongue is tired, my throat is dry, and my chin is weary."

She nervously replied, "Excuse me, I have to go." And that was the end of *that* conversation!

Another month dragged by. I had been locked up in that closet praying for three months. Then the same woman came back and knocked on the closet door.

"Brother Roberson," she said, "you know the church I go to."

"Yes, Ma'am, I do," I replied.

"You know they don't believe in speaking in tongues."

"Yes, I know that."

"Well, my church is holding a laywitness meeting this weekend where laypeople from several states gather together to tell the good things God has done for them. Would you like to come?"

I thought, *You better believe I'd like to come! I would use any excuse to get out of this closet!* I told the woman, "I'll meet you there!"

So I ran home, changed my clothes, and hurried to the house where the people were holding a morning Bible study. I arrived late for the meeting, so I didn't know that the elderly woman who was sitting next to me had walked in using a crutch, which someone had then put in a nearby corner. I had no idea the woman was lame in her leg.

I sat there, waiting for the speaker to begin his message. I was so excited. I had been locked up in a prayer closet for three months. Now I was not only with other people, but I was going to hear a real live message taught by a real live person! I could hardly wait.

Finally the man stood up to speak, holding a huge stack of notes. (If his notes had been a scroll, it could have been rolled out to the back of the house!) He hadn't spoken very long before he had put a new meaning on not being filled with the Holy Ghost!

With elaborate language and a stiff, monotone voice, the man lectured about "Jesus, the great Celestial Go-Between," "the troubled waters of mankind," and "the Omnipotent G-a-w-d." I sat there in my chair, thinking, *What did I get myself into? This is terrible! I'd rather be back in my prayer closet!*

God Shows Up Unexpectedly

My mind floated in and out of the meeting. I didn't know what to do with myself. For excitement, I started to shake my coffee cup so I could watch the coffee rings ripple to the edge of the cup.

Out of sheer boredom, I looked over at this elderly lady next to me. I had no idea anything was going to happen. I felt no anointing. I felt nothing! But when I looked at this woman, suddenly I saw suspended between me and her what looked like an X-ray of someone's hip socket. The socket had a dark substance all around the ball joint, extending three to four inches down the leg.

I almost dropped my cup in astonishment! I blinked, but the X-ray picture remained before my eyes. I looked around to see if anyone else could see what I was seeing. Apparently, no one could.

As I sat there looking at this X-ray, I started praying, *Oh, God, oh, God — what is this? Do you want me to pray for this woman? What in the world do you want me to do?* God remained absolutely silent.

(Later when I was sharing this testimony during a service, the Lord spoke to my spirit, saying, "Son, do you want to know why I didn't speak to you that time —

why I let you go on and disturb the service? Because if I wasn't listening to that man teach, why should I make you listen?" That was a revelation in itself!)

So I leaned over to this elderly lady and said, "Ma'am, you have trouble with your hip!" She turned and studied me for a long moment.

All of a sudden the word "arthritis" just jumped out of my spirit. I blurted out, "It's arthritis in your right hip!"

She studied me for another long moment and then said, "That's what the doctor tells me, young man."

I exclaimed, "Glory to God!"

"Well, I beg your pardon!" she said.

"Oh, I mean, God wants to heal you, Ma'am. May I pray for you?"

The elderly woman just kept studying me. Now, remember, this church didn't believe in speaking with other tongues. So to the woman, my request meant that at some time in the course of my day, I would bow my head and remember her in prayer.

But that's not what prayer meant to me. I was a bench-jumping, chair-leaping, loud-shouting Pentecostal! I believed the louder I shouted, the more power I generated!

Finally the elderly lady answered, "Yes, you may pray for me."

As soon as she said that, I leapt out of my chair, knelt down in front of her, grabbed both of her ankles, and pulled them out toward me. (Meanwhile, that golden-tongued orator was still "orating"!) Then I looked down at her feet and thought, *Oh, oh!* One leg was six inches shorter than the other one!

Oh, no, this is horrible! I thought. *I've never seen the kind of miracle this woman needs!* I was too scared to watch, so I closed my eyes, shouted, *"In the Name of Jesus...!"* and started praying the strongest, hardest, most ultra-Holiness type of prayer I could think of.

Witnesses to the scene told me later that at the very first mention of that mighty Name, the woman's shorter leg cracked and popped; then it suddenly grew out until it was even with the other leg!

The woman had been instantly, totally healed — but I didn't know that! I still had my eyes closed, and I was still praying my strongest prayer. And in my zeal, I almost wrestled that lady off her chair and onto the floor before the others could get me to let go of her ankles!

But God didn't need my help. He popped that leg out without me even realizing it! When I finally opened my eyes and saw the miracle, I was as shocked as everyone else!

About the time I started to pray for the woman, the man who was speaking grabbed his associate and whispered to him, "Go get that guy and break it up!" (I really don't blame him; I was destroying his service with my loud praying!)

The associate started toward all the commotion and, according to those who witnessed the scene, reached us just in time to see the miracle. He was just about to grab me when he saw the woman's short leg suddenly grow out six inches.

So instead of breaking up the disturbance, this man was struck dumb with amazement. He had never seen a miracle before. He didn't even speak in tongues! When it came to the supernatural, this man didn't believe in hardly anything. So when he saw the miracle, he was speechless. Talk about God's timing!

Then the golden-tongued orator ended his message with the question, "What is the most outstanding sequence of events that could possibly be attributed to the God-factor in your life?" While everyone else was wondering what that meant, the associate answered the man's question by pointing to the healed elderly woman and sputtering, "Over here!" The healing of this elderly woman was certainly the most outstanding sequence of events he had ever seen!

After the service, the speaker came over to the little elderly lady and tried to tell her, "Ma'am, God doesn't perform miracles in this day and age."

But the elderly woman replied, "You want to bet, Sonny? You want to bet?" Then she grabbed her crutch and started walking around the room. She swung that crutch back and forth, using it to hold people off while she showed them how well her healed hip was working.

After the house meeting, the congregation all attended a special banquet at the church. For some reason, they didn't invite me. (I wonder why!) But God didn't need me to be invited for His purposes to be fulfilled — the elderly lady went!

Before the people in charge could do anything, that little lady jumped up and gave her testimony at the banquet. After she finished, she shouted, "And what God did for me, He'll do for you!" The place went crazy with excitement.

Later, a woman attending the banquet sought out the elderly lady. This woman had been in a car accident and was now unable to bend over. "Do you think God would heal me?" she asked.

The elderly lady replied, "I think He would. Let's call that man who prayed for me."

By that time, I had gone home, changed clothes, and was busy working in the yard. The phone rang; it was the elderly lady who had just received a miracle. She explained the other woman's condition and asked if they could come over so I could pray for the woman.

I was about to say, "You can bring her and anyone else you can get your hands on!" (I was still lost in the Holy Ghost.) But then the Holy Spirit spoke to my spirit very loudly: "Go to the main auditorium of the church." So I told the woman, "I'll meet you and your friend at the church."

It became very quiet on the other end of the line. After a while, I heard the two women whispering to each other. Then the elderly lady said to me, "Okay, we'll meet you out in front of the church."

When I arrived at the church, the two women met me and tried to take me to a room in the church basement, away from everyone else. But I kept saying what the Holy Ghost was saying to my spirit: "The main auditorium. We have to go to the main auditorium."

Finally, the ladies gave up and took me to the main auditorium, where people were still standing around in little circles, fellowshiping together.

I stood there, looking at the people. I didn't know what to do. I was only there because I was obeying the Holy Ghost. Then the associate who had witnessed the miracle said, "Uh, I think this man wants to say something."

I thought, *I do?* I had never preached before, and I was afraid. Everyone courteously looked at me. Timidly, I began to give the elderly woman's testimony. Suddenly the Holy Ghost fell on me, and I was caught up in the awesome, powerful Presence of God. The gift of faith came on me (although at the time, I didn't understand that), and I heard myself saying things that were so good, I knew it couldn't be *me* preaching; I wasn't that smart. I wanted to step out of my body and take notes!

Then while the gift of faith was still in operation, I looked over at one young man. As I walked over to him, suddenly his shoulder section became transparent like an X-ray, and in the Spirit I saw the shoulder joint and the problem with it. The young man could only lift his arm a little ways.

I said to the young man, "Your shoulder is going to be healed!" The closer I got to him, the more horrified he looked. His eyes got big, and he leaned as far away from me as he could. But it didn't do him any good — I ran over to him and grabbed him by the wrist. Then I said, "In the Name of Jesus!" and jerked his arm straight up in the air.

The young man screamed as his arm went up — then he looked at me in amazement and said, "Why, it didn't hurt!"

"You bet it didn't hurt!" I replied. You see, the gift of faith was on me. I had the mind of God. I was acting with the faith of God, who had totally dislodged that frozen shoulder.

Later that night when the gift of faith wasn't in operation anymore, I lay in bed, thinking, *Roberson, you're so stupid! What if you had broken that man's arm?* I didn't know then that when the gift of faith is in operation, a person thinks like God thinks, and he may do things that just don't make sense in the natural.

Then the woman who couldn't bend her back ran over to me. That same supernatural faith was still on me. I put my hand on the back of her neck and bent her down until she touched her toes. She was instantly healed by the power of God.

The miracles continued. Finally the elders came from every quarter of the church and said, "We're breaking this up! This man is turning this into a holy-rolling, swinging-from-the-chandelier meeting. We're not going to have this!"

But before they could do much of anything, I yelled out, "Does anybody want what I've got?" Immediately all the youth came running over to me, and I began to pray for them. They all started getting filled with the Holy Ghost, speaking in tongues and falling down under the power of God. The adults didn't know what was going on! They went around taking the young people's pulses, asking them, "Are you okay?" (Most of those young people are still serving God today; some have graduated from Bible school.)

People were speaking in tongues all over the auditorium, and the elders were in a frenzy. While they tried to get the situation back under control, I slipped out a side door. I was so lost in the Spirit, I hardly knew where I was. I could hardly walk. I staggered down the sidewalk a little ways until I found an iron post that supported the church. I leaned against the post and cried like a baby.

God had just used me! Because of my background, my mind could not fathom the fact that the God of the universe — the One whom all the ultra-Holiness people had told me dealt out so much punishment — would occupy the same room with me and perform a miracle through me. I can't explain what that felt like. You see, I knew my shortcomings; I knew the real me. To think that God was working with me and through me to establish His Kingdom here on earth was almost more than I could fathom.

Why would He use one such as me? All of my born-again, Holy Ghost-filled years, I had known that I had God's call on my life. And I had always been so hungry to know Him after His power. But no one could tell me how to walk into the power of God on purpose — no one! They could only give me vague generalities that didn't satisfy that deep hunger.

Uncovering a Spiritual Law — By Accident!

Then, as I leaned against that post, all of a sudden prophecy began to flow, and I received the revelation knowledge my heart had been seeking all along. I didn't know enough to speak out loud what I heard in my spirit.

The Holy Spirit said to me, "Son, this anointing didn't suddenly come upon you because it was predestined for this meeting from the foundations of the world. It didn't come on you in respect to your evangelistic call. I wish all My evangelists walked in My power.

"This anointing didn't come on you because of your calling, your creed, your color, or your nation. It came upon you because *you have uncovered a spiritual law: praying in other tongues for your personal edification.* That law carries with it an ironclad guarantee to build you up on your most holy faith in your spirit — that part of you from which faith comes.

"You have found something you can do on purpose to edify yourself — as much as you want to, as long as you want to, whenever you want to. Through praying in the Holy Ghost, you can build yourself up above a walk where your physical senses hold you in checkmate and convince you that God's Word isn't so, to a walk that is vibrant, Spirit-charged, and free in the Holy Ghost."

After being so hungry for God's power for so long, I had accidentally uncovered one of the most important keys to growing in devil-stomping, mountain-moving faith — praying in tongues for personal edification. And do you think that after finding such a major key to unlock divine mysteries, anyone could keep me out of my prayer closet? Not a chance! I had a divine plan for my life to discover!

There is an operation of the Spirit
   you know very little about.
But as you continue to grow and to walk
   in My Spirit,
I will show you things that the Early Church
   walked in.
I will show you things that sparked
   such an operation of My Spirit
   that many came from the cities round about,
   and My power was in manifestation and
   so evident that they were healed,
   every single one.
I will show you the Holy of Holies
   where ministries are born.
I will show you the elements
   that are being left out now —
   elements that men once saw clearly,
   and they pressed in until they had the fullness
   of the Spirit.
I will show you the things men hunger for
   that can only be quenched by a relationship
   with your Lord.

Chapter 3

Spiritual Gifts And Operations

The stairs seemed endless as up and up Rosalie and I climbed. *Hurry!* I kept telling myself, *The seats may be all gone.*

We finally arrived at the top tier. Just a little farther and we could sit down. As I looked for two seats, a flood of people suddenly seemed to gush down each aisle, quickly filling every empty seat in sight. Rosalie and I kept climbing up to the top row, but every seat had already been taken.

At this time, I was still working in the sawmill. The week before, Rosalie and I had heard that the famous evangelist, Kathryn Kuhlman, was coming to our state. We decided it was too great an opportunity to miss. So on the day of the meeting, we drove all the way to Portland from our home in Gilchrist, Oregon (the town we moved to after living in LaPine). But now we couldn't even find two seats! After momentary discouragement, we staked our claim on the two top steps and sat on cold concrete for the next three and a half hours.

'This Is What I Have for You'

The service was more than our hungry eyes and ears could have ever hoped for. I was amazed at the number of miracles and incontestable healings that took place before our eyes. Then Miss Kuhlman gave a passionate plea for people to give their lives to Jesus, and I watched in amazement as a great host of people responded to the promptings of the Holy Spirit.

As I sat there in absolute awe, suddenly I heard someone call my name. I turned and asked Rosalie if she had said something. She shook her head; she hadn't said a word.

Turning again to the stage, I continued to watch everything — the musicians, Miss Kuhlman, the people responding to the altar call — with rapt attention.

"David." There was that voice again! Who was talking at a time like this? Impatiently, I jerked around and glared at a man sitting behind me. He returned my gaze absent-mindedly. His mind was on the meeting, not me.

So I turned again to watch the many people accepting Jesus as Savior up front. Oh, it was exciting! I was filled with wonder. What did you have to do or give up to come to the place in God that Miss Kuhlman had attained, where people so readily respond to the call of the Holy Spirit through you?

"David." My adrenaline was pumping at such a high level from all I was seeing and hearing that I wheeled around and bluntly asked that same man sitting behind me, "What do you want?" The man just stared blankly for a moment. Then with as much interest as he'd give a pebble on a beach, he answered blandly, "I didn't say anything to you."

Then who did? I wondered, exasperated. I turned around to face the stage again. Then I heard the voice one more time — only this time it said, "This is what I have for you." My mind raced as I gazed at the panorama of miracles before me. Could it be? This was beyond belief. This was an anointing and a spiritual gift in action, the likes of which I had never seen in my life.

Surely the voice I had heard wasn't God! Surely it was the devil trying to deceive me. But I wouldn't allow myself to be deceived!

As Rosalie and I drove back to Gilchrist, the memory of the voice rolled over and over in my mind. Then tormenting thoughts of doubt jabbed at my jagged emotions. It was only my mind conjuring up the voice. That was it — vain imaginations! Oh, how I cast down those "imaginations" as I drove home late that night.

Yet somehow deep inside, I knew it really was God. I had heard His voice audibly with my own ears, and His words had struck a chord in my heart.

Oh, God, I prayed, *do you really have a gift for someone like me? How does a spiritual gift happen? Can I do anything to cause it to come to pass?*

The Lord heard the cry of my heart. Later, I would receive the first of many answers to those questions as I leaned against that iron post after "disturbing" the laywitness meeting. There the Lord revealed to me that I had uncovered a spiritual law regarding tongues for personal edification.

I immediately began to take advantage of what I learned that day. And as I continued to pray in the Spirit and study the Word, more revelation came. But the more I learned, the more I came to realize that speaking in other tongues was not only a spiritual law uncovered; it was also a spiritual foundation upon which everything else regarding spiritual gifts and their operation rested.

Understanding Spiritual Gifts

Let's look at the role that praying in other tongues plays in God's government. To do that, we'll have to go to First Corinthians chapter 12, where Paul outlines the operation of the Holy Spirit in the gifts, offices, and callings of the entire Body of Christ. He begins by saying in verse 1:

Now concerning spiritual gifts, brethren, I would not have you ignorant.

Now, I do know this about the Holy Spirit: He would not inspire Paul to make a statement like that and then leave us ignorant! In the discussion following that statement, Paul by the Holy Ghost supplies all the information necessary to eradicate any spiritual ignorance, misconceptions, or religious error we may have concerning the operation of spiritual gifts.

Personally, if there is one subject I don't want to be ignorant about, it is the operation of the gifts of the Spirit. But, to be frank with you, this is one of the areas in which this generation of believers is most lacking. We who are Full Gospel faith people often pride ourselves in knowing a great deal about the gifts of the Spirit. It's too bad we haven't prided ourselves more in knowing how to *operate* in those nine gifts!

Satan, the great deceiver, has successfully spread confusion and division regarding this passage of Scripture in First Corinthians 12 — so much so that

entire denominations have split over different inter-
pretations of the operation of spiritual gifts and the
offices they empower. So it would profit us to make a
careful examination of what Paul is teaching the
Corinthian church in these verses.

In First Corinthians 12:4-6, Paul says this:

> **Now there are diversities of gifts, but the
> same Spirit,**
>
> **And there are differences of administra-
> tions, but the same Lord.**
>
> **And there are diversities of operation, but it
> is the same God which worketh all in all.**

What is Paul saying? Well, we know that the "gifts"
he is talking about in verse 4 are the nine gifts of the
Spirit listed in First Corinthians 12:8-10: 1) the word of
wisdom; 2) the word of knowledge; 3) the gift of faith;
4) gifts of healings; 5) working of miracles; 6) prophecy;
7) discerning of spirits; 8) divers (or different supernatural manifestations of tongues; and 9) interpretation of tongues.

But what does verse 5 mean when it says, **And
there are differences of administrations, but the
same Lord?** To understand what Paul is talking about
in this verse, we have to go to Ephesians 4:8 and 11,
where it says this:

> **Wherefore he saith, When he [Jesus] ascended
> up on high, he led captivity captive, and gave
> gifts unto men....**
>
> **And he gave some, apostles; and some,
> prophets; and some, evangelists; and some,
> pastors and teachers.**

In other words, there are different administrations or offices in the Body of Christ, such as apostle, prophet, teacher, pastor, and evangelist. But it is the same Lord Jesus Christ who ascended on high and gave those gifts or offices to men.

Then in First Corinthians 12:6, it says, **And there are diversities of operations, but it is the same God which worketh all in all.** So Paul is simply saying this: It is the Holy Spirit who determines how the nine gifts of the Spirit and the ministry offices operate. It is Jesus Christ who sets each person into his or her respective office or calling. And it is God the Father who supplied the original plan.

The Gifts Empower and Qualify the Offices

The verses we just read in Ephesians 4 list the "fivefold ministry gifts" that we hear so much about. The nine gifts of the Spirit empower and qualify these five offices. You see, God meant for every person called to one of these ministry offices to preach the Word with signs following (Mark 16:20). God never intended for the preaching of His Word to seem powerless.

The spiritual gifts empower the ministry offices much the same way a power plant supplies power to the various appliances in a home. Each appliance is designed to perform a different function, yet each is hooked up to the same power plant.

In a similar way, one "wire" runs to the apostle, another to the prophet, and still another to the pastor, but each ministry office is hooked up to the Holy Ghost. When God's power is switched on, then just as surely as a toaster acts one way and a blender acts another, the Holy Spirit anoints different offices with particular blends of the nine gifts of the Spirit.

These blends of spiritual gifts working in the fivefold ministry are what qualifies a person to stand in a ministry office and determines which office it will be.

The Eight Operations of God

But the government of God extends itself much further than just the operation of the gifts of the Spirit and the fivefold ministry offices. These nine gifts and five offices are actually all encompassed in eight complete operations of God, which are outlined in First Corinthians 12:28. These operations make up the structure of God's government and include everyone in the Body of Christ.

Now ye are the body of Christ, and members in particular.

And God hath set some in the church, first APOSTLES, secondarily PROPHETS, thirdly TEACHERS, after that MIRACLES, then GIFTS OF HEALINGS, HELPS, GOVERNMENTS, DIVERSITIES OF TONGUES.

— 1 Corinthians 12:27,28

The eight operations mentioned in verse 28 are in divine order. In this listing, the government of God begins with the office of the mighty apostle, the first operation, followed by the prophet and the teacher.

The evangelists and pastors mentioned in Ephesians 4:11 are then replaced in First Corinthians 12 with miracles and gifts of healings. These gifts of the Spirit

53

are the primary ones that empower and qualify the evangelistic and pastoral offices. (The entry level into the fivefold ministry gifts is also at the level of working of miracles and gifts of healings because all five ministry offices — apostle, prophet, evangelist, pastor, and teacher — should be equipped with these two gifts of the Spirit.)

Next is the operation of helps, which handles the physical and material aspects of the ministry. One very important helps calling is what I call the "entrepreneurship of the simplicity of giving." A person called to fulfill this operation is someone of means who has the capacity in his character and his calling to be used by God to pour thousands, if not millions, into the Kingdom of God for the governments of the Church.

Helps is followed by governments or administrations, which includes the organizational skills and gifts needed in the Church. For instance, a person called to this operation may be able not only to organize a massive prayer meeting of ten thousand people, but to make sure that the little believer on the outer perimeter of the crowd has everything he needs to grow in his spiritual walk.

Both helps and governments support those who minister the Word of God by doing many of the natural things that ministers don't have time to do, such as running businesses, etc. Undergirding everything else is the final and foundational operation, *the diversities of tongues.*

So in these eight operations of God, we find not only that the fivefold ministries are all included, but that the nine gifts of the Spirit are also poured out into all the operations, from the apostle all the way to the eighth operation of diversities of tongues.

Where Do You Fit In?

No matter what God has called you to do in life, your calling or "job description" can be found enveloped within one or more of these eight operations of God. And if you are born again, you are called to fill that operation by the power of the Holy Spirit.

"Do you know which operation I'm called to fill, Brother Roberson?" you may ask. No, I don't know. The measure of faith has been placed on the inside of you in seed form (Rom. 12:3). Your calling is hidden in that seed for you, not for me, to discover.

Ephesians 4:7 says, **But unto every one of us is given grace according to the measure of the gift of Christ.** A measure is part of a whole. The "whole" that Paul is talking about here is the Body of Christ. It is a Body with many members in particular, each with an individual calling. Just as a person's physical body has many members with different functions, such as hands, eyes, ears, a nose, and a mouth, Paul says that the Body of Christ also includes different operations that together make up the whole.

What are you separated unto? What is your grace, your measure, your part in the whole operation of the Body of Christ? Whatever it is, God gives you grace for it. That's why Paul said this:

> For I say, THROUGH THE GRACE GIVEN
> UNTO ME, to every man that is among you, not
> to think of himself more highly than he ought
> to think; but to think soberly, according as God
> hath dealt to every man the measure of faith.
>
> — Romans 12:3

In essence Paul was saying, "I'm going to speak to
you according to the separation of God to my apostolic
office. I didn't merit it. I didn't deserve it. God not only
gave me the grace for my office — He gave me the faith
to fulfill it. Therefore, don't think that you're some kind
of special vehicle for God just because you're called to a
certain office."

Some ministers have the attitude, "I'm a mighty
apostle. Get me a Rolls Royce or the Rams football
team to exalt me, you poor, beat-up sheep. I'm a special
calling and gift that is given to you, so you better treat
me right." It's that type of attitude that Paul warned
about when he said, "Think of yourself soberly, realizing that *God* is the One who has dealt to every man the
measure of faith for his calling and his office. In fact,
God not only gave you the grace to receive your calling,
He also gave you the grace to fulfill it."

Certain Gifts Qualify Each Operation

Remember, the nine gifts of the Spirit not only supply the power, but they qualify these eight operations.
Someone may say, "I'm an apostle." But unless a certain blend of the nine gifts of the Spirit is working in
his calling, he is not an apostle.

Or a person may say, "Well, I'm a prophet." But unless he is qualified by the particular blend of the nine spiritual gifts that qualifies and empowers the prophetic office, that person is not a prophet.

In fact, there seems to be a move abroad in the Body of Christ in which many people think they are prophets, but in truth they are not. Others think they are apostles but are not.

These "self-acclaimed" people often attempt to operate in certain gifts of the Spirit to prove their office. But because they haven't been qualified by the Holy Ghost for that office, they mostly operate out of their own fleshly nature. This is something I've found to be true while traveling a long road of observation and experience during more than twenty-five years of ministry.

So we see that you can only qualify for a particular operation if certain gifts are working in your calling. But what about the eighth operation, diversities of tongues? Well, it stands to reason that you can only qualify and fulfill this eighth operation if you are baptized in the Holy Ghost and speak with other tongues!

Diversities of Tongues:
The Foundational Operation

Now that we've looked in a general sense at the eight operations of God in First Corinthians 12:28, let's focus on this eighth and final operation, the diversities of tongues.

I believe diversities of tongues is listed last in this scripture because it is the foundational operation. In the construction of a building, a foundation is the slab built to support the building from underneath. If the foundation is weak, the structure won't stand the test of time nor weather the storms that beat against it. In the same way, diversities of tongues is the operation that the other seven rest upon.

Why do I say that? Well, think about this very carefully: Where is the dividing line between Christians who believe in the power of God and the gifts of the Spirit and those who do not? I can tell you exactly where it is. The dividing line between those who enjoy the power of God and those who don't is in the eighth operation of God, the diversities of tongues.

Have you ever noticed that people who don't speak with other tongues usually don't operate in the other gifts of the Spirit either? On the other hand, people who do speak with tongues are more apt to operate in spiritual gifts. The more you study the matter, the more obvious it becomes: Speaking with other tongues is the dividing line. In fact, within many churches that don't recognize tongues as a manifestation for this day and age, even the preaching of salvation has been lost.

Not only is diversities of tongues the dividing line, but it is actually the entry level to the operation of the spiritual gifts that empower the various offices and callings in the Body of Christ. It is the switch we are looking for that pulls the operation we are called to out of the natural realm into the supernatural power of God.

Why is that? Because speaking with other tongues is designed to equip us from the inside out. It affects the part of us from which all permanent change comes —

the human spirit. So if a person refuses this eighth operation, he won't have the spiritual empowerment to fulfill any of the other seven operations of God — at least not to the depth God desires for him.

For example, someone may be called to one of the ministry offices; he may even be a good intellectual communicator or lecturer about the Word of God. But it is through the diversities of tongues that the power of the Holy Spirit activates the operation he has been called to fulfill. And if he refuses to receive God's gift of speaking in other tongues, he is not allowing himself to become spiritually qualified for his office.

You see, as you pray in tongues, God will build an operation on the inside of you to qualify you for what He has called you to do. As He does, gifts will begin to operate through you that equip you for your particular call.

For example, if *I* pray in the Holy Ghost a lot, God isn't going to train me to be more skillful in carpentry or to perform brain surgery on someone. Those professions are not my calling. He is going to equip me with the graces and gifts of the Spirit that I need to fulfill *my* call, which is to preach the Gospel.

That's why the devil is so afraid of this eighth operation. Throughout history, it is the operation he has always tried hardest to discredit and remove from the Church.

The enemy doesn't want you to pray in tongues. In fact, the less you find out about this foundational operation, the better he likes it. He doesn't care if you play at being an apostle, prophet, evangelist, or pastor — as long as you never qualify for these offices through the power and gifts of the Holy Spirit.

He even rather enjoys deceiving men into building massive organizations of their own making, separate from the calling of God. Men put themselves in charge of these organizations so they can hand down doctrinal rulings as to what is and is not God. With self-deceived pride, they proclaim great, swelling mandates, such as "Tongues are not for today" or "Healing is not for everyone."

The devil is a tactical genius. If he can't remove tongues from some part of the Church, then he goes to step two of his plan: He tries to cause believers to enter into such fanaticism about tongues and hold such unruly, out-of-order services that the sinner doesn't want much to do with them. Satan's strategy is to confuse the use of tongues so greatly that the operation loses its effectiveness and credibility in the eyes of those who have been deceived by its misuse.

Think about it. What is it about tongues that scares the devil so badly? Why has he worked so hard to surround this gift with so much confusion? Paul himself dedicated an entire chapter, First Corinthians 14, to straightening out the error and confusion within the Early Church concerning this gift. No other gift or operation has an entire chapter dedicated to explaining its proper use.

I can tell you why the devil is so afraid: If anything is ever going to build within us an understanding of spiritual matters and to quench our hunger to know Jesus in an intimate relationship, it is this foundational operation of diversities of tongues. And as we have seen, this operation is the supernatural means God has provided for us to become spiritually qualified for any of the other operations that make up His government. Therefore, Satan is very, very fearful of a people who will relentlessly pursue God through praying in tongues.

Divine Help To Find Your Place

Earlier I asked you the question, "Where do you fit in?" Where do you fit in the plan of redemption laid out before the foundation of the world, hidden in a mystery in the heart of God? Are you called to be an apostle, prophet, teacher, evangelist, or pastor? Are you called to administer or to make millions to finance the Gospel?

As I said before, every believer, including you, fits somewhere in the eight operations of God found in First Corinthians 12:28. But how will you know where you fit in? How will you keep from being deceived by the enemy into trying to fill a place in the Body you are not called to or are not yet prepared for?

That's one of the reasons God gave us the foundational eighth operation, diversities of tongues — to help us discover His perfect plan for our lives. Through the supernatural prayer language given to us and prayed through us by the Holy Spirit, God imparts to our spirits the mysteries hidden in Him throughout all the ages — Christ in us, the hope of glory (Col. 1:27). Thank God for divine assistance in finding our place in His great plan!

When I call you and separate you
through ordination
to an operation that I place you in,
My power will qualify you to fulfill that office
from within.
For I have made all things possible to him who
believeth.
Therefore, approach not My Presence
in your own understanding
or in the ideals, creeds, and doctrines
as men would put them forth.
For I place within you an anointing
that cannot lie.
That anointing is truth and will teach you
all things.
Yield yourself to My Spirit for the purposes
of edification,
and I will lift you up.
I will build you into every operation
that I have separated you unto,
and I will qualify you by My power.

Chapter 4

Diversities of Tongues In God's Government

We've seen that the diversities of tongues is an entire operation of God placed into God's government to serve a crucial purpose. To deny it is to deny the perfecting of the Body of Christ.

So let's find out more about the role of diversities of tongues in God's government and the reason God would designate an entire operation to it. I want you to understand what He has made available to us through this awesome gift of speaking with tongues — a gift that Satan has deceived many into believing is either obsolete or insignificant.

The Unique Nature Of Diversities of Tongues

There is only one operation we can fulfill immediately after we are born again: the eighth operation of diversities of tongues. The moment we receive Jesus as Savior, we can also receive the baptism of the Holy Spirit and begin to speak with other tongues, which begins our spiritual qualification for any and all of the other operations to which we may be called.

A person cannot become a mighty apostle or prophet five minutes after he is born again even if that is what he is called to be. He first must become qualified, trained, prepared, and seasoned by the Holy

Spirit before God will separate him to the office he is called to.

That's true with any of the first seven operations listed in First Corinthians 12:28. Not everyone is qualified to teach God's Word. You can tell that by the people who nod off to sleep while some ministers teach! A person can't immediately enter into a full-blown ministry operating in the working of miracles or gifts of healings either.

In every one of the first seven operations, including helps and governments, a person must first be found faithful and receive the equipping of the Holy Ghost before he can fulfill the operation to which he is called.

On the other hand, a person can move into the eighth operation instantaneously with his rebirth.

Suppose the person responds to an altar call and says, "I receive Jesus as Savior." Then someone steps up and says to him, "You just received God's nature. Now you need to be filled with the Holy Ghost."

He asks, "What are you talking about?" He learns that because his spirit just became the receptor of a new nature, he is now able to receive the baptism of the Holy Spirit. "Yes, I'd like to be filled with the Holy Ghost," he says.

"Then receive the Holy Spirit, the promise of the Father."

All of a sudden, the person's chin starts shaking. "Speak it out," he is instructed. His mouth starts forming words, and soon he is speaking in tongues. He dances around for days, speaking in his new language with great joy.

Why did God design it that way? Why are tongues available to us instantaneously with our rebirth? Because praying in tongues has everything to do with our becoming prepared and qualified for our particular calling. And as we pray in tongues, the Holy Spirit is able to build into our heart the understanding of God's will for our personal lives.

Sometimes people get the baptism of the Holy Ghost mixed up with the new birth. However, there is a great difference between being born again and receiving the indwelling fullness of the Holy Spirit's Presence.

The Holy Spirit is a Person just as each of us is a person. When we were born again, we received Him in the creative process that caused us to become new creations. But we didn't receive Him in His fullness until we were baptized in the Holy Ghost. Now He lives inside us, partnering with us in prayer, empowering our lives, and bringing revelation of the Word as we walk in obedience to God.

It is God's will that the moment we are born again, we lift our hands in submission and praise to receive the baptism of the Holy Spirit. That's the very best way to be filled with the Holy Spirit. But the devil has managed to separate the new birth from the baptism of the Holy Spirit through divisions of doctrines so that now, as a rule, the two experiences don't occur together.

The Miracle of Tongues
In the Baptism of the Holy Spirit

Actually, the devil does whatever he can to prevent people from *ever* receiving the baptism of the Holy Ghost with the evidence of speaking in tongues. For example, many times I minister to people who have been in a hundred other prayer lines seeking to be filled with the Holy Spirit, but who have always left disappointed. They respond when I make an altar call, and, like so many ministers before me, I pray for them. Their mouth moves, but they make no sounds.

So I encourage them by saying, "Why don't you just speak out what your lips are already mouthing?" The majority of those who take my suggestion immediately begin to speak in tongues.

Why is that? Because the moment the Person of the Holy Spirit fills a believer, the first thing He does is to start creating the supernatural language of tongues on the inside of the believer's spirit for his own personal edification.

In my own experience, the first evidence that I was baptized in the Holy Spirit was what Isaiah 28:11 called "stammering lips": **For with stammering lips and another tongue will he speak to this people.**

One night when I came to the altar to be filled with the Holy Spirit, something came over me. All of a sudden, my chin, mouth, and tongue all started to move. My mouth seemed to be out of control.

I thought, *What's the matter with my mouth?* I didn't know that the moment I said, "Fill me with the Holy Ghost," the Holy Ghost had begun to create His supernatural words in my spirit. So the words came out in stammering lips because I was afraid to say them out loud. I was sure it would be just me speaking. I didn't realize that my mouth was actually shaping an entire supernatural language of the Holy Spirit.

But later I was worshiping God at home, and the Holy Ghost came upon me again. My mouth began to move the same way it had that night at church.

However, by this time I had learned about Acts 2:4, which says, **And they were all filled with the Holy Ghost, and BEGAN TO SPEAK with other tongues, as the Spirit gave them utterance.** So this time, instead of fighting off the urge to speak out those words, I yielded to the Holy Spirit and began to speak in tongues. And the longer I yielded, the more the Holy Ghost's "rivers of living water" poured out of me.

> **He that believeth on me, as the scripture hath said, out of his belly shall flow rivers of living water.**
>
> **(But this spake he of the Spirit, which they that believe on him should receive: for the Holy Ghost was not yet given; because that Jesus was not yet glorified.)**
>
> **— John 7:38,39**

It wasn't long before I was speaking a full prayer language by the power of the Holy Spirit.

Benefits of Praying in Tongues

Now, if God the Holy Spirit literally creates this language in our spirit, what kind of prayer could it possibly be? What benefits could it possibly hold for us?

We've already seen some of the benefits of praying in other tongues, and we'll discuss several of them in depth later on. But I want to just mention a few of the benefits right now.

For one thing, the Holy Spirit came into our spirit to bring us revelation knowledge of the Cross and everything that Jesus has become to us. Also, on the day you and I spoke with tongues, a viable, powerful working of God's government came into operation within our spirit, designed to give us and cause us to understand what no man can give us through natural means — spiritual authority.

This spiritual power and authority is the means God gives us to overcome torment, worry, fear, and the hopelessness that can take over our lives when we move from one overwhelming situation to another, continually losing ground. Praying in other tongues also supplies the power to overcome character flaws — those deep-seated character traits that keep cropping up and robbing us of our stamina and initiative to overcome in the face of the common testings and trials that precede almost every major victory and promotion by God.

Praying in tongues always affects us in a positive way. God says that it edifies us (1 Cor. 14:4). In Jude 20, He says that it builds us up on our most holy faith. As we faithfully spend time praying in tongues, our lives begin to be transformed. The Word of God begins to come alive as we place our spirit, the "candle of the Lord" (Prov. 20:27), in the hands of the expert Illuminator.

We need to understand the One to whom the Father turned us over for our instruction — the One to whom we can lend our spirit in prayer. Remember, it is the third Person of the Trinity Himself, the Holy Spirit of promise, who has filled us.

We should consider it our privilege and heart's desire to lock ourselves away with the Holy Spirit in prayer. He has no problems or concerns of His own to pray about; He is not the One who needs illumination. Yet He is more than willing to pray through us for all that concerns us. He is eager to teach us and to guide us into all truth (John 16:13).

It doesn't matter what kind of carnal state we are in when we are first born again. It doesn't matter if we've been stealing money, lying, drinking whiskey, or stalking women down dark alleys. When we are baptized in the Holy Spirit, that first simple little gift of speaking in tongues goes into operation for one reason: to edify or build us up. That's why we are not to wait to pray in tongues until we feel sufficiently spiritual.

"But, Brother Roberson, I live a carnal lifestyle." That can change. God wants to bring you from "there to here" — from a life of carnality to a life of freedom and victory. That's why the Holy Spirit came, bringing His supernatural language with Him. No matter how spiritual or unspiritual you may feel, when you start praying in the Holy Ghost, you have begun the edification process.

He Gave Gifts to All Men

So let's go back now to Ephesians 4 to take a closer look at God's design for the working of the Body of

Christ. It will help us understand the role of diversities of tongues in God's government.

(He [Jesus] that descended is the same also that ascended up far above all heavens, that he might fill all things.)

And he gave some, apostles; and some, prophets; and some, evangelists; and some, pastors and teachers;

For the perfecting of the saints, for the work of the ministry, for the edifying of the body of Christ:

Till we all come in the unity of the faith, and of the knowledge of the Son of God, unto a perfect man, unto the measure of the stature of the fulness of Christ.

— Ephesians 4:10-13

During the '80s, I sat under a lot of teaching on this passage of Scripture. This is how I was taught: Jesus ascended on high, and He gave the fivefold ministry offices as a gift to the Church. For what purpose? For the perfecting of the saints so that each and every believer can do the work of the ministry, which then brings edification to the Body of Christ.

Does this interpretation sound familiar? Well, I'll tell you what this teaching did for us ministers: Almost everywhere we went to minister, the congregations treated us as if we were the President of the United States!

I must admit that I didn't mind riding the wave of all that glory, especially in my more carnal early years. I enjoyed the fire out of it! At camp meetings, we ministers would be introduced something like this: "Jesus ascended on high, led captivity captive, and gave gifts unto men. And now let's welcome one of those gifts to the Body of Christ — evangelist and teacher Dave Roberson!"

Somewhere deep inside, a thought lurked that I didn't even articulate to myself: *You poor little peasants. I was singled out as a special gift to you for your maturing so you could do the work of the ministry for the edifying of the Body of Christ. But the whole reason you're being edified and matured is the great gift that resides down on the inside of me.* I began to think I was something special. (Thank God, since then He has healed me of that unhealthy attitude!)

I could always tell which churches had received the governmental teaching on "gifts to the Body of Christ," because I was always treated very respectfully in those churches. For instance, I have had a Rolls Royce assigned to me for my transportation and a man put on duty in the room next to mine just in case I got a whim at two o'clock in the morning for an ice cream cone! I would be lying to you if I said I didn't like that kind of treatment.

But some of us ministers began to expect that kind of special treatment as our God-given right. If everything in the hotel room wasn't just right, we wanted to complain. "Where is my 'super-duper' fruit basket? Where is the guy who is supposed to be in the next room, just waiting to drive me to the meeting?" I can remember feeling insulted if the host church didn't have a car parked in front immediately after the service so I could go out and get in it!

My wife was the first one to really recognize my wrong attitude. We were ministering at a big camp meeting in Omaha, Nebraska, with several big-name ministers. I was the "low man on the totem pole," so I was given the afternoon services — the time when most people want to eat and nap between meetings. But I didn't mind, even though most of the other guest ministers never attended my meetings.

Then God began moving mightily in those afternoon services. The man in charge came to me and said, "We would like you to receive the offerings at every service." So from then on at every service, I would get up and teach a little from the Word and then receive the offering. But the minister scheduled to preach never came into the service until after the offering was taken. It was starting to bother me.

One evening Rosalie and I were riding in the elevator, and someone attending the camp meeting spouted out to me above the heads of the people, "Boy, the other ministers ought to hear you teach!"

I replied sourly, "Yeah, if they hung around long enough, they would." My wife caught the prideful attitude behind my response and took me to task about it later.

But, you see, the teaching I was receiving on God's government wasn't helping my attitude. Every time I heard Ephesians 4 taught that way, my head would get a little fatter as I became a little more convinced that I was a special gift to the Body.

Thank God, if we keep praying in the Holy Ghost and speaking mysteries to the Father, He will straighten us out!

God sent me for a long run on a short rope and jerked the slack out of me regarding my wrong, prideful attitude. He revealed to my spirit the role that the other operations — including diversities of tongues — play in His government. I was so shocked when I first understood what He was saying. I said, "Oh, Lord, You weren't exalting us ministers at all!"

You see, it's good to give honor where honor is due and to show respect to a minister of the Gospel. But if you think that his calling is more honored than yours, think again. God is no respector of persons. You are also a precious gift to the Body of Christ! Whatever your calling or office, it is every bit as important as a minister's calling in God's eyes. You should be treated with just as much respect as any minister is shown.

So what *is* Paul saying in Ephesians 4:10-12? Well, to understand that, you have to look back at First Corinthians 12:27 and 28, where Paul says something very similar. First he says, **Now ye are the body of Christ, and members in particular.** Compare that with Ephesians 4:7: **But unto EVERY ONE OF US is given grace according to the measure of the gift of Christ.**

So in context, Paul is referring to the entire Body of Christ in First Corinthians 12:27. Then in verse 28, Paul says, **And God hath set some in the church....** He goes on to list all eight operations of God. Just as in Ephesians 4:11, he begins with the fivefold ministry. Then he goes on to list helps, governments, and diversities of tongues.

You see, when Jesus ascended on high, He presented His shed blood to the Father for the redemption of mankind, sat down at the right hand of the Father, and said, "It is finished." Then He began to fill all in all — the entire Body of Christ — with His gifts.

Three Categories of Gifts
For Three Purposes

Now let's look at the divine sequence found in First Corinthians 12:28. We know that Jesus only ascended on high once and gave gifts unto men. But for the sake of teaching you how First Corinthians 12:28 ties in to Ephesians 4:11, let's just say that, hypothetically speaking, Jesus ascended on high in three different phases — one time for each of three categories of gifts.

The first time, Jesus grabbed a handful of fivefold ministry gifts and threw them down into the Body of Christ. A whole group of people stood up to receive the gifts.

One said, "My gosh, I'm an apostle to the Body!" Another said, "I am separated to the office of the prophet." Someone else said, "I'm called to be an evangelist." Others exclaimed, "The gift of teaching has landed on me!" or "I'm called to be a pastor!" Those who were called to these ministry offices stood up, recognized their calling, and said, "We have received grace for this."

For what purpose did He give these ministry offices? He gave them for the perfecting, or the maturing, of the saints (Eph. 4:12). Those in the fivefold ministry are supposed to supply the Body of Christ with the revelation knowledge they receive from the Lord. They are to minister the Word of God to bring the saints from spiritual milk to strong meat. In this way, the saints can mature until their transformation is complete.

Then let's say Jesus looked the Body over and said, "The fivefold ministry offices are not enough for the smooth operation of the Body of Christ. I must ascend and grab another handful."

So in this hypothetical illustration, He ascended on high a second time. He grabbed another handful of gifts and threw them down into the Body. This time thousands upon thousands of people stood up and said, "Why, I'm called to helps!" or "I've received the gift of governments." And to these, Jesus said, "Good for you! I have given you your grace, and it is just as much a gift to My Church as the apostle or prophet."

And what do helps and governments do in the Body of Christ? They fulfill the second purpose listed in Ephesians 4:12: They do the work of the ministry.

But as Jesus looked the Body over one more time, He said, "It isn't enough. My people still have to learn to operate out of My Spirit." So He ascended one more time to finish equipping the Body of Christ. This time He grabbed the eighth operation of God — diversities of tongues — and threw it into the entire Body of Christ.

Every person in the Body should have stood up and received this gift. Why? Because the most important manifestation of the diversities of tongues is the direct operation of the Holy Spirit within the believer's spirit to edify himself.

That is the purpose that this one operation fulfills: It is given for the edification of the saints — until what happens? Until we all come into the unity of the faith. Until we quit being deceived by the cunning craftiness of men. Until we fulfill our call, speaking the truth in love.

Every one of us is supposed to receive this operation, because if we are ever going to come into the unity of the faith, we must learn how to release the power of the Holy Spirit, our Teacher who dwells inside of us. He is more than willing to pray hour after hour in divine secrets and mysteries before the Father to help us prepare spiritually for the operation to which God separated us at our rebirth.

So when Jesus ascended on high, He gave three categories of gifts for three separate purposes: the fivefold ministry for the maturing of the saints; helps and governments for the work of the ministry; and diversities of tongues for the edifying of the Body of Christ (*see* chart on page 79). These three categories were given so that we would all come into the unity of the faith and the fullness of the knowledge of the Son of God (Eph. 4:13).

Attaining the Unity of the Faith

The devil has tried to utterly confuse the Church regarding the subject of tongues. He wants us to get so discouraged that we just quit using this divine gift.

Yet of the three categories of gifts given unto men, God designated an entire category to one lone operation, the diversities of tongues! That one operation holds a third of the categories that it takes to bring the Body of Christ into the unity of the faith. (Think about that the next time someone tells you it doesn't do any

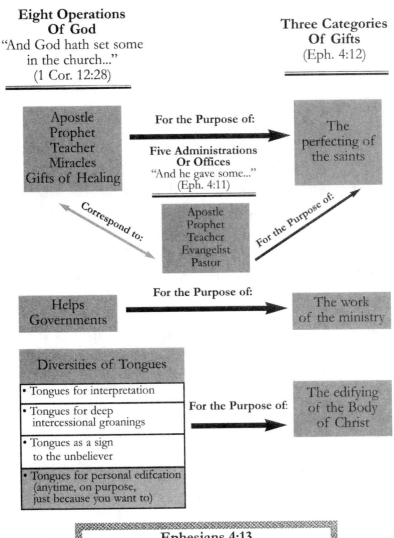

Ephesians 4:8

"He ascended up on high, he led captivity captive, and gave gifts unto men."

Eight Operations Of God
"And God hath set some in the church..."
(1 Cor. 12:28)

Three Categories Of Gifts
(Eph. 4:12)

Apostle
Prophet
Teacher
Miracles
Gifts of Healing

For the Purpose of:

Five Administrations Or Offices
"And he gave some..."
(Eph. 4:11)

The perfecting of the saints

Correspond to:

Apostle
Prophet
Teacher
Evangelist
Pastor

For the Purpose of:

Helps
Governments

For the Purpose of:

The work of the ministry

Diversities of Tongues

• Tongues for interpretation

• Tongues for deep intercessional groanings

• Tongues as a sign to the unbeliever

• Tongues for personal edifcation (anytime, on purpose, just because you want to)

For the Purpose of:

The edifying of the Body of Christ

Ephesians 4:13

"Till we all come in the unity of the faith."

good to pray in tongues or that you can pray too much in tongues!)

Therefore, it would behoove us to find out from His Word the important role this operation is to play in our lives. The truth is, if all we ever fulfilled in the Body of Christ was the eighth operation of diversities of tongues, we would still be a gift to the Body of Christ for the edification of the saints. But no matter what other operation we are called by God to fulfill, we have access to this third category and the edification it provides as we pray in the Holy Ghost.

Yet despite the importance God places on diversities of tongues, many in the Body of Christ want to downplay or even exclude it. But if the category Jesus gave for the edifying of the saints is excluded, how are we ever going to come into the unity of the faith?

It takes all three categories of gifts fulfilling all three purposes listed in Ephesians 4:12 for the Body of Christ to arrive at the place of unity God intended. And as each "measure of the gift of Christ" fulfills his or her call, the Body of Christ will begin to stand up **...unto the measure of the stature of the fulness of Christ** (Eph. 4:13).

Why is all this necessary? Ephesians 4:14 and 15 tells us:

> **That we henceforth be no more children, tossed to and fro, and carried about with every wind of doctrine, by the sleight of men, and cunning craftiness, whereby they lie in wait to deceive;**

But speaking the truth in love, may grow up into him in all things, which is the head, even Christ.

Isn't it interesting why we need these gifts that Jesus gave unto men? We need them so we won't be deceived by the cunning craftiness of men. We also need them so we can be purged of all lying and start speaking the truth. When we are speaking the truth in purity of spirit and we're not being deceived anymore, we can then start the qualification process for our calling — the empowerment of spiritual gifts.

Keep on praying, saith the Spirit of Grace,
    and entering into Me,
And I'll deliver things to you.
It will cause you and your loved ones
    to be set free.
Just release Me, saith the Lord,
And you'll soon see
    that when I move in My power,
    I can set people free.

Chapter 5

The Four Basic Diversities Of Tongues

When I first became a Christian and then subsequently received the gift of speaking in tongues, I was taught that I could *only* pray "in the Spirit" when a strong unction of the Holy Spirit overpowered me and drove me to nearly shout in tongues. I later learned that this is not so.

The truth is, not much is taught on the diversities of tongues because within the Church, not much understanding exists regarding the workings of the Spirit.

The operations of the Spirit cannot be understood with the natural mind. For instance, it is foolishness to the natural mind to think that speaking in a language that neither you nor anyone else understands will not only edify you and enlighten you to the things of God, but will launch you into fulfilling your divine call.

The Different Supernatural Flows of Tongues

So let's explore further this little-understood eighth operation of God. The word "diversities" simply means *differences*. Therefore, the terms "divers tongues" and "diversities of tongues" tell us there are different supernatural flows or manifestations of tongues.

The reason the church world is so confused over the subject of tongues is that believers generally try to impose the same set of rules on all the different operations or manifestations of tongues. To do so causes mass confusion among believers and misuses the gifts of the Spirit so that instead of being drawn to Jesus, the world doesn't even want what we have to offer.

Although many diversifications of tongues occur as the Spirit wills, four basic manifestations are outlined in the Word:

1. *Tongues for personal edification* (1 Cor. 14:4)

   This is the supernatural language the Holy Spirit prays through us that we can use to pray hour after hour as we desire. It accompanies the baptism in the Holy Spirit.

2. *Tongues for interpretation* (1 Cor. 14:5)

   This manifestation of tongues is normally presented in a public assembly, accompanied by interpretation by the same or another person.

3. *Tongues of deep intercessional groanings* (Rom. 8:26)

   This diversification of tongues empowers the believers to stand in the gap for their own lives, their families, their church, their city, their nation, etc. God may also call on them to intercede for someone or for some situation that is totally unknown to them.

4. *Tongues as a sign to the unbeliever* (1 Cor. 14:22)

This is the phenomenon that took place on the Day of Pentecost (Acts 2:4-11). It occurs when the Holy Spirit transcends the intellect and all language barriers by empowering a believer to preach, teach, or testify about Christ in some language of men of which the believer himself has no knowledge.

The rules that govern the operation of tongues for personal edification are as different as night and day from the rules that govern tongues for interpretation. For that matter, the rules governing the deep intercessional groanings of the Spirit are completely different from either one of the other two manifestations of tongues. And the diversity of tongues that presents itself as a sign to the unbeliever has very different rules from the other three!

Of these four different manifestations of tongues, two are designed to be used in the individual prayer life of a believer: tongues for personal edification and tongues that extend into the deep intercessional groanings of the Holy Spirit. The other two, tongues for interpretation and tongues as a sign to the unbeliever, are normally for use in public assembly. As a believer begins to understand and yield to these four different manifestations of the diversities of tongues, it will completely transform his life.

Tongues for Personal Edification

The most common, yet perhaps the most unique, manifestation of diversities of tongues is *tongues for personal edification*. This is the prayer language each of us receives when we are filled with the Holy Ghost.

It is used by God to transfer divine secrets and mysteries from His Spirit to ours.

In my earlier hypothetical illustration, Jesus ascended on high the third time to gather armfuls of the diversities of tongues. Then He threw that operation into the Body of Christ, and every believer received the potential for tongues for personal edification. If any believer will step out and receive that gift by faith, it is his.

Tongues for personal edification is the most basic foundational operation of God, because it is designed by God to do for you what no preacher or teacher can do. It edifies you by building into your spirit godly traits such as love, divine insight into God's Word, and wisdom to know right from wrong and truth from falsehood.

You see, a teacher can tell us that we should walk in love, but he can't give us the strength to do it. That strength comes only from our reborn human spirit, and praying in tongues provides the means by which the Holy Spirit can build that strength into our spirit.

Praying in tongues is as supernatural as raising the dead, because it doesn't originate with you. The source of both the raising of the dead and this supernatural language is the power of the Holy Spirit. The only difference is the availability of the gift.

You see, all nine gifts of the Spirit, the first seven operations of God as listed in First Corinthians 12:28, and three of the four diversities of tongues are all given as the Holy Spirit wills. But there is one diversity of tongues that you can operate at will — anytime you want to, as long as you want to — immediately after being filled with the Holy Ghost, and that is tongues for personal edification.

I wish I could operate in the mighty working of miracles or the discerning of spirits anytime I wanted to. But I cannot, because all the gifts of the Spirit flow through me severally as He wills for the edification of other people.

But there's one simple gift that flows to me to build me up and edify me. God has done with this simple gift what He has done with no other, because He has made me the steward of my own edification.

It is a remarkable truth that we have been given stewardship of the operation of this simple gift called tongues. Now with our own free will, we determine how much or how little we want to be edified by allowing the Holy Spirit to pray through us.

Anytime we want to pray in tongues, all we have to do is reach out momentarily with our faith. The Holy Spirit will immediately respond and begin to create that supernatural language down on the inside of our spirit. And He will continue to do so hour after hour, as long as we want to stay in the prayer closet. We could pray for twelve hours, and it would do nothing but permanently benefit us in our climb toward becoming qualified for God's call on our lives.

You see, contrary to what some people say, praying in tongues does not make us strange. Any kind of prayer within the guidelines of Scripture can do nothing but exalt the Word of God within us. Remember, the Spirit and the Word are one (1 John 5:7).

Praying in the Spirit never takes away from the Word. Instead, it builds up our spirit by giving us greater understanding of the revelation knowledge already contained within the Word. Why? Because as the Holy Spirit prays through us, He is always in total agreement with the Word.

Therefore, it is absolutely impossible to pray too much in the Holy Ghost. Tongues for personal edification does nothing but enhance the working of the Word on the inside of us, causing us to receive and walk in more of God's power as we become more yielded to Him.

So after receiving this first diversity through the baptism of the Holy Spirit, we begin our climb into the spiritual qualifications for any or all of the other seven operations of God. As we pray in tongues for our own personal edification, the Holy Spirit releases the Father's perfect plan for us. The Spirit of God is certainly the One most able to qualify us for that plan.

As we pray in tongues, the Holy Spirit prays through our spirit for needs in our lives that we aren't even aware of. You see, God knows what lies in the deepest recesses of our being, and He through the Holy Spirit prays for us.

In this edification process, spiritual authority grows and our faith is built up. We can reach the place where so much authority is released as we line up against the devil and bind him in Jesus' Name that our commands of faith literally shake the enemy's kingdom.

But we aren't going to cause the devil's kingdom to crumble and fall when our faith is still shaken over a credit card balance that we can't pay! That's a lesson that even the prophet Elijah had to learn. After defeating the prophets of Baal on Mount Carmel, he sat and whined under the juniper tree that the evil Queen Jezebel was going to take his life until God dealt with him and got him back into faith (1 Kings 18 and 19).

God has created a place of peace that we can enter into in prayer. This is the place where we can "count it all joy" when we fall into different temptations, tests, and trials (James 1:2). Why can we do that? Because we have grown in our spiritual authority, building up ourselves on our most holy faith by praying in the Holy Ghost (Jude 20). We have begun to learn how to change circumstances arrayed against us rather than to have circumstances rule over us.

Tongues for personal edification also develops our character, which is of utmost importance. God requires holiness, because His power operating through unholy character will eventually destroy the vessel through which the power flows.

I once prayed for a little girl in a service who greatly needed a creative miracle but didn't instantly receive one. I was bitterly disappointed, knowing that God wanted to see that little girl whole. After the service, I went to my hotel room perplexed and sad, asking God why no miracle had occurred.

The Lord told me that He cared for both the little girl and for me. He said that until my character was further developed in Him, He had to withhold the kind of power necessary to cause that kind of creative miracle. If I had received that level of His power at my level of spiritual maturity, it would have destroyed me.

Until there is nothing more important to us than seeking first God's Kingdom and His righteousness, His power will do us little good. As we mature in Him, we will become more and more of an asset to Him. Tongues for personal edification is the only diversity of tongues that we can operate "on purpose," just because we want to, in order to arrive at that mature state.

Tongues for Interpretation

Tongues for interpretation occurs when a message is given in an unknown tongue and then interpreted in our native language as a divine message to the church body. We cannot operate in tongues for interpretation anytime we choose. Some people claim to be able to do that, but I know from experience that I cannot. I know when that particular gift of the Spirit comes upon me. It is different than when I pray in tongues for edification.

Many times I have desired to operate in this diversity of tongues at will, but that doesn't mean I can make it happen. I can pray or ask God that I might interpret, but that doesn't mean I will always be able to do it.

There will be times when God slides us into interpretation when we are praying in the Spirit. However, we cannot operate in interpretation just because we want to.

Tongues
Of Deep Intercessional Groanings

Tongues of deep intercessional groanings is another diversity that God moves us into as we allow Him to transform us into the image of His Son. It is the third main diversity of tongues. Again, it cannot be generated by our own will.

We can pray in our understanding and intercede for those we know. For example, if I know that one of my sons is going to a job interview, I can pray in my understanding for favor and wisdom as he meets his prospective employer and answers his questions.

However, if the devil has laid plans to take his life by having a semi-truck flatten his small car on the way to the interview, I have no foreknowledge of that. It is during a time like this that the Holy Spirit will draw me into intercession with deep groanings. I don't know how to pray, but He does.

If we are yielded to God, the Holy Spirit will lead us into intercession for those in our family, in our circle of friends, and even for those we may have never met.

God has called us to be people who will ask for bread on behalf of another. In Luke 11:5-8, Jesus has just finished teaching His disciples the Lord's Prayer. In this passage of Scripture, He continues to teach without changing the subject of prayer.

And he said unto them, Which of you shall have a friend, and shall go unto him at midnight, and say unto him, Friend, lend me three loaves;

For a friend of mine in his journey is come to me, and I have nothing to set before him?

And he from within shall answer and say, Trouble me not: the door is now shut, and my children are with me in bed; I cannot rise and give thee.

I say unto you, Though he will not rise and give him, because he is his friend, yet because of his importunity he will rise and give him as many as he needeth.

In intercession, we become the man in the middle, asking bread for a friend. We are the one who stands in the gap. We aren't asking for ourselves. If the friend hadn't come to our home, we would be asleep because we had no needs. We are a go-between for the needs of our friend. This by definition is an intercessor.

Many pastors and teachers who have realized that this passage of Scripture teaches something about intercession often label the man behind the door as a type of God. However, this isn't so. The man behind the door is a picture of you and me in our fleshly nature. It is a man with wrong attitudes that Jesus could then directly contrast with what God is really like.

The man behind the door isn't like God, because he doesn't want to give the bread to his friend. But we know from Luke 11:13 that God is more than willing to give us anything we ask for:

If ye then, being evil, know how to give good gifts unto your children: how much more shall your heavenly Father give the Holy Spirit to them that ask him?

So as we yield ourselves to the Holy Spirit, allowing Him to use us in deep intercession for our unsaved loved ones, friends, and fellow Christians, God will answer our prayers.

We have to realize that although our mind may not understand, we are producing results as we intercede. Our Heavenly Father is more willing to flow through our intercessory prayer than we are willing to receive that particular manifestation of tongues. He is willing to give us bread on behalf of others.

First John 5:16 says that if we see a brother sin a sin that is not unto death, we can ask God to give us life for him:

> **If any man see his brother sin a sin which is not unto death, he** [the man who saw his brother] **shall ask, and he** [God] **shall give him life for them that sin not unto death. There is a sin unto death: I do not say that he shall pray for it.**

That scripture really didn't make a lot of sense to me for a long time. I thought I understood that the only way to receive God's forgiveness is to confess our sin and repent. When we say, "God forgive me," He does forgive.

It seemed strange to me that someone else could sin, and I could ask for his forgiveness. I came to understand that if a person does me wrong and I ask God to forgive him, God will forgive him for his offense against me. However, if the person harbors other sin in his life, he will still have to go to God himself.

For example, if you are walking in unforgiveness, you will have to deal with God yourself. However, I can make intercession for you until the devil's hold is broken and you make the necessary decision to come to God and take care of the problem.

Thank God that He will use us to intercede for those who sin a sin that isn't unto death. He will cause us to stand in the gap, taking authority against the works of darkness in our brother's life.

Jesus Himself said, **Greater love hath no man than this, that a man lay down his life for his friends** (John 15:13). If you are willing to be used not only to stand in the gap, but to stand against what the enemy will try to throw at you, God will use you.

For example, my associate in the ministry once became deathly ill. I was on vacation at the time and was unaware of his life-and-death struggle. Yet although I didn't know about the situation, the Holy Spirit prayed through me for a full day in heavy intercessional groanings.

I was experienced enough to know that I was in a crucial battle in the spiritual realm. But I had no idea that the crisis was so close to home. I found out later that the hour I began to sense a release and a lifting of the burden, his fever lifted and the horrible pain began to subside.

The Holy Spirit is faithful, and He knows what to pray for even when we don't! What a priceless gift from the Father!

However, it is important to understand that a person cannot slip into the deep groanings of intercession anytime he wants to. Some people think they can, so they try to groan out of emotions. But there is a difference between that kind of fleshly manipulation and an honest heart saying, "God, I just want to stand in the gap for this situation."

In the latter case, God will often slip that intercessor between hell and the people who are trying to get there or between Satan and the people the enemy is trying to steal from and destroy.

When God puts you in that place of intercession, your heart cries out, "If you are going to hell, you'll have to go around me to get there!" And many times, those you're praying for would have reached that destination, except that you were in the way and they couldn't get past you!

Another fact we must realize is that God loves you just as much as the people for whom He wants you to intercede. And He knows that when He slips you into true intercession to stand in the gap, you are going to attract the power of hell. The devil will come against you because you are blocking his plans for those people's destruction.

You must be in a place of strength so you can stand up to the devil's onslaught. Jesus said that the man who digs deeply into the Word of God is like a man who dug deeply until he found rock and then built his house upon that rock. When the rains came and the floods washed around the house, the house wouldn't fall because it stood on the rock (Matt. 7:24-27).

We won't fall if we are established on the rock of doing God's Word. The storms will come, and the enemy will attack those who are standing in the gap. But Jesus said that the devil isn't powerful enough to cause the fall of one whose house is built on the rock of doing God's Word.

Tongues as a Sign to the Unbeliever

When I was young in the Lord, I thought "tongues as a sign to the unbeliever" occurred during those wild

Pentecostal services my church sometimes had in my ultra-Holiness days.

But I reconsidered my conclusion after witnessing many variations of this scenario: Someone brings a visitor to church. The visitor is just sitting there, taking in the service. Suddenly, Sister Chicken Walker jumps up and starts screaming in tongues while jerking her head like a hen looking for kernels of corn on the ground!

"What's wrong with that woman?" the visitor asks.

"Oh, the Holy Ghost came on her; she's just being blessed."

Later on in the service, someone asks the visitor, "Would you like to be filled with the Holy Ghost?"

"Oh, no," he says. "I have neck trouble. I don't know if I could survive being blessed by the Holy Ghost!"

I finally came to realize that tongues aren't a sign to the unbeliever unto salvation in that kind of situation; they are a sign that makes unbelievers think Christians are crazy!

So I began asking God, "When *are* tongues a sign to the unbeliever?"

The Lord showed me the answer to that question as I gained some experience in the ministry. Now I can tell you exactly when tongues are a sign to the unbeliever: when the Holy Spirit transcends your intellect, empowering you to speak, preach, or teach in any language on the face of this earth of which you have no previous knowledge.

For instance, if I were preaching in an Indian village and my translator suddenly died and went home to be with Jesus, I would have a choice of believing for a major or a minor miracle. I could choose the major miracle and grab him by the shirt, jerk him upright, and say, "Nobody gets out of my service that easy! Return to life — you have a job to do!" Or I could ask the ushers to carry the interpreter out and hope that the Holy Spirit chooses to move upon me, enabling me to preach the rest of the message in the people's dialect.

The latter miracle, my friend, happens only as the Holy Spirit wills and is an example of tongues as a sign to the unbeliever. To date, this particular diversity of tongues has happened in my ministry nineteen times. For example, I've preached in an Indian dialect, in French, in Spanish, in Arabic, and in German. Each time I had no idea what I was saying.

The first time it occurred, I was a guest on a Christian talk show in San Jose, California. Somewhere in the midst of the interview, the host asked me, "Brother Roberson, what has most changed your life up to this time?"

Well, I had just had a profound experience in my walk with the Lord that had made the love of God very real to me. So I answered, "My friend, it's the love of God. It has so changed me..."

All of a sudden before I knew what was going on, tongues started rolling out from deep inside of me. I could have stopped them, but the unction was so strong, I sensed that I needed to let that supernatural language flow out of me.

Then I panicked, thinking, *This station is half-owned by a secular company! I don't even know if speaking in tongues on the program is legal!*

I glanced over at my host. He didn't act as if he was going to stop me. I thought, *It's okay, because when I get through speaking with tongues, God will give me the interpretation.* But when I finished speaking, I just sat there looking at the camera. No interpretation came, and I couldn't interpret the message in tongues just because I wanted to.

I thought, *What do I do now? Lord, don't fail me now!*

We completed the program, acting as if nothing had happened. Everyone was ignoring the incident. But as I stepped off the set, a woman came running over to me. A German immigrant from the old country, she said to me with a broken German accent, "Brother Roberson, Brother Roberson! How long have you been speaking accented German from the old country?"

"Ma'am, excuse me," I replied, "but I barely speak English from the new country!"

"Then you know not what has happened," she said.

"What has happened?" I asked.

The woman explained, "Suddenly you stopped speaking in English, and you began to address the German community in perfect accented German from the old country!"

Dumbfounded, I said, "I didn't know that's what I was doing!"

She continued, "A German woman who lives in Sacramento just called our hot line, and since I'm the only German telephone counselor, I talked to her.

"This woman was dying of a terminal disease, and you told her what to do in German. She obeyed your instructions and then fell under God's power in her living room. When she got up, she was absolutely healed! She called us to testify of the miracle that had taken place. You know not what has happened, Brother Roberson!"

I replied, "No, but if I'm the last one to find out about this one more time, I'm going to ask God for a raise!"

The next time this phenomenon of tongues as a sign to the unbeliever occurred in my ministry was in Anaheim, California. While ministering in a service, I called out a little Catholic Spanish woman sitting on the edge of the aisle. I began telling her by revelation what was wrong with her body.

This woman was a very reverent Catholic who spoke almost no English. To her, I was a man of the cloth, a man of God. So although she didn't understand what I was saying as I told her what was wrong with her body, she would respond to everything I said, "Sì, man of God. Sì, man of God."

Then suddenly tongues burst out from my spirit. I wasn't surprised, because tongues for interpretation often manifests when I am ministering to someone. Then the interpretation comes immediately afterward to help me know how to minister accurately to the individual.

But this time before I could even listen for an interpretation, this little bitty Spanish woman said something back to me in another language! When she finished speaking, tongues rolled up out of my spirit again. Then the Spanish woman said, "Ahhh!" and fell down on the floor under the power of God.

I thought, *Hmmmm, I guess she's healed!*

Later that night, I was eating at a Chinese restaurant when one of my staff members caught up with me. "You know that Spanish woman who got healed at tonight's meeting?" he asked.

"Yes," I said.

"Well, I talked to some of the church members, and they said you don't realize what happened. She doesn't speak English."

"Yes, I know that," I replied.

"But did you know that you suddenly began to tell her everything that was wrong with her in Spanish? And when you paused for a moment, she asked you a question in Spanish — which you then answered in Spanish!"

"I did?" I asked, amazed.

"That's what they told me," the staff member said.

"That's it," I said. "If I'm the last one to find out about this one more time, I am *really* going to ask God for a raise!"

I'll tell you one more example of this diversity of tongues from my own experience. This time the manifestation came in a different way.

I was holding a meeting in Florida, preaching up a storm. But I noticed that every time I made a statement of revelation knowledge, a man about three rows from the front would bend over and whisper to the man next to him. My righteous indignation began to get stirred up; I was getting irritated!

I thought, *If they're going to interrupt the service, the least they could do is sit in back!*

Somewhere in the middle of my message, the two men stopped whispering to each other, which helped me concentrate. God performed all kinds of miracles that night. After the service, I was in the back room recovering when the pastor came in to talk to me.

She said, "Did you notice those two men who were whispering to each other during the service?"

"Yes," I replied. "They talked about a third of the way through the message and then stopped."

"Well, one of them only speaks French. He brought his own translator so he could enjoy the service."

I thought, *Uh, oh.* But just as I started to feel badly for my irritation with the two men, the pastor interrupted my thoughts.

"This Frenchman said that one third of the way through the service, you stopped preaching in English and started to preach in French."

"But I didn't preach in French!" I protested.

"Well, he says you did."

"Okay," I said. "Have someone ask the Frenchman who can't speak English what I preached in French."

Someone talked to the man and found out I had preached the exact same message in French that I had preached in English!

Now, it's one thing for the Holy Ghost to move through you and inspire you to preach what He wants you to preach. But it's another thing for the Holy Spirit to take the message you received by revelation and translate it for you into French. That means your revelation is right on! (And the message I was preaching that night is the same one I am discussing in this chapter!)

Now, I wish I could move in the deep intercessional groanings of the Spirit or tongues for interpretation anytime I want to. But I cannot, for these diversities of tongues manifest severally as the Holy Spirit wills. I wish that I could operate in tongues as a sign to the unbeliever anytime I decided to, but I cannot. It manifests only as He wills and moves upon me. There is only one diversity of tongues that I can operate at my own will, and that is tongues for personal edification.

Do All Speak With Tongues?

Now that you understand the four basic diversities of tongues, you can better understand what Paul was talking about in First Corinthians 12:29 and 30 when he asks several questions. He starts out by asking, **Are all apostles? are all prophets? are all teachers? are all workers of miracles?** (v.29). The correct answer to all these questions is, "Of course not."

Who are these "workers of miracles" that Paul is talking about? They are those who operate in the working of miracles, one of the gifts of the Spirit that qualifies the fivefold offices.

No, not everyone is called to have that gift of the Spirit operating in their lives to the extent that it qualifies them for the fivefold ministry. But everyone in the Body of Christ *is* called to fulfill the commission of the believer found in Mark 16:16-18: to speak with new tongues, lay hands on the sick and see them recover, and cast out devils. And at times, as the Spirit wills, that does include the working of miracles!

Some examples of fivefold ministers who have been qualified by the Spirit in the working of miracles include William Branham, George Jeffreys, Maria Woodworth-Etter, and Kathryn Kuhlman. Each of these ministers of the Gospel stood in an office ordained of God that was empowered by a certain blend of the nine gifts of the Spirit.

So when Paul asks, "Are all workers of miracles?" the answer is no. Then in verse 30, he goes on to ask, **Have all the gifts of healing?** [No, of course not.] **do all speak with tongues? do all interpret?**

At one time I wished Paul had left out the question about tongues. In fact, a lot of people who don't believe in speaking in tongues in this day and age use this verse as an argument for their case.

The last time I encountered someone who did that was at a wedding. Without meaning to, I locked horns with a fiery grandma. She got right up in my face and asked, "What faith are you?" She was concerned because I was the minister marrying her grandson to his bride.

I mentioned the names of a few well-known preachers of the time, thinking the grandma would recognize them. She had not heard of any of them. So I asked her if she had heard of a certain denomination. She said, "Oh, yes, the Charismatic people. You're one of those. Well, you have your place."

I asked, "What do you mean, Ma'am?"

She explained what she had learned through her church background. She had been taught that according to First Corinthians 12:28 and 29, God placed some in the Body as apostles, prophets, and teachers, but that not all are called to each office.

Then she got to First Corinthians 12:30: **Have all the gifts of healing? do all speak with tongues? do all interpret?** I asked her, "Well, do all speak with tongues?"

She answered, "No, it's listed right here with all the other offices. Everyone isn't supposed to speak with tongues." It was her understanding that we are all called to our special unique place in the part of the Body in which we feel comfortable.

I said, "No, Ma'am, we are called to the same Body. It is men who have brought divisions."

"Well, then," she replied, "why does it say, 'Do all speak with tongues?' Paul wouldn't have asked that question if we were all supposed to speak with tongues!"

I must admit I had no answer for that little grandma at the time. And as I said, I thought it would have been better if Paul had left that question out of the verse. But he didn't, so eventually I had to deal with it.

I finally noticed the next question Paul asks in verse 30: "Do all interpret?" and realized that Paul was talking about *the second diversity of tongues, tongues for interpretation.* He was *not* referring to the gift of tongues for our own personal edification.

So Paul is asking, "Do all operate in tongues and interpretation in a public assembly?" The answer is a definite no. Not everyone is called to operate in that diversity of tongues. But all *are* called by God to speak with tongues for personal edification, which is the number-one diversity of tongues.

Those who will obey Me and hear My voice
    are those whom I will take
    from glory to glory.
But remember, your time is not the way
    I gauge time,
    for My time is eternal.
I will wait as long as necessary,
    but your time is placed within the time span
    of men and women.

Sometimes there were those
    who spent their lives in prayer
    and then others harvested from their labor.
But as you desire to see My glory,
    even in your life span I will move this way.
The intensity of seeking Me
    is how you free Me.

Chapter 6

Paul's Source of Revelation

The Apostle Paul actually received from God the blueprint for the foundation of the Early Church. That includes the gifts, offices, and operations of the Spirit in First Corinthians 12 that we already discussed.

The Extent
Of Paul's Revelation Knowledge

As I study the Pauline epistles, I am absolutely amazed to see the extent of detail that God revealed to Paul's spirit regarding the complete foundational structure for the Church.

It becomes obvious that the revelation Paul received is every bit as powerful and detailed as what Moses received on Mount Sinai when God gave Israel the Law. The revelation given to Moses as he stood in God's Presence included not only the Ten Commandments, but the intricacies of the Law in all of its meticulous detail and administration.

With the exception of Jesus, Paul undoubtedly received more direct revelation from God than any man since Moses. Once I realized that, I became fascinated with the search to discover Paul's source of revelation knowledge. I found the answer in the Book of First Corinthians, and now I want to show you how to tap into that same source to receive every good thing God has planned for your life.

You see, Paul didn't receive revelation knowledge just because he was an apostle. He received revelation because he decided for himself to go into God as far as he could go to receive everything God had for him. Jesus said, **For many are called, but few are chosen** (Matt. 22:14). Those who are not only called but chosen make the same decision Paul did.

Paul's Definition of the Carnal Christian

The entire Book of First Corinthians was written to Christians who feed only on the milk, not on the meat, of the Word. Paul classified this kind of Christian as "carnal":

> **And I, brethren, could not speak unto you as unto spiritual, but as unto carnal, even as unto babes in Christ.**
>
> **I have fed you with milk, and not with meat: for hitherto ye were not able to bear it, neither yet now are ye able.**
>
> **— 1 Corinthians 3:1,2**

Paul was saying to the Corinthians, "Look, there are so many things I want to tell you, but I can't. You are carnal. You are not yet able to bear the meat of the Word."

Then Paul went on to write the entire book to what he labeled as the carnal mind — a mind not yet capable of really receiving, discerning, and understanding spiritual matters.

(That's a little scary when you consider how few preachers in the Church actually understand, much less walk in, the "milk" of First Corinthians! No wonder the Church walks in so little of the power of God. No wonder the world looks at most believers as not having the answers it needs.)

Then in First Corinthians 3:3, Paul defined what constitutes carnality:

For ye are yet carnal: for whereas there is among you envying, and strife, and divisions, are ye not carnal, and walk as men?

In other words, Paul was saying, "Do you not walk as mere natural men instead of as those who have received the power of God in a new nature?"

It doesn't take a super-spiritual Christian to understand that if envying, strife, and divisions exist among a group of people, they are walking as carnal men. Who wouldn't accuse someone who walked in envy and strife of being carnal?

God once told me, "Do not hurt people. Do not in any way destroy them — not for any reason." Interestingly, it seems irrelevant to our Heavenly Father what people do to us. He simply said, "Don't hurt *them.*"

The more I attempt to know God, the more I find out that He wants His love, outlined in First Corinthians 13, to be fulfilled in me. That includes thinking no evil and having no regard to the evil done to me. I am also finding that the further I go into the realm of First Corinthians 13, the more peace, confidence, and assurance in my Father I experience.

If we are full of envy and strife, the world labels us as carnal. But if we begin to walk in the maximum degree of love and say, "I will not hurt another man," the world says we are eccentric. That's why we should only want to please Jesus. The world won't be holding our hand on the day of reckoning. We will stand alone before Jesus, accountable for our own actions.

So Paul labeled envyings and strife as carnality. I can understand that. The more kindly we treat people — the more we let God love others through us — the more real His Presence becomes to us.

But notice something else that Paul labeled as carnal in First Corinthians 3:4 and 5. He said we are carnal if we *run after men*:

> **For while one saith, I am of Paul; and another, I am of Apollos; are ye not carnal?**
>
> **Who then is Paul, and who is Apollos, but ministers by whom ye believed, even as the Lord gave to every man?**

In other words, Paul is saying in verse 5: "God gave us our ministry, and because of that ministry you believed unto salvation. But He has given *every man* a ministry." Then in verse 6, Paul goes on to say, **I have planted** [you received salvation through my ministry], **Apollos watered** [he came along to instruct you]; **but GOD GAVE THE INCREASE.**

Only God Can Give the Increase

Paul was trying to get the Corinthian church to look past the ministry of men and to focus on the ministry of the Holy Spirit within them — the only ministry that could actually transform their lives and cause them to walk in the biblical principles that they were learning from their teachers.

Notice the terminology Paul used when he said, "I planted." He was speaking of his apostleship, his proper gift of God. He had pioneered the original ground for the Corinthians.

So Paul was saying, "I came and got you born again. I planted you into God's Kingdom. Later I sent Apollos, and he watered your life by teaching you about faith and your inheritance in God.

"But who are we but men by whom you have heard the Gospel? I can't heal you. I have only my gift from God. I can only preach salvation and healing to you, but God is the One who saves and heals you. Although I have sown and Apollos has watered, it is God who must come and work inside of you to give you the increase."

Then Paul went on through the entire Book of Corinthians to outline many spiritual principles that will take us out of carnality if we apply them to our lives. He dealt with important issues such as brothers in Christ suing one another; marriage problems; the callings, offices, and anointings of the Church; walking in the love of God; the resurrection of the dead; and questions regarding Communion. Although all these issues fall under the category of "the milk of the Word," they still have to be spiritually discerned.

In essence Paul was saying, "All we preachers can do is to lay out these basic principles that are designed to take you out of carnality. But if you won't allow the Holy Spirit's ministry in you to transform you according to the principles you are hearing, we can't do anything about it. That's where our ministry ends."

You Are God's Building

Then in First Corinthians 3:7-11, Paul says this:

So then neither is he that planteth any thing, neither he that watereth; but God that giveth the increase.

Now he that planteth and he that watereth are one: and every man shall receive his own reward according to his own labour.

For we are labourers together with God: ye are God's husbandry, YE ARE GOD'S BUILDING.

According to the grace of God which is given unto me, as a wise masterbuilder, I have laid the foundation, and another buildeth thereon. But let every man take heed how he buildeth thereupon.

For other foundation can no man lay than that is laid, which is Jesus Christ.

What are you? You are one lively stone in a vast spiritual structure called the building of God. As a lively stone, you are called to fulfill a unique ministry as a colaborer in the Body of Christ, always building on the foundation that Paul laid as a wise master builder — the revelation of "Jesus Christ, and Him crucified" (1 Cor. 2:2).

So where does my ministry as a minister of the Gospel end and the Holy Spirit's ministry take over? Well, I can instruct you in your inheritance in God. I can give you an occasional word of wisdom or word of knowledge as the Spirit wills. I can teach you about faith, love, and the anointings of God.

But I cannot give you the anointing and the equipping for your individual call as a lively stone in the building of God. You are going to have to go to God for what no man can give you. It is the Holy Ghost and His personal involvement on the inside of you that brings the increase.

And I'll tell you this: You cannot spend time praying in the Holy Ghost without praying the plan of God and coming forth better equipped for your contribution as a lively stone in His building.

My ministry ends with giving you knowledge. I can sow you into the Kingdom and water you with instruction, but I cannot give you the increase. Only God can give you that.

That's why Paul told the Corinthians, "I have received grace from God to be the master builder. I have received a mystery from God and have laid the foundation of Jesus Christ crucified.

"You may as well know that as you answer God's call and fulfill your ministry, there is no other foundation than the one I have laid. When your life takes shape and you make your contribution to the Body, you become an addition, another layer, to God's building. But you better take heed how you build upon the foundation that I have already preached to you. Why fulfill your ministry in a way that produces only wood, hay, and stubble [1 Cor. 3:12]? Why would you do that when you could go to the Source?"

Discovering Paul's Source Of Revelation Knowledge

Paul wouldn't have called others carnal had he not been able to show them a way out of that carnal state.

117

It wouldn't do Paul any good to reprimand believers for running after men instead of God unless he went on to show them how to personally enter into God's Presence to be transformed and to receive God's increase.

So in the second chapter of First Corinthians, Paul revealed his source of revelation knowledge and of a Christian walk of power — the way out of carnality, envy, and strife.

Remember, this book is directed to the carnal mind of the baby Christian. Paul wanted the baby Christian to learn how to tap into the same source of revelation knowledge he had found. He wanted to encourage Corinthians to take their Christianity beyond a carnal walk of the senses into a vital relationship with God.

Paul was saying, "I can reveal to you my source — where I received the understanding of these divine mysteries. If you can understand what I tell you, you don't have to remain carnal."

Well, personally, I don't want to stay carnal. I want to keep myself in a place of humility where I am qualified to be taught by Paul.

If I can jump into the same spiritual "river" he frequented to receive revelation knowledge, I want to do it, because ministers can only give me so much. They cannot give me an anointing. They can't give me my call. They can teach me about faith and joy and peace, but they cannot give those spiritual treasures to me.

It is Jesus Christ through the power of the Holy Spirit who has given all the gifts and who is all in all. So I'm going to discover the same source Paul went to and learn how to allow God to transform me according to the Word that I've been taught. I'm going back to the second chapter of First Corinthians and jump in!

Paul's Source Revealed

So let's discover Paul's source of revelation knowledge. Then we can go to God ourselves to receive from Him what no man can give us. Notice what Paul said in First Corinthians 2:7 and 8:

> But WE SPEAK THE WISDOM OF GOD IN A MYSTERY, even THE HIDDEN WISDOM, which God ordained before the world unto our glory:
>
> Which none of the princes of this world knew: for had they known it, they would not have crucified the Lord of glory.

When Paul talks about a mystery, he uses the term in the same sense it is used for the legendary detective, Sherlock Holmes. When Holmes solved a mystery, he did so by finding isolated clues that weren't obvious to the casual observer. Then he put them together in such a way that he came to the correct conclusion.

Well, in the case of God's plan of redemption, it was necessary for the Cross to be hidden in God as a mystery. It wasn't as though the clues didn't exist; they are scattered throughout the Old Testament. But the clues weren't obvious enough to solve the mystery of Christ crucified.

Why is that? Because if the princes of this world had known that mystery, they wouldn't have crucified the Lord of glory — and it was necessary for Jesus to die and be raised to life again.

119

This is why Paul said what he did in verse 9 about the Old Testament saints:

> **But as it is written, Eye hath not seen, nor ear heard, neither have entered into the heart of man, the things which God hath prepared for them that love him.**

Then the most incredible thing happens between verses 9 and 10: There is a change of covenants! Look at what First Corinthians 2:10 and 11 says:

> **But GOD HATH REVEALED THEM UNTO US BY HIS SPIRIT: for the Spirit searcheth all things, yea, the deep things of God.**
>
> **For what man knoweth the things of a man, save the spirit of man which is in him? even so the things of God knoweth no man, but the Spirit of God.**

Verses 8 and 9 speak of Jesus Christ crucified; then in verse 10, the Holy Spirit has been given to the Church. The change in covenants has taken place. At this point, Paul begins to reveal his source of knowledge.

Now that Jesus has died for the sins of every person, Paul explains, God wants every person to hear what was once necessarily hidden. These mysteries have now been released in full-scale revelation to the Church, made available to every believer who will yield himself to the Holy Spirit. That's what verse 12 is talking about:

> **Now we have received, not the spirit of the world, but the spirit which is of God; that we might know the things that are freely given to us of God.**

The Holy Spirit came all the way from Heaven to solve the greatest mystery of all time. His commission is to take the wisdom of God — the same wisdom that was hidden in God in a mystery since before the foundation of the world — and reveal it unto us.

The Old Testament saints were only given glimpses into this hidden wisdom.

Receiving the end of your faith, even the salvation of your souls.

Of which salvation the prophets have inquired and searched diligently, who prophesied of the grace that should come unto you:

Searching what, or what manner of time the Spirit of Christ which was in them did signify, when it testified beforehand the sufferings of Christ, and the glory that should follow.

Unto whom it was revealed, that not unto themselves, but unto us they did minister the things, which are now reported unto you by them that have preached the gospel unto you with the Holy Ghost sent down from heaven; which things the angels desire to look into.

1 Peter 1:9-12

But through the ministry of the Holy Spirit, God has purposely revealed the mysteries of His wisdom to every one of us who believe in Jesus. Hebrews 8:11 says that under the New Covenant, we can be directly taught by the Holy Spirit concerning spiritual matters:

And they shall not teach every man his neighbour, and every man his brother, saying, Know the Lord: for all shall know me, from the least to the greatest.

This verse outlines the difference between God's dealings with Israel as a nation under the Law and His dealings with us who have received the Holy Spirit. The Law consisted of the Ten Commandments, various ordinances, and the blood sacrifices.

Under the Old Covenant, people didn't have the recreated nature of the new birth. And since it is impossible for a spiritually dead man to know God, everyone had to be taught to know God through the Law and the sacrifices.

But now we can know God from the least to the greatest, because He wrote His laws in our heart and put them in our mind. He gave us the same Source of revelation knowledge He gave Paul: the Holy Spirit, who searches the deep things of God with the intention of revealing them to us.

The Link Between Tongues
And Revelation Knowledge

But what did Paul do that was so different from anyone else who was filled with the Holy Spirit in his day? Other apostles were called; they had the same Holy Ghost. What caused Paul to be more equipped and gave him access to more revelation knowledge than any other man alive?

In studying and meditating on all the Pauline epistles, I have found a common link between the revelation knowledge that Paul understood and established in his life and something he did.

Paul made this key statement in First Corinthians 14:18: **I thank my God, I SPEAK WITH TONGUES MORE THAN YE ALL.**

Now wait a minute, Paul. Let's get all the Corinthians and line them up for a survey.

"Hello, Father Corinthian, how much are you praying?"

"Oh, on the way to work on my camel."

"Okay. How about you, Mother Corinthian?"

"Well, I pray as I take my bread out of the oven."

"Oh, really."

Paul probably didn't conduct such a survey; nevertheless, he could truthfully say, "I thank God I speak in that supernatural language of edification that encompasses the entire revelation of Jesus Christ more than you all."

Do you think it was a coincidence that, number one, Paul operated in more revelation knowledge than anyone else of his day; and, number two, he prayed in tongues for personal edification more than any other Holy Ghost-filled person in the Corinthian church? No! I can guarantee you it wasn't coincidental.

There is a spiritual link between tongues and revelation knowledge. As I said earlier, tongues is the dividing line between those who walk in the miraculous and those who don't. This also seems to be the dividing line for the reception of revelation knowledge.

Paul prayed in tongues more than any other man, woman, or child in the Corinthian church — probably more than any other man alive in the church world of that day. And Paul was responsible for three-fourths of the revelation knowledge contained in the New Testament that constitutes the foundation of the Church.

Where did Paul get such astounding revelation knowledge? Well, what do you think he was doing as he walked through the wilderness and from city to city? What did he fill his days with during those long hours of travel?

He spent hour after hour after hour communicating the mysteries of Christ before God. And God answered his prayers, bringing him into the fullness of his divine call as the apostle to the Gentiles as He caused the revelation of Christ to be born in his spirit — so much so that Paul orchestrated the entire foundation of the Early Church!

I can just imagine him walking down the dusty road, speaking in tongues. His camel driver asks, "What did you say, Paul?" Paul replies, "I'm not talking to you."

Then at night, Paul pitches his tent and falls asleep. All of a sudden he is awakened. The Holy Spirit is revealing another mystery to him. He grabs his quill and inkwell and starts writing a letter to one of the churches as fast as he can.

God thought so much of Paul's letters that He made them a permanent part of His Word; now we call them the Pauline epistles. Contained within those epistles are divine secrets — the mysteries that were once hidden in God but that now lie recorded in that Bible on your shelf.

The Holy Spirit revealed to Paul those mysteries of the Gospel as an apostle "born out of due time" (1 Cor. 15:8). He wasn't taught as the other twelve who had fellowshiped personally with Jesus. What he received from God came by direct revelation.

After fifteen years, Paul conferred with those who had been made apostles before him. Later he said, "They added nothing to me. Quite the contrary, it seems that the apostleship of ministry to the Gentiles has been committed unto me" (Gal. 2:6,7).

Speaking Divine Mysteries

The spiritual link between praying in tongues and revelation knowledge is in the understanding of the word "mysteries." To help us understand this link, Paul mentioned this word three times between chapters 2 and 14 of First Corinthians.

We have already read the first mention in First Corinthians 2:7:

But WE SPEAK THE WISDOM OF GOD IN A MYSTERY, even the hidden wisdom, which God ordained before the world unto our glory.

The second time Paul mentioned "mysteries" is in First Corinthians 4:1:

Let a man so account of us, as of the ministers of Christ, and STEWARDS OF THE MYSTERIES OF GOD.

So in the same letter that Paul told the Corinthian church he was thankful he spoke with tongues more than all of them, he also stated that he had been made a steward of the mysteries of God.

A steward is an administrator. A rich man of that day would employ a steward, who acted as an administrator over the rich man's wealth and goods. The steward guarded the rich man's goods against waste, misuse, and thievery.

In order for Paul to be a good steward of the mysteries of God, he had to protect those mysteries against infiltration of false doctrine, legalism, Satan's hatred for the Church, etc. How did Paul do that? By allowing the Holy Spirit to pray these very same mysteries through him hour after hour in tongues. He knew it would affect his spiritual understanding of the revelation of Christ to the Church.

The third time mysteries is mentioned is in First Corinthians 14:2:

> **For he that speaketh in an unknown tongue speaketh not unto men, but unto God: for no man understandeth him; howbeit IN THE SPIRIT HE SPEAKETH MYSTERIES.**

Notice that the moment you start praying in tongues, you put yourself in the Spirit. The Holy Spirit bypasses your flesh, soul, and intellect and goes right to your spirit. There He starts creating that supernatural language as soon as you open your mouth, and you begin to speak mysteries to God.

But what mysteries is Paul speaking about in this verse? Well, the word "mysteries" basically means *divine secrets.* These divine secrets aren't the kind that can never be told; rather, they are secrets that are hidden on the inside of God. These secrets have been made accessible to us by the blood of Jesus and the power of the Holy Spirit.

W. E. Vine in his *Expository Dictionary of New Testament Words* gives another good scriptural definition for these mysteries: "...that which, being outside the range of unassisted natural apprehension, can be made known only by Divine revelation, and is made known...to those only who are illumined by His Spirit."[1]

So suppose you spent eight hours praying in the Holy Ghost, speaking mysteries that are out of the range of unassisted natural apprehension and that can only be known by divine revelation to those illuminated by the Holy Spirit. Well, I can tell you this much about those mysteries you're praying: They're certainly not for God's benefit!

Are you going to sneak up on God's blind side and whisper some deep spiritual secret in His ear that He didn't know at least a couple of millennia before this planet became graced with your presence? No, I don't think so.

So if these mysteries are not for God's benefit, they must be for ours. Therefore, praying in tongues must be like any other kind of prayer in that it is designed by God to be answered — just as much as is the mighty, mountain-moving prayer of faith or the "I'll go where You want me to go" prayer of consecration.

John 16:13 says this:

---

[1] W. E. Vine, *Expository Dictionary of New Testament Words* (Old Tappan, New Jersey: Fleming H. Revell Company, 1966), p. 97.

> **Howbeit when he, the Spirit of truth, is come, he will guide you into all truth: for he shall not speak of himself; but whatsoever he shall hear, that shall he speak: and he will shew you things to come.**

The Holy Spirit is the intermediary between us and Jesus, and He will only speak what He hears. His commission as the Spirit of Truth is to glorify Jesus by receiving truth from Him and then transferring these mysteries of Christ from His understanding to ours through the supernatural language of tongues.

Also, Hebrews 7:25 says that Jesus our High Priest "ever lives to make intercession" for us. So the Holy Spirit hears the intercession Jesus is making for us and then pours it through our spirit as we pray in other tongues.

What else can we know about those mysteries or divine secrets that First Corinthians 14:2 says we speak as we pray in the Spirit? I meditated and prayed and studied in my search to find out what that verse meant. I discovered that the word "mysteries" in this verse is the exact same Greek word as the one used for the hidden mysteries that are now available to us through the ministry of the Holy Ghost in this dispensation of grace.

I was amazed. I asked, "Lord, do You mean that the mysteries that were hidden in You since before the world began are the same mysteries I penetrate the throne room of grace with every time I pray in tongues?"

The Lord said, "You got it!"

That's why your faith is increased every time you pray in tongues. You don't receive some electrical, tangible charge from speaking a bunch of syllables in the air. The reason you are edified is that you are speaking the same mysteries Paul wrote about: the mystery of healing, the mystery of righteousness, the mystery of redemption. You are speaking them before the throne room of grace, and God answers them as He does every prayer.

You see, the word "tongues" is an old King James English word for "language." Like any other language, the Holy Spirit's supernatural language carries within it thoughts, expressions, and entire sentences. Actually, His language is more articulate than any man-created language on the face of the earth. God uses this language of edification to increase your spiritual understanding regarding the mysteries of everything that Christ, the Hope of Glory, is in you (Col. 1:27).

You see, when the Holy Spirit is able to express these mysteries through your spirit, eventually they will manifest themselves in your understanding. Tongues literally free the Holy Spirit to move on your mind with revelation knowledge, insight, wisdom, and understanding of spiritual matters.

That's why the devil has removed tongues from three-quarters of the Church. It's much easier for believers to be deceived by the ever-changing doctrines of man when they have been separated from one of the primary teaching tools that enables them to learn from the Holy Spirit Himself!

My Personal Discovery
Of the Spiritual Link

When I first began to pray in tongues in my prayer closet for hours every day, I was so naive that I didn't know why I was being edified. I only knew that praying in tongues was doing something positive to me. So I stayed in the closet and prayed day after day, and my times of prayer kept getting better the longer I stayed.

I had been praying in my closet about two months when a logger friend of mine named Earl Hitson called me. Earl stands six feet three inches tall and has a chest as big as a barrel. He's a big, burly man, but he has one of the most tender hearts for the Lord I've ever encountered.

Earl had heard that I had resigned my job and was locking myself in a closet to pray every day. He had some time on his hands, so he asked me, "Davy, would you mind if I come over there and pray with you?"

"No, I don't mind, Earl. Come on over."

So Earl began to join me for prayer. We would pray in English first. Then when we ran out of things to pray about in English, we'd start praying in tongues, Earl in one corner and me in another.

But besides praying with me, Earl was also working long hours. So after a while, he'd start to get tired. Finally he would fall asleep and snore away for a couple of hours. Then he'd snort and wake himself up. The first thing he'd do is slit his eyes open and peek over at me to see if I had noticed that he had fallen asleep. I never let on that I knew.

Earl may have had a hard time staying awake during prayer, but as the months went by, he became one of my spiritual mentors. It was he who lived the life of faith before me. He is the one who introduced me to some truths about faith, which set the foundation for my own walk of faith.

Anyway, I had been praying in tongues for about three months when something unusual happened. One day I was reading a passage of Scripture that I had read a hundred times before. Suddenly it seemed that those particular verses lifted off the page, and the understanding of the passage exploded in all directions inside of my spirit.

The moment before, I had no idea what it meant, and the next moment I understood it for the first time. The anointing within that teaches us all things explained those verses to me!

But the anointing which ye have received of him abideth in you, and ye need not that any man teach you: but as the same anointing teacheth you of all things, and is truth, and is no lie, and even as it hath taught you, ye shall abide in him.

— 1 John 2:27

I was so amazed! I thought, *Oh, Lord, what's going on here? I always thought these verses meant something else!* (I had learned a very different interpretation from my ultra-Holiness days.)

This same experience started to happen to me frequently. Every time the Holy Spirit would give me more revelation of God's Word, I would wait impatiently for Earl to come so I could tell him about it.

I'd ask, "Earl, have you seen this verse?"

"Well, yes, Davy."

"But do you know what it means, Earl?"

Earl would start explaining it to me with the confidence of a spiritual mentor. "Well, Davy, it means this and this." I'd wait for him to get just far enough into his explanation to make sure he didn't know what I knew. Then I wouldn't be able to stand it anymore.

I'd interrupt, "No, Earl, this is what it means!" Then I'd tell him what the Holy Spirit had just taught me.

Earl would look at me and ask, "How did you get that?"

"I don't know, Earl. There is just something that goes off inside of me. I don't even know how or why it happens, but suddenly I understand these scriptures."

At that time, neither of us knew why I was suddenly getting all this revelation knowledge. We tried to reason it out.

"I think I know, Earl," I said. "I just left my job to go full time in the ministry a few months ago. I have no income and nobody to preach to. So God must be filling me up with revelation knowledge because I'm a preacher! If He doesn't do it, what would I preach?"

So I came to the conclusion that God was giving me revelation knowledge because I went full time in the ministry. But later I sure discovered the fallacy in that way of thinking! I know preachers who have been in the full-time ministry all of their lives, and they've still never said anything worthwhile!

Later on, the Lord gave me the revelation of what was bringing the revelations: He was communicating with me the same way He will communicate with any person who prays out the mysteries in tongues before His throne.

As I prayed out divine mysteries every day, God answered my prayers by helping me better understand the mind of Christ. The Word of God began to come alive in me. And that, my friend, is an important part of edification.

Here's a natural illustration of what happens when we receive revelation knowledge that may help you understand the process better: You can equate praying in tongues to downloading information onto a computer chip. What's the computer language? Tongues.

So hour after hour, you pray in tongues, constantly feeding divine mysteries into that "computer chip." Then at some point, the Holy Spirit instantaneously "installs" the contents of that computer chip into your spirit, releasing the entire revelation that it contains in a millisecond.

Suddenly your spirit understands an entirely new aspect of the Scriptures that you never understood before. It would take you months to teach others every-thing you received in one millisecond. Why? Because your spirit is capable of understanding and receiving hundreds of thousands of bits and pieces of information in a second. It's the natural mind that gives you trouble. Your brain is limited; it can only assimilate one "paragraph" of revelation at a time.

The more you pray in tongues, the more you "download" divine mysteries onto that spiritual computer chip. And when the Holy Spirit "installs" it into your spirit and releases the revelation, suddenly you begin to understand the mind of Christ. The mystery of Christ in you, the Hope of Glory, begins to be born in your spirit, accompanied by great faith.

So Paul's source of revelation knowledge and his means of receiving it are both revealed in the Book of First Corinthians: The Holy Spirit revealed hidden mysteries of divine wisdom to him through tongues for personal edification. And the very same gift the Apostle Paul used to receive revelation knowledge is available to you and me. It is a gift that we can exercise at our own volition, *on purpose*, just because we want to!

Offer yourselves a living sacrifice
  through the eternal Spirit,
  saith the Spirit of Grace.
For I do desire even this day
  that you be not conformed to the world
  and its systems, but be transformed
  by the renewing of your mind
  that you may prove
  the good, acceptable, and perfect will
  that I have separated you unto
  from the foundations of the earth.

Oh, that you might enter into the delicacies
  of the Spirit,
  that precious place of fellowship with Me,
  that dormitory of understanding
  where I invite you in to fellowship with Me,
  where things are seen
  through the eyes of the Spirit,
  and your understanding
  is charged with My understanding.

And I would say unto you
    that in this secret place of the Most High
    dwells the understanding
    and the power for your transformation.
Therefore, pray and utilize the forces
    and the power of the Spirit within,
And pray, edifying yourself,
    that you may enter in.

Chapter 7

Praying Out the Mysteries Of God's Plan

What if you had a prayer partner, someone who was your friend, who was so knowledgeable of God that he *never* prayed amiss? What if he always knew the beginning from the end and knew God's will for you in every circumstance?

What if this prayer partner spoke with such wisdom that he was always one step ahead of the devil and *never* prayed in unbelief because he knew the mind of God so thoroughly? What if he knew what God has called you to do in minute detail and never, ever in the history of all creation had one of his prayers fail?

Would you like someone like that praying for you? And if you had someone like that, how much would you let him pray for you? Three minutes a day, or as much as He wanted to?

Well, you can have just such a prayer partner. Just open your mouth and say, "Hello, Holy Ghost!"

Finding God's Perfect Will for You

Every time you spend an hour or a day praying in tongues, you are praying out the mind of Christ that encompasses the full foundational revelation of the Church — the mystery of everything that Christ the Hope of Glory is in you, to you, and through you.

But as you continue to pray out those mysteries, the Holy Spirit also expresses the mind of Christ for you on a very personal level, helping you find and walk in the absolute perfect plan of God for your life.

That's one of the Holy Spirit's most crucial roles in your life. Why? Well, are you sure that you know exactly what your calling is in the Body of Christ? Did you know that you can flounder around all of your life under the ceiling of the flesh and never find God's perfect will for you? (For instance, if you stop along the way to fight with people, you will go no further than that fight until you deal with it according to the Word.)

That's why the Bible says there is a *good* and an *acceptable* and a *perfect* will of God for your life (Rom. 12:2). Jesus also talked about different types of "ground" in people's hearts: One type yields thirtyfold, one sixtyfold, and another a hundredfold of the Word that is sown (Mark 4:20).

Many people never leave the "thirtyfold" stage of God's plan for them. They spend their entire lives cheated out of their reward because they don't know how to release the power of the Holy Spirit inside of them. If they understood how to do that, then every day would bring them closer to God's perfect plan. Next year would be different than this year, and five years down the road, they'd be able to look back and know that they hadn't wasted that time.

I went on a personal search to discover from the Word of God not only how to *find* the perfect will of God for my life, but how to go on by the power of the Holy Spirit to *pursue* it. I found my answer in the Book of Romans. And now there isn't a thing this side of hell that the devil can do to stop me, because greater is He who is in me than he that is in the world (1 John 4:4)!

The Good, Acceptable, And Perfect Will of God

Let's look at what Paul said in Romans 12:1,2 about the good, acceptable, and perfect will of God:

> **I beseech you therefore, brethren, by the mercies of God, that ye present your bodies a living sacrifice, holy, acceptable unto God, which is your reasonable service.**
>
> **And be not conformed to this world: but be ye transformed by the renewing of your mind, that ye may prove what is that good, and acceptable, and perfect, will of God.**

These verses say that somehow through the offering of my body as a living sacrifice, I will go through a process that causes me to no longer be conformed to this world — its way of thinking and what it does. Somehow I will experience transformation by the renewing of my mind to prove not only the good, but the acceptable, and finally the absolute perfect will of God.

So my question to God was this: "What 'perfect will' are You talking about? I mean, if I'm going to offer my body as a living sacrifice and, as a result, find Your perfect will, I'd like to know what 'perfect will' I'm looking for."

I went to someone known to be knowledgeable of the Scriptures and asked him, "What perfect will of God is the Bible talking about in Romans 12:2?"

He asked me, "What is your spiritual background, Brother Roberson?"

"Oh, my background is ultra-Holiness. We believed that it was a sin to wear jewelry and that women shouldn't cut their hair. We had a lot of legalistic do's and don'ts because we thought that pleased God. We also thought God sent disease to teach us lessons and gave us poverty to keep us humble."

"Well, do you still believe that way?"

"No," I replied. "I believe that Jesus Christ bore my sicknesses and carried my pains, and I don't have to be sick anymore. It would be a miscarriage of justice for God to put a disease on me when He already laid it on Jesus. And I believe it is His good pleasure to bless me materially and financially, not to keep me broke."

The man said, "That's right. You see, you're being transformed by the renewing of your mind as you learn more of God's Word. You're finding the good, the acceptable, and the perfect will of God."

My friend's explanation is in part what that verse is saying. But later I found out that when verse 2 isn't taken out of context, it is easier to see exactly what it's talking about. The good, acceptable, and perfect will of God refers to your call in the Body of Christ that God has given you by grace. And if you ever learn to offer your body as a living sacrifice, you will find not just the good, not just the acceptable, but the *absolute perfect* will of God for your life.

"Prove that to me, Brother Roberson." I'll be glad to! Let's look at Romans 12:4-8:

For as we have many members in one body, and all members have not the same office:

So we, being many, are one body in Christ, and every one members one of another.

Having then gifts differing according to the grace that is given to us, whether prophecy, let us prophesy according to the proportion of faith;

Or ministry, let us wait on our ministering: or he that teacheth, on teaching;

Or he that exhorteth, on exhortation: he that giveth, let him do it with simplicity; he that ruleth, with diligence; he that sheweth mercy, with cheerfulness.

Within this many-membered spiritual body called the Body of Christ are many graces and callings that differ from one another, whether they be apostle, prophet, teacher, pastor, evangelist, helps, governments, or the diversities of tongues. So this passage of Scripture, taken in context, is saying that if I ever learn how to offer my body as a living sacrifice, the result will be that I find God's particular grace and calling for my life.

How Do We Offer Our Bodies As Living Sacrifices?

The reason some people don't experience many faith victories in their lives is that they are *not* fulfilling their call. They aren't finding what God wants them to do. They aren't pursuing Him to discover what His absolute perfect will is for their lives.

I am personally so hungry to know God's perfect will for my life that I'll do whatever is necessary to attain that goal. I want to know to the "nth degree" what Jesus has called me to do, for what purpose I was born, and what anointings are available to me.

So in my search, the question for me was not whether I would offer my body as a living sacrifice. I was too hungry for God to refuse. My question was this: Is there a way I can find out *how* to offer my body as a living sacrifice? If so, somebody please tell me how — and then turn me loose!

I want my day in court. If I fail to fulfill my call, don't let it be because you taught me wrong. Don't put me in a holding tank where some powerless doctrine like "Tongues aren't for today" takes away my victory until I have no reward left.

Show me how I can walk all the way into God and receive the best God has for me. Just give me my day in court. Then if I fail, it won't be because someone else took my victory away from me.

Well, I kept on searching and studying for the answer to my question. Then one day I discovered I didn't have to look any further than the Apostle Paul and the Book of Romans to find out how to present my body as a living sacrifice.

Every Condemning Sentence Canceled

Notice that in Romans 12:1, it says, **I beseech you THEREFORE, brethren, by the mercies of God....** The word "therefore" means "Based on what I've already said." In other words, Paul is saying, "Use the information I taught you in the previous chapters to go on and offer your body so you can find the perfect will of God."

Well, we don't have to go back very far to find out where Paul taught us how to offer our bodies as living sacrifices. The eighth chapter holds our answer.

Let's start at Romans 8:1:

There is therefore now no condemnation to them which are in Christ Jesus, who walk not after the flesh, but after the Spirit.

That word "condemnation" is being used in the same way we say a criminal is condemned to die.

So Jesus has given me a promise through Paul's teachings. He has delivered me from every condemning sentence against me, whether of the flesh, the devil, the world, sickness, pain, poverty, or disease. None of these hell-inspired things can be carried out in me anymore — *if* I meet one condition: I must walk after the spirit and not after the flesh.

Paul is actually speaking of walking according to the new nature, the reborn human spirit we received when we were born again. The Holy Spirit has been sent to teach our reborn human spirit all truth:

Howbeit when he, the Spirit of truth, is come, he will guide you into all truth: for he shall not speak of himself; but whatsoever he shall hear, that shall he speak: and he will shew you things to come.

— John 16:13

The Holy Spirit teaches my reborn human spirit that I am no longer under the condemning sentences of sin, sickness, and poverty. I no longer have to walk as an unregenerate man in the flesh. I am to walk after my reborn human spirit as I am taught and led by the Holy Spirit.

The devil condemned me to die in my sins so that for all eternity, hell would be my home. But Jesus stepped into my shoes and took my place. He took that condemning sentence unto Himself. Now because Jesus was condemned, I can go free. He was made to be sin for me that I might be made the righteousness of God in Christ (2 Cor. 5:21).

I was condemned to die under the penalty of every damnable disease known to mankind. But Jesus Christ stepped into my shoes as my Substitute. He bore my sicknesses and carried my pains (Matt. 8:17), dying under the condemning sentence of my diseases. Now as long as I walk after the Spirit, that condemning sentence can no longer be carried out in me.

I was condemned to die in poverty. But Jesus Himself by the grace of God took the condemning sentence of poverty upon Himself: **For ye know the grace of our Lord Jesus Christ, that, though he was rich, yet for your sakes he became poor, that ye through his poverty might be rich** (2 Cor. 8:9). Now if I ever learn to walk after the Spirit and not by the dictates of the flesh, that condemning sentence can no longer be carried out in me.

So we who are born again have a promise. All condemning sentences by the flesh, the devil, or the world are canceled if we walk not after the flesh but after the Spirit.

How To Walk After the Spirit

That brings me to this question: *How* do I walk after the Spirit? Paul wouldn't make the statement he did in Romans 8:1 without going on to tell me how to leave behind the walk of the flesh and begin to walk after the Spirit.

In the verses that follow, Paul differentiates between the walk in the Spirit and a walk in the flesh. Notice in verse 13, he says, **For if ye live after the flesh, ye shall die:** [Don't you wish Paul wasn't so plain about it?] **but if ye THROUGH THE SPIRIT do mortify the deeds of the body, ye shall live.**

So now Paul is telling me that to walk after the Spirit, I must somehow mortify, or put to death, the deeds of the body through the power of my reborn spirit as it is edified and built up by the Holy Spirit. This is starting to sound like Romans 12:1. There it tells me to offer my body as a living sacrifice. But back in Romans 8:13, it tells me that I can't do it through will power, the energy of the flesh; it has to be *through the Spirit.*

We're going to talk more about mortifying the deeds of the flesh later. For now, the question remains: How do I release the Holy Spirit to edify and build up my reborn human spirit to mortify the deeds of the flesh and offer my body as a living sacrifice so I can find God's perfect will for my life?

The Holy Spirit Helps Our Infirmities Through Prayer

To find the answer to that question, skip down to verse 26. Paul is still dividing between a walk of the Spirit and a walk in the flesh. But now he's going to tell us how to offer our bodies as a living sacrifice.

Likewise the Spirit also helpeth our infirmities: for we know not what we should pray for as we ought: but the Spirit itself maketh intercession for us with groanings which cannot be uttered.

Paul begins with the word, "likewise." In other words, he is saying, "In this manner" or "This is how the Holy Spirit helps our infirmities, or our weaknesses." The word "infirmities" refers to our inability to produce results because of the limitations imposed on us by our flesh. So the Holy Spirit was sent to help us in our inability to produce results in our own strength.

Let me break down the meaning of this verse a little further. Suppose a damnable disease brings normal life to a standstill. I can't get the disease out of my body, and it's in the process of killing me. That, my friend, is an infirmity.

Or suppose poverty tracks me down and cancels out anything I'm doing for the Kingdom of God. It brings my forward progress to a standstill, and there doesn't seem to be anything I can do about it. That, too, is an infirmity.

But, thank God, the Bible promises that "likewise the Spirit helpeth mine infirmities" — my inability to produce results because of the limitations imposed on me by the flesh!

What is your infirmity, your weakness? Is it anger? No love for people? Do you scream at your wife at home? Whatever it is, the Holy Spirit has been sent to help your weaknesses. He's going to show you how to mortify the deeds of the flesh.

The Holy Ghost knows how ignorant we are. He knows we don't know how to pray as we ought. He knows we really need to have our soul bypassed when it is being whipped by the devil. So, thank God, He bypasses our soul and the fight the devil wages with it. And He brings an entire language of edification with Him — a language so articulate that it makes the English language we speak look like we are playing with linguistic Tinker Toys!

When we pray even just one sentence in tongues, it is for edification, because God is the origin of it. The Holy Ghost can express with one paragraph what would take us all afternoon to say!

It is an awesome language, and the Holy Spirit uses it to express not only the mystery of what Christ is in us, but the call of God that we cannot fulfill in our own strength. He steps in with groanings that cannot be uttered and makes intercession for us according to the will of God.

So enter into the closet and say, "Take over, Holy Ghost. My soul has been sabotaging me lately, but I don't mind spending a day with You!"

The Mind of the Spirit

Now look at verse 27 to see what the Holy Spirit is doing to help us in our infirmities:

And he that searcheth the hearts knoweth what is the mind of the Spirit, because he maketh intercession for the saints according to the will of God.

Notice it says that the Holy Spirit searches the *hearts*, plural. That means the Holy Spirit has the power to search the hearts of the entire Body of Christ and represent each person before the Father's throne, all at the same time. This ability is what makes Him God.

As the Holy Spirit goes into my heart to search it, He already knows something very important: the mind of the Spirit. That's why He can make intercession according to the will of God as He searches my heart.

For a long time, I searched out that scripture, asking God, "What does it mean when it says, 'the Holy Spirit knows the mind of the Spirit'?" I would pack a pile of Greek books in my suitcase and take them on the road with me, searching the Scriptures to find out what the mind of the Spirit is. But I couldn't seem to find the answer.

Then one day the Lord spoke the revelation to my spirit. I had been praying in tongues all day long, and at the end of the day, He whispered to me the answer to the mystery, taking me back to Romans 8.

In Romans 8:20-21, Paul says that all creation was subjected to corruption (at the fall of man) in hope of being delivered from bondage to freedom. Paul went on to say that we who have been born again and filled with the Holy Ghost also groan in our spirits, longing for the glorification of our bodies and of the Church (v. 23).

Paul is talking about God's plan for mankind in these verses — a plan that spans the approximately seven thousand years of man's existence on this earth (including the millennium). This is the context in which he talks about the mind of the Spirit in verse 27.

But why is the term "*mind* of the Spirit" used? Well, God has something different in His mind for each generation born. God's plan of redemption spans seven thousand years, but He who searches the hearts knows what God's mind is for your generation, for your church, and for your life within that great plan. He knows what God called and predestined you to do before the foundation of the world. That is what enables the Holy Spirit to be your Representative, your Champion, as He makes intercession for you according to the will of God.

The Conference Table of God

For the sake of our finite minds, let's imagine the conference table of God in eternities past. At the head of that great conference table sat God the Father. At His right hand sat Jesus Christ, and at His left, the Holy Spirit. The subject of the conference: the planning of creation.

God laid everything out on the table included in His great plan. He said, "We'll create this, and We'll create that, and then We'll create people." Then He started going down through the generations, looking ahead to

His plan for each person to be born on this earth. Finally, He reached Dave Roberson's name.

God laid out His plan for Dave on the table, from Dave's birth through every great thing He had called him to do to fulfill his calling. Then Jesus (who at the time was known as the mighty Logos, the Word of God) stood up and said, "Knowing what will happen at the appointed time, I will go forth and redeem Dave."

Next the Holy Spirit stepped up and said, "At the appointed time, I will go forth and baptize Dave's heart. I will also take a supernatural prayer language with me to help Dave pray out the mysteries of God's plan, because I was here with the Father when He planned Dave's life from the beginning."

God planned not only my life at Heaven's great conference table, but your life as well. He planned not only your life, but even the lives of all the female babies of various tribes and peoples who were killed because they were the firstborn and not a male. God had a carefully laid-out plan for each one of those little unwanted babies. In fact, there has never been a person born on this earth for whom God neglected to plan his or her life from beginning to end.

And who knows God's plan for you? Who better than the Holy Spirit, who was with God the Father when He planned it? And now the Holy Spirit lives within you and searches your heart to find out if you're on the wrong or the right path.

Your natural mind can't tell you if you're on the right path. But the Holy Spirit says, "If you will release Me, I will help your weaknesses and begin to make intercession for you according to the will of God. I will work God's plan for your life."

Nothing Can Separate You From God's Plan

I can't spend six hours praying in the Holy Ghost and worshiping God without the Holy Spirit taking the plan of God — His perfect will for my life — and enforcing it out ahead of me. As I pray, the Holy Ghost will lay hold of and remove every boulder and every mountain that stands in the way of my fulfilling the perfect will of God. And who is a match for the Holy Ghost?

That's why Romans 8:28 goes on to say this:

And we know that all things work together for good to them that love God, to them who are the called according to his purpose.

Why will all things now work together for good? Because the Holy Ghost is the One who seizes hold of everything that is contrary to God's will for my life and uses His power to replace it with God's perfect plan. And He does it because I have found out how to release the perfect will of God into my life.

Now you can see why Romans 8 ends with such a note of triumph:

Nay, in all these things we are more than conquerors through him that loved us.

For I am persuaded, that neither death, nor life, nor angels, nor principalities, nor powers, nor things present, nor things to come,

> **Nor height, nor depth, nor any other creature, shall be able to separate us from the love of God, which is in Christ Jesus our Lord.**
>
> **— Romans 8:37-39**

How can I be so convinced that neither height, nor depth, nor any creature, nor things present, nor things to come can separate me from God's plan and His love for me? Because I discovered how to walk after the Spirit and not after the flesh. I found out how to allow the Holy Spirit to work God's plan in my life as I pray much in the Holy Ghost.

Yielding Your Authority To the Holy Spirit

This is where I get excited. In His infinite wisdom, the Holy Ghost knew what to target in order to help us in our infirmities. Certainly He wasn't going to try to conquer our soul, our mind, our will, our intellect, or our emotions first. Most of us have proven beyond any reasonable doubt that we can be pushed around in those arenas. We get mad at each other; we fall into sin; we live on the edge of carnality; we can't overcome our soul enough to pray as we should.

So the Holy Spirit just bypassed all that mess — our wavering soul, our defeats, our up-and-down emotional roller-coaster rides, our whimpering, our swelled speeches of doctrinal error, our lying down in defeat, and our little deceptions. Instead, He went straight into the depths of our spirit — the new creation that contains all the authority Jesus transferred to us:

And Jesus came and spake unto them, saying, All power is given unto me in heaven and in earth.

GO YE therefore, and teach all nations, baptizing them in the name of the Father, and of the Son, and of the Holy Ghost.

— Matthew 28:18,19

Then the Holy Spirit said to each of us, "Look, little one, you're being whipped because you're puny and weak and your spirit has no understanding of revelation. But your spirit man does have a new nature, a capacity to understand spiritual matters, and the spiritual authority I deposited in you when you were born again.

"So, excuse Me, but I'm here now, and I would like to borrow your authority from you. You see, I need a conqueror. And although I am the all-powerful Holy Spirit, I can't do anything in your life without your authority.

"First of all, I need your permission and authority to pray through you. Will you give that to Me and let Me help you fulfill God's perfect will for your life?"

You see, the Holy Spirit has a handicap — *us*. He would have finished taking care of mankind's mess a long time ago if it wasn't for His handicap. He can't even pray through us until we give Him that authority! Only when we yield our authority to Him will He transfer His supernatural language to our spirit man, giving us utterance to pray mysteries before the throne of God.

If we are wise, we will lend our authority to the wisest, most powerful Being in the universe, the One who moved on the face of the deep and separated the upper and lower firmaments. He who has all that power needs only our authority to operate it in our lives.

The moment we start praying in the Holy Ghost, we give Heaven the authority to create that prayer in our spirit so we can pray the mind of Christ. As we yield our authority to Him by praying in the Holy Ghost, we turn Him loose to move us into God's perfect will for our lives!

Watering the Seed of God's Plan

Don't you wish there was a Book of Roberson, a Book of ____ (insert your name!), that followed the Book of Revelation? If there was, I could look up the chapter that represented the particular year I was living: "Let me see, this is the fifty-third year of my life, so I'll turn to the fifty-third chapter. Look here, I'm supposed to go to this city and preach at this church next month. Glory be to God, thank You, Father, for the Book of Roberson that has Your plan for my life in it!"

There is no such book in the Bible. But such a book does exist! The moment you were born again and the Holy Spirit came to dwell within you, that book was deposited on the inside of your spirit. That book is God's perfect will for your life in seed form.

On the inside of that seed is the "DNA" programming for God's entire plan for you. And if you'll yield to the Holy Spirit, He will bring forth its contents, causing it to grow into a strong, deeply rooted tree of blessing and divine purpose. He will continually work God's plan, searching your heart moment by moment and praying the will of God for your life way out ahead of you.

You see, the leadership of the Holy Spirit is not a whim or a passing thought. When you're following His direction, your life will not be like this: "Oh, I think God wants me to go to that city tomorrow." Then the next day, "Oh, I'm not sure whether or not He wants me to go." And the following day, "Oh, I think He really does want me to go."

The Holy Spirit doesn't run things the way a natural man does. He doesn't play with your life. He is out for your success! But you have to cooperate with Him by allowing Him to pray through you.

When Jesus said that out of your innermost being shall flow rivers of living water (John 7:38), He was speaking of the Holy Ghost. So the more you pray in the Holy Ghost, the more you water the seed that contains God's plan. As you continue to pray and sow to the Spirit, you will eventually reap from the Spirit, for the seed will sprout and grow into the will and the direction of God for your life. The more the seed grows, the more prevalent God's plan will become.

As you continue to walk after the Spirit, that divine direction will become so strong in your life that it will be almost impossible for you to walk in the wrong direction. God's direction will no longer be hard to *catch*; it will be hard to *miss*. You will literally have to get past God to fail!

God's wisdom and guidance will gradually consume and overtake you, until the voice of the Holy Spirit becomes louder than the enemy who surrounds you with adverse circumstances and proclaims you are going to fail. And at every level of God's plan that you attain, the anointing of His Spirit will be there to give you the grace to fulfill His perfect will.

I'm telling you, the devil is so afraid that you're going to get hold of this message and run with it. I don't think you have any idea how afraid the devil is of prayer. You see, he knows he has only one chance to keep you from fulfilling the purpose you were born to fulfill: He has to get you out of prayer so that you stop allowing the Holy Spirit to work God's plan for you. Other than that strategy, the devil doesn't have a chance, because greater is He who is in you than he that is in the world (1 John 4:4)!

'Well Done'

So why is it so vitally important that you learn how to release the power of the Holy Spirit in your life to walk in God's perfect will? Because just as sure as you breathe, at the appointed moment in God's time scale that all creation has longed for, Jesus will split the eastern sky at the sound of a great trumpet.

On that day, when you behold Jesus face to face, what will He say to you? Will you be able to stand there knowing that you chose to believe in God enough to abandon your life to Him while it still made a difference? If so, you will hear the words, "You did a job well done, My good and faithful servant."

I'm trying to help you understand the value of the Lamb's reward for fulfilling your call. On the day you stand before the Master, you will trade everything you possess for just one nod of approval, one look from His eyes, that says, "Well done." You will trade it all to know that *He* knows the hell you went through to give your whole life to your call; He sees the multitudes you took home to Heaven with you. Nothing can replace that reward.

Someone may say, "But I don't have time to pray." Of course, you don't, because you've never taken your Holy Ghost "calculator" and calculated what your lack of prayer has cost your character and your life. If you ever did, you'd say instead, "I don't have time *not* to pray!"

Whatever you are not doing, you are not doing it because you don't want to. If you aren't praying as you should, the reason is simple: you don't want to.

"Well, I have a career. I don't have time to pray that much." But you are in that situation because it is what you chose.

"Can I have a career and a strong prayer life as well?" You don't know what a career is until you release the Holy Spirit to help you fulfill it by His power.

You have a call. No one else has it. God would have to arrange something else for the Body of Christ if you failed to find and fulfill what God has called you to do.

But you *can* find your divine call. You're still on this earth; you're still breathing. You still have the opportunity to release the Holy Spirit in prayer to help you find and fulfill God's perfect will for your life. Are you going to let your lazy flesh cheat you out of hearing those words, "Well done"? I don't think so!

For you desire to be led by the Spirit.
You desire to be led from this natural place
    to that natural place.
But know this: Long before I lead you
    to be a force for Me in the natural,
I begin to lead you in the spiritual.

For I lead you from glory to glory,
    from a place of unrest to a place of rest
    so that when I give you
    what I would have you do,
    it will stand the fire and pass the test.
So enter into My grace.
You have yet to experience the best that I have.
For it is a place of rest,
    saith the Spirit of Grace.
It is My best.

Chapter 8

The Channel Through Which The Holy Spirit Speaks

We can never receive enough teaching on an intellectual level to make us victorious in life. Therefore, if we don't learn to fellowship with the Godhead in the realm of the Spirit, we will never progress very far in fulfilling our divine call.

We've seen that it's our awesome privilege to have the third Person of the Godhead living inside us to oversee God's plan for our personal lives. But in order to take advantage of the Holy Spirit's expert leadership, we have to understand *how* He communicates with us as we pray in other tongues.

You see, the Holy Spirit always speaks through the same channel. We need to become familiar with that channel so we can differentiate His voice from every other voice, thought, and impression.

First, we must understand that God always communes with our *spirit*. If we don't know how to identify the difference between God communing with our spirit and the devil fooling with our mind, we will walk in the wrong direction most of the time. Why? Because *the devil has studied mankind for six thousand years*, and he has learned some unique ways to set us up and keep us walking around in circles in our lives.

The Spirit, Soul, and Body of Man

In order to discern the voice of the Holy Spirit in your daily life, you first have to understand the operation of the spirit, soul, and body of man.

I have sat under many teachers on this subject. Most isolate all the verses they can pertaining to the spirit, the soul, and the body. Then they may draw three little circles on a chalkboard and outline the characteristics of the three parts of man, saying, "This is your spirit. This is your soul. And this is your body."

I didn't have too much trouble understanding the operation and characteristics of the body. But I had a hard time grasping the difference between the soul and the spirit.

According to the great Bible teachers of our day, the soul consists of a person's mind or intellect, his will, and his emotional faculties. It is the part of man that needs to be renewed by the Word. I totally agreed with this. And I knew that when man's spirit departs from his body, his soul goes with him. But beyond that, I couldn't quite understand how man's spirit fit into the picture.

So as I tried to understand this subject, I asked God, "Lord, what is the difference between me and a dog?" Now, I like dogs, but they don't have a spirit. They don't go to Heaven the way people do.

Animals do exist in Heaven, but they didn't go from here to there. They were created in Heaven. They live there. As far as anyone knows, animals born here on earth just return back to the dust after they die.

But evidently, dogs do have a soul, because they have intellect, emotions, and a will. So what is the difference between a dog's soul and mine? It is this: My soul finds immortality within an immortal spirit.

When God created my emotions, my will, and my intellect, He held these forces in His hand and said, "This is the soul of man." But within what confines would He house these forces that make up the essence of who I am?

This is where the operation of the spirit came in. God created these forces that make up the soul and placed them in an eternal substance called the spirit. It is the immortal spirit encompassing the soul that gives the soul its eternal nature.

Characteristics of Man's Spirit

We can gain some insight into the spirit of man by looking at what Jesus said in Luke 16:19-22:

> **There was a certain rich man, which was clothed in purple and fine linen, and fared sumptuously every day:**
>
> **And there was a certain beggar named Lazarus, which was laid at his gate, full of sores,**
>
> **And desiring to be fed with the crumbs which fell from the rich man's table: moreover the dogs came and licked his sores.**
>
> **And it came to pass, that the beggar died, and was carried by the angels into Abraham's bosom: the rich man also died, and was buried.**

Even though the rich man died and was buried — even though his flesh or his body was in the grave — in verse 23 it says that his spirit went somewhere else:

And IN HELL he lift up HIS EYES, being in torments, and SEETH Abraham afar off, and Lazarus in his bosom.

There it is in black and white — the spirit man has eyes!

Notice it also says that the rich man was "in torments." That is speaking of strong emotions. So the rich man's spirit man also had emotions.

Now look at verse 24:

And he cried and said, Father Abraham, have mercy on me, and send Lazarus, that he may dip the tip of his finger in water, and cool my tongue; for I am tormented in this flame.

My goodness, people in Heaven have fingers, and people in hell have tongues! We better think about this for a moment. Either our spirit man possesses all the rest of the body parts as well, or there is a bunch of spiritual tongues and eyeballs lying around in hell while spiritual fingers float around Heaven!

It stands to reason that if my spirit man has a spiritual finger, tongue, and a pair of eyes, he also has every other body part as well. That is basic.

In fact, let's take it a step further. If I were to separate my inner man from my outer man and leave the two standing next to each other, my physical body and my spirit man would look a lot alike — except for the fact that my spirit would be without defects. In fact, all the defects that were programmed into the human race when Adam fell would be gone.

Now, if my outer man were to hold up his finger and say, "What is my finger made out of?" you would say, "It's made out of flesh." If you answered in more detail, you'd say, "It's made of cells, blood, bone, and many small compounds."

Well, if my physical man is made out of physical material that you can name, what about my spirit man? What if my inner man held up his finger — which the passage in Luke 16 proves the spirit man has — and asked, "What is my finger made out of?" You would say, "Well, uh, a heavenly substance. Hmmm, let's see — spirit." You wouldn't be able to break it down any further.

So my inner man fills my outer man finger for finger, hand for hand, arm for arm, leg for leg. I have physical eyes and spiritual eyes. My spiritual eyeball fills my physical eyeball.

Let's take this a step further. Within my inner man is the nature of the new creation, containing such spiritual forces as love, peace, joy, and dominion. The inner man is my stabilizer in life. He never fluctuates up and down. His only inclination is to go up higher in the realm of God.

The part of me that fluctuates between up and down is the emotional make-up of my soul through which my spirit man operates. My emotions want to go to the highs of extreme happiness one day and to the lows of deep depression the next. But my spirit man never wants to go anywhere but up into the high places with God.

My inner man fits into my outer man, and one day my old outer man is going to say, "I quit." At that moment, I — my spirit man — will step out of my body and go home to Heaven. It will be glorious!

So I have a spiritual brain that fits into and operates through my natural brain in this physical body. It is within my spiritual brain that the soul is housed.

Identify the Channel of Communication

In the natural, you don't hear with your ear one day and with your big toe the next. In the same way, your spiritual anatomy isn't designed for God to communicate with different parts of your spirit man depending on what day it is. Every time God talks to you, He will communicate through the same channel. Therefore, if you can isolate and identify that channel, you can open a door to a spiritual treasure house that no man can close.

When we hear God's voice, it seems as if it comes from somewhere deep down in the center of our being and rises to our mind. Most of us have enough sense to know it doesn't originate in our natural mind; it comes up to our mind.

I always wondered where that deep inner well was that God's voice came from. I wanted to discover how to uncap and monitor it so I could listen to the Holy Spirit on purpose, just because I wanted to hear Him.

Well, in First Corinthians 14:14, it says that if I, Dave Roberson, pray in an unknown tongue, my human spirit is doing the praying under the influence of the Holy Spirit. I came to realize that if that's true, then somewhere within my spirit the Holy Spirit has to bring that supernatural language into existence and then deposit it in my spirit. A transfer of those tongues has to take place from the Person of the Holy Spirit to my human spirit. Otherwise, it wouldn't be me doing the praying.

The Lord once gave me an inner vision to show me how the Holy Spirit transfers His supernatural language to my spirit. In the vision, I saw the outer man and the inner man. The outer man, the fleshly man, was the darkest of the figures. The soul was another shade lighter, and the spirit man was absolutely light.

I saw the Holy Spirit literally creating or bringing into existence His supernatural language in my spiritual mind, which was actually encased within the natural mind of my outer man.

What science has labeled the subconscious is actually the spiritual mind. Scientists say that it possesses incredible ability that far exceeds the operational capacity of the physical brain.

So when the Holy Spirit creates His supernatural language in you, those tongues originate way down deep in your spirit and then come up into the recesses of your spiritual mind, which lies within your physical mind. This explains the fact that when the Holy Spirit speaks, it is not a surface speaking. It comes from the depths of that spiritual mind and bursts outwardly into your intellect.

That's why if you don't let the tongues come out of your mouth, those supernatural words will bypass your mouth and drift up to your thoughts, and you'll "hear" the tongues in your natural mind.

Now, as long as you let the supernatural language that the Holy Spirit creates come out of your mouth, your mind is free to think of other things. For instance, I've made it a regular practice to read the Word while I pray in tongues.

But what if you stop that flow and stop speaking those tongues out? Can you pray in tongues in your mind? Not effectively, because you actually complete the channel of prayer by allowing the Holy Spirit's language to come out of your mouth.

If you don't speak out that language (and it can be just a quiet whispering under your breath), eventually your mind will shift over to something else and dismiss the tongues, and you'll find you have stopped praying. You have cut short the flow of prayer coming through God's channel of communication.

The Door to Another World

When you pray in tongues, you immediately put yourself in the Spirit, because you open the door to another world. You have opened the channel to your own human spirit, giving yourself direct contact with the Holy Spirit. So let's isolate the door through which God's voice comes so you can recognize when He is speaking to you.

After the vision that showed me how the Holy Spirit transfers His language to the human spirit, the Lord instructed me to do something very unusual. (During this experience, I was under a heavy anointing, unaware of my physical surroundings. It sounded like His voice was coming from everywhere.)

He said, "Son, now I want you to learn to locate the channel through which I communicate with you." (Most of us operate out of that channel without any idea where it is!)

Then the Lord instructed me, "Pray in tongues for a while." I obeyed until He told me to stop. Then He said, "Now listen."

As I kept quiet and listened, the tongues continued to come up from my spirit and explode across my intellect. Even though I wasn't speaking the tongues out of my mouth, I could "hear" them loud in my mind. I realized then that the channel through which the Holy Spirit creates His supernatural language is the same channel through which He brings revelation, visions, prophecy, and so forth, to my mind.

Get Acquainted With God's Channel Of Communication

I'll tell you the truth — the only reason I can teach on these matters in detail is that the Holy Spirit taught them first to me in detail. And He couldn't have done that unless the channel of communication between me and God had opened up so I could accurately discern His voice.

You see, it is as you pray in tongues that the channel is actually opened through which God communicates. This is what happens when tongues for interpretation operates. The tongues open the channel for what is about to come. Once that channel is open, the Holy Spirit can send the interpretation through in the same manner He sent the tongues.

Then the more you pray in the Holy Ghost, the more familiar you become with that channel and the greater your ability to recognize when God comes across the same channel with a vision or with revelation knowledge in your native language.

As you consistently give yourself to praying in tongues, that channel of communication will become increasingly clear and definite. You'll find it easier and easier to enter into the rest of faith as you learn to shut out the world and hear the voice of God within. It won't be long before you'll immediately know the difference between mental energy and the inspiration of the Holy Spirit.

But if you're not consistently allowing the Holy Spirit to create that supernatural language in your spirit as you speak it out of your mouth, it will become much more difficult to shut out external circumstances. You won't find it easy at all to monitor your spirit for what God may be saying to you.

As I faithfully kept praying in tongues, I learned how to listen to that channel. I know now where His voice comes from. I know where visions come from that burst suddenly across my mind. I also know where revelation knowledge comes from, because all of these things originate in the same part of my spirit.

I know how to shut down in the middle of all kinds of chaos and monitor that channel through which God communicates. I may receive an inner witness, a check or warning signal, or a vision. I may hear Him speak to me in English. No matter what turmoil is going on around me, I can shut it out and wait for whatever I need to come through that channel of divine communication — and you can do the same!

What You Have
That the Old Testament Saints Didn't

As you begin to pray out the mysteries of Christ in other tongues, what happens? You open up the channel. Now you can experience direct communication with God — something the Old Testament saints longed for but couldn't experience.

Jesus said concerning John the Baptist that there had never been born of a woman a greater prophet than John (Matt. 11:11). I read that years ago and thought, *How can that be? What about Elijah? John the Baptist didn't have the miracles in his ministry that Elijah had.*

I thought Elijah was quite a great prophet. Think about what he accomplished in his ministry: raising the dead, stopping armies with fire from Heaven, flying off in a chariot. Those are some great exploits! But Jesus said that John the Baptist was greater. Why? John didn't perform miracles. All he did was eat wild locusts and honey and tell people to repent.

So why would Jesus say that about John the Baptist? Because of all the prophets under the Old Covenant, this man had more knowledge of Christ than any of them. God chose him to be the forerunner who would preach about the coming Messiah.

Then Jesus made an even more remarkable statement. He said that the least in the Kingdom of God is greater than John the Baptist! Imagine — Mary

Wallpaper and Joe Public are greater than the greatest prophet under the Old Covenant!

Why is that? Because the prophets of old weren't born again. They hadn't received the new nature or the baptism in the Holy Spirit. They didn't have unlimited access to God. But as a tongue-talking, praying believer, you do!

When we were born again and received the nature of God, the most important thing we received was the capacity to understand spiritual things. That's why Heaven sent us the Teacher of all teachers to come and make sure we attained the discernment, wisdom, and understanding of everything that God is.

I have the Teacher living inside of me, and my channel is open. Now He is going to teach me how to go all the way in to attain the highest God has for me.

He has bypassed all the trash in the soul and the flesh and has deposited Himself in my "power plant," my spirit man. Now He says, "I want to teach this man his authority in Christ. He keeps praying in tongues, so he must want Me to teach him about it!

"So I'm going to bring his new nature forward with all the authority that has been given to him. And anything in the flesh or soul realm that gets in the way is going to end up looking like it's in the undertow of the Titanic!"

The Four Ways
The Holy Spirit Communicates

Having located the channel through which God speaks to us, let's discuss the four basic ways the Holy Spirit uses that channel to communicate.

First, He communicates by the *inner witness*. The Bible says that the Kingdom of God, which is within us, is righteousness, peace, and joy in the Holy Ghost (Rom. 14:17). The Holy Spirit who dwells inside of us is a continual Source of absolute peace. He will continually pour His peace throughout our being if we will let Him.

Therefore, the inner witness is often manifested as a disruption to that flow of God's peace, alerting us to a wrong turn, a problem, an obstacle, etc.

Second, the Holy Spirit communicates by *revelation*. The reason God communicates with our spirit and not our physical mind or intellect is that our spiritual mind has the capacity to receive and store millions of bits of information per second. That kind of reception is in God's class!

When the Holy Spirit speaks to us in our native language, He has slowed Himself down to ultra-slow motion, such as the way a camera is set when filming a plant's growth. That's what it's like for the Holy Spirit when He has to slow down to speak to us in the language we understand.

So the Holy Spirit loves to communicate by revelation. He likes to encapsulate an entire revelation and send it through that same channel. All of a sudden, the revelation hits your spirit and explodes outward. You receive the entire revelation in a hundredth of a second.

For instance, you may be praying in the Holy Ghost, meditating on the Word regarding a pressing problem in your business. All of a sudden a revelation capsule explodes inside and you exclaim, "My gosh! I know what to do for the next ten years! And I got it in half a second!"

So you call all your business partners together, and it takes you fifteen days to lay out the plan you received in a half a second by revelation. Why? Because your spirit has to feed one little piece of revelation knowledge at a time to your intellect, which then converts it to your native language.

Do you want to increase these types of experiences in your life? Then spend time praying in the Spirit. You will keep the channel wide open and promote peace and edification in every area of life.

Third, the Holy Spirit communicates by the *audible voice*. You may be thinking about something else, when suddenly He says something in your spirit that seems audible to you. You hear it as clearly as if someone were standing next to you speaking.

I wish God would communicate to me this way all the time so I could hear Him that clearly. But He doesn't. In fact, I have only heard God audibly one time in my entire life — at the Kathryn Kuhlman meeting that I related earlier. He called my name three times and then said something to me about my ministry.

Other than that one time, the Lord has always communicated to me inside of my spirit. It was just a matter of developing my ability to know when it was Him and when it wasn't.

The fourth and less common way that the Holy Spirit communicates is by *vision*. For example, the Lord sometimes communicates to me through what I call "teaching visions." These types of visions assist me at times in understanding the Word of God.

I usually only receive these teaching visions when I am praying in tongues while meditating on the Word, or when a strong anointing comes on me as I'm testifying or preaching. When the visions occur, they explode across my mind with lightning speed.

So whether by inner witness, revelation, audible voice, or vision, the Holy Spirit always communicates through the same channel — that supernatural doorway into another world. Our part is to open that channel by praying in the Holy Ghost so we can begin to learn how to discern the voice of God.

The Anointing Within:
Inoculation Against Deception

I'll tell you another important benefit of becoming familiar with the way God communicates: When you go into a meeting where someone is teaching false doctrine, that wrong teaching won't be able to penetrate into your spirit. You'll be able to discern what is going on as you sit in a meeting. Is the devil attacking the service and the Holy Ghost fighting for it? Or is a "wolf" behind the pulpit, trying to steal the wool off the sheep?

You see, developing the ability to discern what is not true, even if it is spoken from behind the pulpit, is one of the first results of consistently praying in tongues. Praying in tongues is an inoculation against deception.

Jesus said that when the Holy Spirit came, He would guide us into all truth (John 16:13). No wonder John later said this about the Holy Spirit:

175

These things have I written unto you concerning them that seduce you.

But the anointing which ye have received of him abideth in you, and ye need not that any man teach you: but as THE SAME ANOINTING TEACHETH YOU of all things, and IS TRUTH, AND IS NO LIE, and even as it hath taught you, ye shall abide in him.

— 1 John 2:26,27

What did John mean when he said that you have no need that any man teach you? Well, the truth is, most deception takes place behind the pulpit. That's where great religious movements are born that deny half of the Bible. For instance, when the devil talks church leaders into removing the right to speak in tongues out of their bylaws, that particular denomination takes a step into deception.

Just because someone stands behind a pulpit doesn't make him right. He is only right if his teaching lines up with the Word of God. Truth is truth and stands by its own merit.

So how are we going to know when someone is teaching wrong doctrine, whether intentionally or out of ignorance? By the anointing inside of us that is truth and does not bear witness to lies.

In the legalistic, ultra-Holiness church where I was first born again, the people would do all sorts of things to raise money for the church, such as selling "anointed" pieces of a cut-up preaching tent (I was first in line to buy one of those!), "anointed" oil, water from the Jordan River, and even wallets that were never supposed to go empty. (I went broke buying that wallet — and then I even lost the wallet!) Or sometimes we were told to give a love offering to prove God for our lost loved ones or to have a visiting prophet prophesy over us.

But the Gospel is not for merchandising, and none of the things of God are for sale — absolutely *none* of them.

So after praying in tongues every day for a year, I went back to visit my old Holiness friends. But when they started using the familiar "gimmick" tactics, urging the congregation to give a love offering to "buy" some coveted blessing, my spirit went dead. I thought, *What's wrong with me? I used to get all excited just like everyone else when they talked about this kind of thing. Have I backslidden without knowing it?*

No, I hadn't backslidden. The Spirit of Truth inside of me, my Teacher who cannot lie and bears witness only to the truth, had been activated through many hours of praying in tongues. He was causing me to discern the lies that had deceived me in the past but could not deceive me anymore.

This is just one more reason why I strongly disagree with people who say that if you pray too much in tongues, you'll get "weird." A person who makes a statement like that is void of understanding. He would never say such a thing if he understood the role this basic gift plays in hearing the voice of God and becoming familiar with the channel through which He speaks. No one who loves people would deliberately deprive the Body of Christ of such a blessing!

The Candle of the Lord

Let's look at one more scripture regarding how the Holy Spirit communicates with us. Proverbs 20:27 has something profound to say about the subject:

The spirit of man is the candle of the Lord, searching all the inward parts of the belly.

What an incredible statement! My human spirit is the part of me that is created in God's image; it is the candle of God. In other words, it is the part of me that the Holy Spirit ignites to illuminate my understanding of Himself, imparting unto me revelation knowledge.

What do we do with a candle? We don't have much use for one in a bright room. We light a candle when the room is dark. We put it on a tabletop, and it throws illumination into the entire room.

With God's candle, our spirit man, the Holy Spirit searches out all the inward parts of the belly — all the dark places in our lives that need the light of His truth. This is the same searching process that takes place in us as we pray in tongues. He who searches the heart knows the mind of God and makes intercession for us according to the will of God (Rom. 8:27).

The Holy Spirit teaches us everything we cannot discern. He shows us mysteries and divine secrets we need to know about God and His ways. He is our first and foremost Teacher.

If we let the Holy Ghost teach us, at times we will enter into different realms of anointings during prayer, such as tongues for interpretation or the deep groanings of intercession. There will be times when He will teach us mysteries during our prayer vigils. But no matter what happens in prayer, we will always come out the beneficiary if we yield our "candle" to the Holy Spirit, allowing Him to illuminate our inmost parts with the light of His truth.

You have desired to know Me.
You have desired the intimacy of the Spirit
    that can only come through edification
    and worship.
Hear what the Spirit would say.
For I desire to fellowship with you.
I desire to operate through you in My power
    so that others might be blessed.

Come aside and come up higher.
Begin to fellowship with Me,
    and I will begin to fellowship with you.
And even though the path grows narrower,
I will take you into a holy communion
    with Myself,
        for it is through My fellowship with you
        that your hunger and thirst is quenched.

Chapter 9

The Edification Process

Are you beginning to grasp just how wide and deep and high this subject of tongues really is? Well, there is much more territory to explore! Let me take you further now into the edification process that occurs as you allow the Holy Spirit to pray through you.

What Does It Mean To *Edify* Your Spirit?

First Corinthians 14:4 tells us what happens when we pray in tongues for any amount of time:

> **He that speaketh in an unknown tongue EDIFIETH HIMSELF; but he that prophesieth edifieth the church.**

The word "edification" is derived from the word "edifice," which means *a massive, magnificent building.* So when you pray in tongues, you are actually erecting a superstructure, a divine operation, on the inside of your spirit to house the anointing of God and to qualify you for your divine calling.

Most of the time when ministers preach on the subject of tongues, they emphasize the fact that when you pray in tongues, you charge up your spirit the way you would charge up a battery in the natural. They tell you that your spirit is actually receiving a spiritual charge, a tangible force or anointing something like electricity. Then later when you lay hands on someone, that tangible force goes "pow!" and the power of God goes into that person to heal, deliver, and set free.

Well, that's true as far as it goes. However, before that tangible anointing is manifested through a person, he must go through the edification process that causes it to manifest. Not many Christians seem to know anything about that process. Often they think that they receive some kind of "magical" charge from praying in tongues that will immediately begin to operate through them.

I used to believe like that. I thought God would anoint me just as I was. Little did I know that He wasn't at all intending to leave me in my carnal state! That isn't what edification is all about.

I remember what a surprise it was to me when the Lord started to use me after I had spent several months praying in my prayer closet. The second meeting I ever held, the Holy Spirit prompted me to call a woman out of the audience. I was scared; this was all new to me. I told the woman, "Ma'am, you have something wrong with your body, and God wants to heal you."

Then I laid my hands on both sides of her face, closed my eyes, and began to pray my hardest prayer. But in the middle of my prayer, this lady left! Talk about humiliating! I was too embarrassed to open my eyes. Here I was, standing in front of a crowd of people, and the woman I was praying for had just left!

When I had exhausted everything I could think of to pray and finally got brave enough to open my eyes, I looked around to see where the woman had gone — and there she was lying on the floor! I thought, *Oh, Lord, look at that! That must be what it means to receive a charge from praying in the Holy Ghost!* I didn't know what to do. But when the woman got back on her feet, she was healed!

For a long time, that was all I thought being edified in the Holy Ghost meant — God was charging up my spirit, pouring a powerful anointing into me to use when ministering to others. But as I kept praying in tongues, I began to realize that there was much, much more to this edification process than anyone had ever told me.

The Devil Can't Understand the Mysteries

Some people wonder what effect we are having on the devil and his plans when we pray in tongues for edification. One thing we are *not* doing is ordering the devil around. He doesn't even understand what we are saying.

The Word says that when a man prays in an unknown tongue, he isn't talking to men; he is speaking with God (1 Cor. 14:2). If *I* don't understand what I am praying, why would it be the devil's business to know? Why would God allow him to have the upper hand on me? If the devil understands the mysteries and I don't, then he has an edge on me.

That's why I can't accept the idea that the devil can understand us when we pray in tongues. When we begin to pray in tongues for personal edification, we enter into a holy "closet," and our born-again, recreated, seated-in-heavenly-places-with-Christ-Jesus spirit is locked in a divine communication with God Himself. It is a personal communication, a holy communion, and the devil cannot enter there.

If I were to call the President of the United States and he personally answered the telephone, you would find me passed out on the floor from shock! The President is much too busy of a man to talk to me.

On the other hand, my Heavenly Father is continually administrating over the life of every believer both in Heaven and on earth. Yet when I speak with tongues, I immediately enter into divine communication with God Himself. He picks up the "red telephone" on the other end and says, "I know that's you, Roberson, and I know what you want. And because the Holy Ghost in His wisdom is praying this prayer in your stead, I want you to know that the answer is on its way — and there is nothing the devil can do about it!"

That's why the devil *hates* praying in tongues — because he has absolutely no idea what we're saying to God, and it makes him nervous!

Why doesn't he understand? Well, look back at the temple built under the Old Covenant. Within the temple was the outer court, where the people sacrificed to God; the inner court, where the priest offered sacrifices to God on behalf of the people; and finally, the Holy of Holies, where God's Presence dwelt. Only the high priest was allowed in the Holy of Holies once a year to present the blood sacrifice for the Israelite people.

If the devil had ever had the audacity to try to break through that veil and penetrate the Holy of Holies, he never would have made it. It was completely out of his jurisdiction; he had no access there.

The temple is a shadow or type of the believer. As a believer, my body is the temple of God because the Holy Spirit has come and made His abode on the inside of me. My flesh is the outer court; my soul the inner court. But my born-again, recreated spirit is a type of the Holy of Holies — and nobody, but *nobody* except my High Priest is allowed inside there.

So when I pray in tongues, Satan has no idea what God is saying to me. Why? Because the Holy Spirit creates that supernatural language within my Holy of Holies, and it is outside of all satanic jurisdiction.

I know a man whose sister was in a car accident. She was transported to the hospital, her life hanging by a thread. This man was a faith man. As he headed for the hospital as fast as he could drive, he confessed over and over, "My sister will live and not die; she will live and not die!"

But every time this man would make his confession, "She'll live and not die," something would shatter his emotions so badly that it just shook him up from the top of his head to the bottom of his feet. Then the thought would hit, *She'll die!* This happened again and again as the man sped toward the hospital. It was really shaking him up.

Then suddenly through the gift of the discerning of spirits, God opened this man's spiritual eyes. (The discerning of spirits allows you to see into the realm of the spirit, whether angels or demons.)

When God opened this man's eyes, he saw two demons — one sitting on his left shoulder, the other on his right. Every time the man would make his confession, "She'll live and not die," one demon would scream through his ear to the other demon, "She'll die! She'll die!"

Then the Lord spoke to the man in his spirit: "Make your confession, and then begin to pray in tongues." So the man made his confession one more time and began to pray in tongues. After a while, one of the demons looked around the back of the man's head at the other demon and said, "What do you think he's saying?"

The other devil said, "I don't know, but is it burning you the way it's burning me?"

"Yes," the other demon answered. "Do you think we should leave?" So they left. And you may as well know, the man's sister lived and did not die!

Building Yourself Up On Your Most Holy Faith

So what happens when I pray in tongues for personal edification, which I can do at will, anytime I desire? Why is this, the most "foolish" of all gifts to the natural mind, so important and so powerful?

Let's look at Jude 20 and 21 to discover more of our answer:

> **But ye, beloved, building up yourselves on your most holy faith, praying in the Holy Ghost,**
>
> **Keep yourselves in the love of God, looking for the mercy of our Lord Jesus Christ unto eternal life.**

We know that God is only pleased by and only moves in response to our faith. In Romans 10:17, Paul tells us, **So then faith cometh by hearing, and hearing by the word of God.** But we also know that we can hear and hear and hear the Word and yet not see any change in our lives. We still have to get that Word planted in our spirits and then find some way to release the faith that the Word has produced.

Thousands of people around the world are filled to overflowing with God's Word. Yet still, for the most part, the Church does not experience the miraculous results found in the Book of Acts. So there must be a missing ingredient most believers are unaware of.

The truth is, any minister, no matter how anointed and full of the Word he may be, can only tell you what he has learned through experience and as the Holy Ghost has taught him in his own times of meditation on the Word. But that teaching will not profit you if you don't find some way to mix faith with it. You must personally get that Word into your spirit and then let the Holy Spirit teach *you.*

That's why Jude says we are to build ourselves up on our most holy faith by praying always in the Holy Ghost. It is only as we willingly and freely present our bodies as a living sacrifice and take the time to endure in prayer that the Holy Ghost can begin to reveal to us the mysteries of Christ. Only then can He release the faith in our hearts that is needed for God's power to operate in our lives.

Hungry for God's Power

Ever since I was born again, I've been so hungry to know God in His power. At first, I thought there was something wrong with me because I encountered so many groups of believers who just didn't seem to be hungry. They just didn't seem to care that they lived such powerless lives.

I would wonder, *Lord, why aren't more people hungry for Your power like I am? Is it the call You have on my life to operate in miracles that makes me different?*

I was so hungry for God's power when I was first born again that I would try anything that I was told would help me walk in more power. If it promised to satisfy the hunger on the inside of me, I would do it.

One person said to me, "No wonder you're not walking in the power of God."

I asked, "Why not?"

"Because of the jewelry you're wearing."

"You mean, if I take this jewelry off, I will walk in God's power?"

"That's right."

So I took off my jewelry. What happened? Well, before I took off my jewelry, I was a powerless jewelry wearer. And after I took it off, I became a powerless non-jewelry wearer! It didn't make a bit of difference.

Then later when I moved to Oregon and hooked up with another group of believers, someone told me, "No wonder you don't walk in the power of God."

"Why not?"

"Well, how were you baptized?"

"I was baptized in water in the Name of the Father, the Son, and the Holy Ghost."

"Well, no wonder!" the person exclaimed. "You were baptized in the name of three Gods, and there is only one God!" (This particular group believed there is only one God, whose Name is Jesus.)

Well, then," I said, "I'll just get rebaptized!" (As I said, at that point in my Christian walk, if I thought something meant more power in my life, I was all for it. Get rebaptized? Just name the place!)

We were in the middle of an Oregon winter at an elevation of 4,800 feet. It was snowing, the ground was frozen, and the two ponds were covered with a thick layer of ice. After building a bonfire beside the upper pond, a group of us were baptized in the freezing water that flowed through the flume (an artificial channel built to transport logs by water) between the two ponds. The preacher and I were first to step down into the frigid water. (I was too ignorant to know that I could have been baptized in a warm bathtub!)

It was so cold, my legs started to turn blue. I felt like I was freezing to death — but I was determined to go under the water and get rebaptized so I could have more power in my life!

The preacher asked me, "Are you ready?"

With chattering teeth, I stammered, "Okay, baptize me." So he dunked me in the icy water, baptizing me in the Name of Jesus.

Well, in the months that followed, I came to realize that before I was immersed in that freezing water, I was a powerless Pentecostal boy supposedly baptized in the name of three Gods. Then that preacher shoved me under the icy water and baptized me in the Name of Jesus — and I became a powerless Pentecostal boy baptized in the name of one God! Once again, it didn't make one bit of difference.

It wasn't until later — the day I discovered I had "uncovered a spiritual law" — that I learned a vital key to releasing God's power in my life.

"Oh, Brother Roberson, can you teach *me* to walk in power?" Oh, yes, I can. And I don't care if your name is Susie Wallpaper or Joe Public either. This key isn't reserved for an elect few.

Just keep on reading this book, and I'll teach you how to walk *out of* everything that Jesus said you've been delivered from. I'll also teach you how to walk *into* everything He said you could be in your life — on purpose, just because you want to go there! The answer is just as available to you who want it as the air you breathe.

Contending for the Faith

When the Holy Ghost began to reveal to me the treasures hidden in the Book of Jude, I realized I had discovered an important key in my search to know God in His power. First, I latched onto verse 3:

> **Beloved, when I gave all diligence to write unto you of the common salvation, it was needful for me to write unto you, and exhort you that ye should EARNESTLY CONTEND FOR THE FAITH which was once delivered unto the saints.**

I was so excited when I read that we should earnestly contend for the devil-stomping, mountain-moving kind of faith that was once delivered to the saints. Why was I so excited? Well, one thing I had learned about God's Word was this: God wouldn't tell me to contend for the faith without then going on in minute detail to teach me *how* to contend. I was on the right trail, tracking down my answer!

You see, it wasn't enough to know I should contend for the faith. The cry of my heart was, "For God's sake, can someone teach me *how*? Don't wave a delicious steak in front of my face and then not give it to me!"

Once I was discussing this passage of Scripture with another minister, and he asked me, "What is your background on the subject of faith?"

I answered, "The Word of God is my only background on the subject of faith. I am a faith man. I take God's Word for what it says. I'm not moved by what I see, hear, or feel. I'm not moved by disease or financial lack. Only one standard controls my life, and that's what the Word of God says about my problem — not the devil, not the circumstances, only the Word of God."

"Well, then," the man said, "if you believe all that, you already have more faith than the Early Church had."

"I beg your pardon," I replied. "If I'm going to have *more* faith than the Early Church had, it seems to me I am first going to have at least *as much*! If I remember correctly, during one of Peter's revivals, people lay the sick and dying in the streets near the meeting because those on whom Peter's shadow fell were getting healed!

"Now, correct me if I'm wrong," I continued, "but I didn't notice anyone laying the sick on the street near this meeting in the hope that *our* shadow would fall on them and heal them! It seems to me that we need to contend for that kind of powerful faith that was once delivered to those early saints!"

Then in verse 4, Jude tells us what happened to the mountain-moving faith in which the Early Church operated:

> **For there are certain men crept in unawares, who were before of old ordained to this condemnation, ungodly men, turning the grace of our God into lasciviousness, and denying the only Lord God, and our Lord Jesus Christ.**

Certain men had crept into the Church unawares. Whoever these men were, to a large extent they stole the faith of the Early Church.

So I conducted a study on these men from the Book of Jude, if for no other reason than to find out what path I should *not* take. I didn't want my faith to suffer the same fate as the early believers — stolen from me by dead religion.

Jude compared these ungodly men to **raging waves of the sea, foaming out their own shame...** (v. 13). What was he talking about? Well, a wave rises out of the ocean, and for a moment, puts on a display of foaming glory. But just as quickly as it appears, it disappears back into the sea.

Jude also compared these men to "wandering stars." You and I know these phenomena in the heavens as shooting stars. All of a sudden, a shooting star will flash in the night sky in a spectacular blaze of glory and then quickly disappear back into the darkness from which it came. Similarly, these wandering stars, after appearing as bright lights of truth for a short season, would slink back into the "blackness of darkness" that was reserved for them forever.

These men are also called "clouds without water" (v. 12). Throughout the Bible, water is used as a type of the Holy Ghost. For instance, we saw earlier that Jesus likened the Holy Spirit to rivers of living waters, flowing from our innermost being (John 7:38).

So these clouds without water were men who stole the power of God from the Early Church. They crept in unawares, using doctrines of men to steal the faith of believers until there was no faith left — until the Church plunged into the Dark Ages, having lost her faith to a large extent for hundreds of years. No wonder Jude compared these men to clouds without water!

In a drought, a cloud without water may come over the horizon looking promising. It may put on a good show as it drifts overhead. But when it comes to producing needed rain, that cloud is powerless to do so because it has no water.

So the first criterion to walking in the power of God is that I must be a cloud *with* water. In other words, I must be filled with the Holy Spirit. But evidently, just having the Holy Spirit isn't enough.

I used to think that the baptism in the Holy Ghost was all I needed to automatically see God's power released in my life. Wrong. I know people who have been baptized in the Holy Ghost for forty years. But if you measured the power of the Holy Spirit by the fruit of their lives, you would come to the conclusion that the Holy Spirit had no power at all!

I finally came to the conclusion that even though I was a cloud with water — even though I had been filled with the Holy Spirit — there still must be something *I* had to do to walk in God's power. Just having the Holy Spirit wasn't enough. There had to be a way to release Him on the inside of me. There had to be a way to get all that Holy Ghost power out of my spirit and onto the problems that needed to be overcome.

At times as I sat in a service listening to a minister preaching the Gospel, I wanted to raise my hand and say, "Excuse me, Mister Evangelist, but the Holy Spirit you're talking about — the One who moved on the face of the deep — is He the same One who now abides on the inside of me?"

"Why, yes, Son," he would say.

"Well, then, Mister Preacher, could you please tell me how to get all that power out of my spirit and loosed on the problem? Because until now, the common cold has whipped me!"

I knew there had to be a way to release the power on the inside of me — and later, I found out there is! And it is just as deliberate and as power-releasing as you want it to be in your life!

Rising Above a Carnal, Sense-Ruled Walk

Jude had more to say in verse 19 about those "clouds without water" who had crept into the Church unawares:

These be they who separate themselves, sensual, having not the Spirit.

These ungodly men were sensual, or sense-ruled. That means they were dominated more by the carnal appetites of the flesh than they were by the Word of God. It goes on to say that they "had not the Spirit." These men did not have the Holy Ghost in operation in their lives. Therefore, they were separated from truth by the devil and by carnality and the lusts of the flesh.

So, evidently, being filled with the Holy Spirit must have something to do with not being dominated by the flesh. It must have something to do with whether disease stops me or I stop the disease. Somehow there must be a way to release the Holy Spirit in my life so that instead of poverty paralyzing my progress, I can turn around and stop financial lack in its tracks.

I'm not a cloud without water. I've been baptized in the Holy Ghost. I'm a tongue-talking, devil-stomping, mountain-moving, faith-filled believer! I don't have to be like those who separated themselves.

Why don't I? The next verse follows the same line of thought as verse 19, and it tells me why: "But, you, beloved — you who do have the Holy Ghost — build yourselves up on your most holy faith. Build yourself up above a walk that is dominated by the senses by praying in the Holy Ghost!"

This edification process of Jude 20 delivers us from the strife-filled, carnal condition described in Jude 19 and enables us to live continually in Jude 21: **KEEP YOURSELVES IN THE LOVE OF GOD, looking for the mercy of our Lord Jesus Christ unto eternal life.** In other words, praying in tongues is the bridge between a state of strife and sensuality and the love of God.

Oh, how much we have sought God for that elusive increase of the faith God deposited on the inside of us — and here was this verse all along, giving us in black and white an ironclad guarantee that we can build ourselves up! Up where? Up above a walk where disease brings us to a standstill. Up above a walk where poverty reigns in our lives. Up above a walk where our children are lost to the world forever. Up above this sense-dominated realm where we are more moved by what we see, hear, and feel than we are by the Word of God.

We can release the power of the Holy Ghost in our lives as we build ourselves up on our most holy faith. How? By praying in the Holy Ghost!

Pray Until the Power Comes!

Mark 11:23 says that I can say to a mountain in my life, "Be removed and be cast into the sea," and if I don't doubt in my heart, I'll have what I say with my mouth. The condition that must be met here is that *I do not doubt in my heart.*

Then in verse 24, Jesus states that I shall have whatever I desire when I pray believing that I have received my answer. So once again, the only stipulation —

other than that my prayer must be according to the will of God — is that I must not doubt in my heart.

Well, that makes this fact very significant: I've found something I can do on purpose, as much and as long as I want to, that carries God's guarantee to edify me and to build me up on my most holy faith *within the part of me where He said I must not doubt.*

Therefore, when I speak to the mountain, the only question left between me and a walk of devil-stomping, mountain-moving power is this: Do I have the guts to pray until the power comes? Because it's not a question of whether or not the power will come. It *will* come. The only question is, do I have the guts to stay in there until it does?

"But, Brother Roberson, I'm a businessman." Then the Holy Spirit will come in power to your business. "I'm a preacher." Then He will come in power to your ministry.

The question is *not* "Will the power come?" When Jesus inspired these words in Jude 20, He took it out of all golden-tongued, speculative theology and put it into the realm of fact. And if Jesus said it, it is so whether you believe it or not. This isn't a democracy. Jesus didn't ask you for your vote. Your job is not to change God's truth, but to find it.

Jesus inspired Jude to write verses 19 and 20. So Jesus is saying there is a key that, when acted upon, will build you up above a sense-dominated walk where everything you've been delivered from defeats you. Instead, this key will cause you to walk in power on your most holy faith. What is the key? Using that supernatural language called tongues.

Why Are We Edified?

So we know from First Corinthians 14:4 and Jude 19 that we are edified when we pray in tongues. But my question to God is this: "*Why* are we edified?" I mean, if I'm going to spend three or four hours praying in the Holy Ghost, I want to know why it edifies me.

To know that you should pray in tongues isn't enough. If you really believed it edifies you and qualifies you to fulfill God's call on your life — the very thing you desire most in your heart — no one could keep you out of your prayer closet!

Many Christians know what First Corinthians 14:4 says, but they still spend most of their time starting man-made programs and trying to figure out God's plan for their lives in their heads. So, obviously, they don't really believe that their answer lies in stopping long enough to edify themselves by praying in an unknown tongue.

Therefore, knowing I should pray in tongues isn't enough. I want to know *why* I am edified. Why am I built up on my most holy faith when I speak a bunch of syllables in the air for two or three hours that I don't understand with my natural mind?

I told God, "Maybe if You could help me understand why, I could help Your people understand it too. Then they could also enter into a walk of the Spirit in power." You can imagine how I felt when one day the Lord opened up the Scriptures to me and showed me the *why* behind the edification process of tongues. He took me back to First Corinthians 14:2-4:

For he that speaketh in an unknown tongue speaketh not unto men, but unto God: for no man understandeth him; howbeit in the spirit he speaketh mysteries.

But he that prophesieth speaketh unto men to edification, and exhortation, and comfort.

He that speaketh in an unknown tongue edifieth himself; but he that prophesieth edifieth the church.

Notice that Paul says in verse 4 that he who prophesies edifies the church. Why? Because through the simple gift of prophecy (which is equivalent to the gift of tongues and interpretation operating together), suddenly the mind of Christ for that day and hour is made known to that particular public assembly.

A person who prophesies speaks to men unto edification, exhortation, and comfort (v. 3). But all exhortation has to be based on a scriptural foundation, or there is nothing to exhort about. For instance, I can't exhort on Jesus stopping off at the moon to have breakfast on His way down to earth, because that's not in the Scriptures! Therefore, sometimes the Holy Spirit will unveil a mystery through prophecy, illuminating the mind of Christ regarding a scripture that hasn't been understood.

And after the Holy Ghost prophesies through someone unto edification and exhortation, a divine comfort comes to the body of believers that is different than an emotional high. They are comforted in a way that is stronger than emotions. The prophecy picks them up in the Spirit and gives them a sense of "Everything is going to be okay" that can stay with them for days.

So when a person prophesies, it edifies the church *collectively*, and when he prays in tongues, it edifies him *individually*. However, the reasons why either the body of believers or the individual is edified are the same: In both cases, the mind of Christ is revealed.

Prophecy causes the mind of Christ to be manifested collectively to the church. On the other hand, praying in tongues causes the mind of Christ to be manifested in you as an individual, for the Holy Spirit will begin to take the mysteries you've been praying before the throne of God and communicate them back to you by revelation. *That's* why you are edified through praying in tongues!

Therefore, spending three hours praying in the Holy Ghost would be one of the wisest moves you've ever made. And if you do it every day — look out, devil! You're building yourself up on your most holy faith, receiving greater and greater revelation of the mind of Christ — and the devil has no idea what you're saying. He just has to watch it happen!

For when My Spirit is free to move,
I can remove those things that have taken root
   in you.
In a moment's time, I can do those things
   that take years to attain.
For it is not by your power nor by your might,
But it is through My Spirit
   that I do mortify these things.

So yield yourself to Me,
And declare yourself free.
And I will do this work in you,
   saith the Spirit of Grace.

Chapter 10

Purging and Mortification

People are looking for help to change. Most have character flaws they don't like in themselves, but they don't have any idea what to do to get rid of those flaws.

So these people keep on plugging away in a religious system that demands more and more out of them so that new buildings can be built and new programs can be started. Finally, spiritual exhaustion sets in, and they give up the fight. They resign themselves to always remaining the way they are and view God as the head of organizationalism. Assuming that their relationship with God is based on their relationship with an organization, they are left faithless and frustrated.

But God never intended for us to live futile lives of frustration. That's why He gave us the Holy Spirit — to reveal the mysteries of Christ in us and to perfect change. So let's take a closer look at the ministry of the Holy Spirit on the inside of us. Let's see how, through the edification process, He takes us from where we are into everything He said we could be.

No 'Quick Fix'

Even Christians who believe that praying in tongues edifies them often don't understand how the edification process works.

Let me paint a picture of what many believers think the edification process is: Before a person is baptized in the Holy Ghost, he is like a dirty old crow eating some dead animal off the road on a cloudy day. Then he starts praying in tongues. All of a sudden, the sun comes out from behind the cloud and shines its bright rays on the crow. Instantaneously the lowly bird is transformed into a grand, golden eagle that takes off soaring in the air, never to have another problem!

Wrong. That's not how the edification process works. At the same time the Holy Spirit builds you up in your spirit to understand revelation knowledge in God's Word, He also strengthens your born-again spirit with the power to mortify or put to death the deeds of the flesh (Rom. 8:13).

The Purging Process

Jesus said, "If you bear fruit, I will *purge* (or prune) you" (John 15:2). Whether we like it or not, if we bear fruit as a branch connected to the Vine, we are going to undergo purging. Why? So we can bear more fruit.

So beware: You're going to provoke an internal war when you begin to consistently pray in tongues, because impurities will soon start to surface that you don't want to get rid of. God will endeavor to purge those impurities off your life so you can fulfill your divine call without being destroyed by the devil.

The Holy Spirit pulls out the dead limbs that serve as a ceiling in our lives, preventing us from climbing higher in our walk with God. Every time God wants to use us, the devil walks out on those limbs and tries to stop the move of God in our lives through our finances, our wrong attitudes, our unforgiveness, etc. And if we don't allow the Holy Spirit to cut those dead limbs off, the devil will keep us sitting on a "do-little pile" the rest of our lives.

But I can assure you of this much: The Holy Ghost will not immediately try to purge every dead limb your flesh is clinging to. He will wait until you have built yourself up to a place high enough in the Spirit through praying in tongues that you can handle the emotional war that will result when He cuts each dead limb out of your life.

The purging process may not always be fun, but it is always necessary, because one way or another, we *will* be purged. We can choose to have all of our short-comings and faults pruned away now. Or we can wait until the Day of the Judgment Seat of Christ when our works will be tried as by fire (1 Cor. 3:12-15). On that day, all of our fleshly works that we failed to mortify in this life will be purged for us.

But here is the good news! We're not left to ourselves to mortify the deeds of the flesh. According to Romans 8:13, God has given you and me the Holy Spirit to strengthen us and to help purge us of anything that could rob us of our reward:

> **For if ye live after the flesh, ye shall die: but if ye through the Spirit do mortify the deeds of the body, ye shall live.**

You see, Satan's most powerful weapon is decep-tion. His goal is to steal our reward by keeping us in the dark about what Jesus has called us to do with our lives. The devil knows that when all is said and done, the one thing you and I will be rewarded for is how much of God's personal plan for our lives we have managed to fulfill.

Therefore, I don't want to wait until the Great Judgment Seat of Christ to have all of the fleshly works that hinder my walk with God purged out of me. I want to know how the Holy Spirit works in my life *now* to prune me in preparation for my divine call.

The First Step:
Waking Up the Conscience

So just accept it: You can't be charged up and edified in your spirit man without also undergoing a purging process in your life. It is impossible to rise upward in God without cutting off the things that are holding you down.

Therefore, the first thing the Holy Spirit does as you keep praying in tongues is to wake up your conscience. It becomes much more difficult to do the fleshly things you used to do.

For instance, if someone makes a cutting remark to you, you just smile and praise God for his deliverance. You think, *I wouldn't have done that last year. I would have slapped him out of his shoes!* Something has changed. It's the edification process at work.

When the Holy Spirit wakes up your conscience to something you are doing wrong, that means He is there with the power to put it to death. When you add your faith and begin to resist it, mortification takes place and the Holy Spirit cleanses you from it. *That* is edification.

Things Hidden in Darkness Revealed

Remember what I said earlier: The mysteries you pray out in tongues are for your benefit, not God's. Every time you pray in the Spirit, you communicate up before God's throne the mysteries of Christ in you, the Hope of Glory. When God starts to answer those prayers, you begin to receive insight into His Word. The understanding of everything that Jesus is in you starts to come forth on the inside.

At the same time these mysteries are revealed to your understanding, the Holy Spirit also casts a brilliant light on spiritual roadblocks that are hidden in darkness — those sins, faults, and shortcomings that keep you from producing a hundredfold harvest of God's plan for your life.

This is what Jesus is talking about in Mark 4:20-22. After describing the different types of bad ground in people's hearts, He says this:

> And these are they which are sown on good ground; such as hear the word, and receive it, and bring forth fruit, some thirtyfold, some sixty, and some an hundred.
>
> And he said unto them, Is a candle brought to be put under a bushel, or under a bed? and not to be set on a candlestick?

So Jesus calls me "good ground" if I receive God's Word — both the written Word and the mysteries of His personal plan for my life — and then bring forth the fruit of that Word thirty, sixty, and a hundredfold.

Then Jesus asks the question, "Is a candle lit to be hidden under a bushel or under a bed?" The answer is no. Can a lighted candle be brought into a dark room without shining its light on that which is hidden in darkness? No. Is the Word of God given to you *not* to understand? No!

Jesus then makes this statement in verse 22:

For there is nothing hid, which shall not be manifested; neither was any thing kept secret, but that it should come abroad.

In other words, when the Holy Spirit begins to illuminate your spirit by the Word of God, it is like walking into a dark room with a lighted candle. Every obstacle in the room that is hidden in darkness will be revealed by the light.

Jesus happens to be talking about your life. He happens to be talking about uncovering the things hidden in darkness that prevent you from producing a hundredfold walk.

You see, the candle of your spirit was lit when you were born again, and you cannot pray in tongues without causing that lit candle to burn brighter and brighter. That, my friend, is when that internal war begins! Why? Because the flesh doesn't like its deeds exposed to the light. The flesh is just like those little cockroaches that live in cheap motels. When the light is turned on, they scurry for cover. They love the cover of darkness.

So it is with your flesh. I guarantee you, your flesh isn't going to want to get rid of everything the Holy Spirit shines a light on!

Inward Transformation
Before Outward Change

Before I understood the dynamics of that internal war, it was a great mystery to me why so many people, although hungry for more of God and stirred up in their spirits to pray much in the Holy Ghost, gave up before any noticeable results had occurred. Then I realized that most of those people had given up because they were looking for their answers in the wrong place.

Let me give you an example. Suppose a believer gets all excited about praying in tongues. He decides, *Look out, devil! I'm going to lock myself away somewhere and pray in tongues an hour every day. And woe to the man who tries to get in my way to stop me! He'll have boot marks on his back end!*

So this man marches to his prayer closet with a ten-pound Bible under his arm. Yes, sir, he's going to pray in tongues an hour every day. There's just one problem. He's coming into this commitment as a manic-depressive suffering from a terminal disease who is in the process of filing bankruptcy!

But this man doesn't care, because he's found the answer. He thinks, *I've found Someone who knows my weakness and will pray for my problem. Everything is going to be different now!*

One month goes by. This believer prays in tongues one hour every day. No change. Two months go by. He's still praying in tongues. No change. Three months go by. Now he's out watching the horizon.

"What are you looking for?"

"Oh, not much. But, you know, I put my time in. I've been praying in tongues for three months! If anyone should receive an answer, it's me!"

I'll tell you what that man is doing. He's out looking for the spectacular and missing the miraculous! In other words, he's expecting God to answer the mysteries he has prayed out in tongues by changing his outward circumstances in some magnificent way. Meanwhile, he is oblivious to the miraculous work of the Holy Ghost that is taking place inside of him.

Perhaps this believer imagines a big, white stallion with flaming, red eyes riding over the horizon and thundering down into the valley to his house. As the stallion approaches, he recognizes who is in the saddle.

"Oh, boy, it's Jesus! Wow, this praying in tongues stuff really works!"

Jesus reins in His stallion next to the believer and says, "First of all, give Me a list of everyone you owe money to." The man gives Him the list, and Jesus gallops off on His horse, leaving a cloud of dust behind Him. Jesus is back in a half an hour and tells the man, "Every bill is paid off."

Then Jesus says, "Excuse Me a minute," and takes off after the spirit of poverty that He has just spotted slinking around in the shadows. The big stallion stomps on that slimy devil until he's just a miserable heap on the floor — and instantly poverty is broken in the believer's life!

Jesus trots back on His stallion and dismounts. Then He walks over to the believer and lays hands on him — and the disease and manic depression immediately disappear! The believer exclaims, "Oh, my! I've been made a new person, and I only prayed for three months! This stuff really does work!"

Jesus gets back on his horse and begins to ride off. All of a sudden, He stops and rides back. He says, "By the way, I forgot this." He reaches into His pocket and pulls out an envelope containing ten thousand dollars. "This is for eating and fellowshiping in restaurants after church services," He informs the delighted man.

Then Jesus rides off toward the horizon. Silhouetted by the setting sun, He rears up on his stallion, shouts, "Hi ho, Holy Ghost, and away!" and gallops off. The believer sighs, wipes his forehead with the back of his hand, and says, "Now *that* was a real deliverance!"

Many people make the same mistake as that man did. They pray in tongues, looking for their outward circumstances to suddenly change. But they miss where the supernatural transformation actually takes place — in their spirit. And too often they give up before God can finish working in them the most important changes of all. They look for the spectacular but miss the miraculous.

Remember, *praying in tongues is like any other prayer — it is designed to be answered!* But because it is our human spirit doing the praying (1 Cor. 14:14), it is also our spirit man receiving the answer to our prayers.

Now let me show you how the spirit man receives the answer to the mysteries prayed out in the Holy Ghost. Let's just suppose that I hold a crusade where hundreds of people get excited about praying in tongues. In fact, they are so excited that even after I leave town, they decide to spend a certain amount of time in prayer every day.

But after a few weeks of seeing no apparent changes in their circumstances, one by one they begin to drop away. Finally, there is only one person left who is still keeping his commitment to pray in tongues every day.

Let's say this one man hangs on to his commitment for several months, praying in the Holy Ghost and looking for change. Gradually something very miraculous begins to take place inside of him.

Something happens to his insight into the Word. Scriptures he never understood before come alive. In casual conversation with his friends, he can suddenly explain verses that used to be a mystery to him. When people come to him with their problems, he wonders, *Why don't they do this and this?* because it all seems so clear to him.

This man is experiencing the effect that praying in tongues has on his spirit. He is experiencing the way God answers this kind of prayer.

In this same way, your spirit can begin to receive wisdom and direction to fulfill God's special plan for you. You can develop a kind of "know-so" whereby you just somehow *know* what God wants, even though at times you don't know *how* you know.

Now, all this doesn't mean that noticeable results won't begin to show up in external circumstances. *They will!* The most unexpected, incredible things will begin to take place. God will work in your job, in your family, and in your body. Friends and loved ones will notice the difference in you as faith and assurance begin to radiate and flow out from your life.

I have seen many miracles take place as a result of perseverance in praying in the Holy Ghost. But, you see, first faith must come by hearing and hearing by the Word of God (Rom. 10:17). And as insight into the Word begins to increase, so does the purging process that transforms a person from the inside out. *Then*, according to God's divine order, outward circumstances begin to line up with the changes that have already occurred in the hidden man of the heart.

Deal with the Root — Not the Bad Fruit

God used a house in a neighborhood near my home to teach me a lesson along this line. Everyone hates this house. As you drive through this neighborhood of elegant homes, suddenly you turn the corner and here's this dilapidated house.

Trash is piled knee-deep all over the yard. The house is in dire need of a paint job. The screen door is cocked sideways. The lawn is overgrown. Several old cars with no tires are scattered around. All of this in the middle of a very nice neighborhood!

Everyone who lives in the area is angry at the man who lives in that house, but no one has convinced him to do anything about its appearance. "I lived here first before any of these other houses were even built," he says, and he refuses to change.

One day I looked at this house as I drove by and thought, *Oh, my Lord, what a mess!* Then the Holy Spirit took advantage of the opportunity to teach me something. He spoke to my spirit, saying, "Did you know that the outside of that house is an exact picture of the inside of the man who lives in it?"

Whoa! With that revelation fresh in my mind, the first thing I wanted to do when I arrived home was mow my lawn!

But, you see, the Holy Spirit was pointing out a mistake that most Christians make: They are always trying to pick the bad fruit off the tree of their life without dealing with the root that caused the bad fruit to grow in the first place!

For example, people are often coaxed through their emotions to respond to an altar call. "Run up here and leave all of your bad fruit at the altar," the preacher says. So they kneel at the altar and think, *Okay, I'm not going to slap my wife anymore. I'm not going to drink alcohol anymore.*

So they pick off their bad fruit, leave it on the altar, and go home. Now, it's good that they have repented and made a commitment to God never to commit such sins again. However, there is a big problem. If they don't deal with the root of the problem — those spiritual roadblocks hidden within them in darkness — that bad fruit will simply grow back.

Will Worship vs. Mortification by the Spirit

But you can't discover the root of fleshly works in your life on your own. The Holy Spirit is the only One who can search the innermost parts of your heart to find the root. Then He edifies your reborn human spirit to rise up and put to death the deeds of the flesh on a daily basis. That's why the baptism in the Holy Spirit takes place in the human spirit — because that's where all permanent change comes from.

I've been in the ministry now for more than twenty-five years, and I have found that people can't change themselves. For example, when I rededicated my life to the Lord at that ultra-Holiness church, people preached at me all the time about what I was supposed to be and what I was supposed to do. They told me to quit sinning and gave me a list of all kinds of do's and don'ts.

But it wasn't until I found out how to release the power of the Holy Spirit inside of me that I was able to put to death that old man's fleshly deeds. Then finally, *finally*, Jesus, the Man of Compassion, could begin to come forward in my life.

You see, the natural mind is only familiar with trying to change through *will worship*. Do you know what will worship is? It is when you endeavor to discipline yourself against the problem as hard as you can using your own will. "I will not sin anymore. I will not sin anymore," you say with gritted teeth. But try as you might, sometimes you just can't break a fleshly habit using the strength of your own will.

On the other hand, mortification through the Spirit is the process by which the Holy Spirit rises up on the inside of you to destroy the hold that the flesh has had over you. Instead of the sin having dominion over you, you gain dominion over it!

The Cart Before the Horse

But how do we loose that power on the inside of us to mortify the deeds of the body? Earlier we saw that Romans 8:26 gives us the answer:

> **Likewise the Spirit also helpeth our infirmities: for we know not what we should pray for as we ought: but the Spirit itself maketh intercession for us with groanings which cannot be uttered.**

So the key that releases the Holy Spirit's power in our lives on a personal level to mortify the deeds of the flesh is *the supernatural languages of tongues.* The Holy Spirit says, "Excuse me, but I'd like to help you. If you'll let Me make intercession for you with groanings that cannot be uttered, I'll break the hold of those roadblocks that stand in the way of God's best for you."

The ultra-Holiness church I attended as a young man didn't understand that key. They taught the doctrine of "the three works of grace" — first saved, then sanctified (which means separated from the filthiness of the world), then filled with the Holy Ghost. They told me, "You need to be born again."

"Thank you, I am."

"Now you need to get sanctified."

"Sanctified from what?" I asked.

"From smoking, drinking, chewing tobacco — all that sort of thing."

"Then I can receive the Holy Ghost?" I asked.

"That's right."

"You mean, I can't get saved first, filled with the Holy Ghost second, and sanctified third?"

"No way! Do you think God is going to baptize a tobacco-mouth, alcohol-breath, unsanctified Christian?"

"Oh," I said. "I guess not."

But those folks had the cart before the horse! The Bible says it is *through the Spirit* that you mortify the deeds of the body.

The Holiness folks said to me, "You have to become good enough to receive the Holy Spirit."

I replied, "Yes, but I need the Holy Spirit to become good enough!"

So they said, "Then you can't have Him!"

But despite what those folks thought, I got filled with the Holy Ghost anyway! I came up to the altar one night at church, and the Holy Spirit came on me. Out of ignorance, I fought off the urge to speak out the supernatural words He was creating on the inside of me.

But later as I worshiped God at home, the Holy Ghost came on me again. This time, I lifted my hands and began to yield to Him. I fell down on the floor under the power of God and got up speaking with tongues — and I've been doing it ever since!

But I couldn't even tell those church folks I had received the Holy Spirit, because I still smoked my pipe and watched Star Trek! Then the Holy Spirit told me, "Let me step in, Son. I'm the power that has been sent to help you out of your weaknesses."

So I just kept praying in tongues. I'd smoke my pipe on the way to church Sunday morning. Then I would be under such conviction on the way home from church that I'd throw my pipe out the car window.

But on Monday morning at work, I'd buy another one. I'd smoke my pipe on the way to the Wednesday evening church service. Then on the way home from church, I'd throw it away. The purging process was well underway; I had provoked that internal war through praying in tongues!

But I found out that mortification through the power of the Holy Spirit goes for the root, and then the bad fruit just falls off. I can't tell you the exact time that the pipe and the tobacco just fell off my "tree." All I know for sure is that once my reborn human spirit had been built up sufficiently by the Holy Spirit, it struck the root, and the bad fruit dried up and fell off the limb for good. It beat anything I had ever seen!

The Parable of Sister Diet

You may be able to better understand the difference between willpower and mortification through my little parable about Sister Diet. For Sister Diet, every January starts the same thing all over again: "I'm going to lose thirty pounds of this unsightly heaviness. No more MacDonald's. No more pies and cakes. I'm just going to eat salads, and I'm going to start a big exercise program!"

Sister Diet stirs up her emotions and gets her willpower kicked in. Then on January 1, she starts her diet. She holds on for two months, stretching her willpower like a tight guitar string. By the third month, it's "Oh, God! Another salad!"

Then one day, the pastor receives a call from the local pie factory. "Pastor, we have a woman down here who claims to be one of your parishioners, and she just raided our pie factory. She says her name is Sister Diet. Do you know her?"

"Yes, I do."

"Well, she's babbling out of her mind — something about her will breaking."

"What happened to her?"

"I don't know. Have you ever seen those Bugs Bunny cartoons where the Tasmanian Devil whirls through like a tornado, eating up trees and anything else in his way? Well, Sister Diet just chewed her way through the door and the pie case and ate half of everything in the pie case. Then she chewed her way through the steel door of the freezer — and she's still in there! We have her in two straitjackets. Can you come and get her?"

So the pastor comes to retrieve Sister Diet. As he half carries her out of the pie factory, she continues to mumble incoherently, "My will broke. My will broke."

The parable of Sister Diet is a little extreme, but you get the point. Will worship can only take you so far in your battle to overcome the deeds of the flesh. The only true way to put those fleshly works to death once and for all is *through the Spirit*.

Willpower Can't Change a Marriage

I'll give you another example of how flesh can take back its ground when change is attempted through willpower alone. When a husband and wife are having marital problems, family counseling can be a real help. The counselor teaches both the husband and the wife how they are supposed to fulfill their roles in the marriage. He tells them, "If you'll do these things, it will change your marriage."

It's easy to tell people what they need to do to change their marriage. But if the counselor doesn't teach the husband and wife how to find the root of the problem — how to allow the Holy Spirit to purge them of the weaknesses that caused the problems in the first place — then all he has done is to give the couple some great but ineffective speeches.

So the husband and wife leave the counselor's office all stirred up in their emotions and determined to change their marriage. The first thing the wife does is to buy the recommended book *Do Yourself a Favor and Love Your Spouse* and read it.

The husband comes home from a hard day at the office. The wife is scantily dressed, candles flicker on the table, and the aroma of pheasant under glass fills the air.

He asks, "Where are the kids?"

"Never mind, Sweetie," she says.

He thinks, *My Lord, I have a new wife!*

Later the wife conveniently leaves the book *Do Yourself a Favor and Love Your Spouse* lying on a table in plain sight. The husband finds it and reads it. Later he comes home holding a red rose and greets her with "Hello, my dearest." He begins to go out of his way to do all those tender, loving little things that mean so much.

On Saturday morning, the wife wakes up to a kiss. The husband sets a breakfast tray on her lap with a red rose lying next to the food. "I have myself a new husband!" she exclaims.

Both husband and wife are in seventh heaven for a while. But about three months later, the will to keep up the effort of being a loving spouse is stretching thin.

It's Saturday morning again, and the wife wakes up to a kiss and another breakfast tray with a red rose lying next to the food. She says grumpily, "Oh, don't they have anything down at that flower place but red roses?"

The husband snaps back, "I'm going to slap you clear out of bed, woman!" And the battle of the sexes is resumed full force!

Whether it's smoking, eating too much, arguing with your spouse, or any other deed of the flesh, the principle is the same: Relying on sheer willpower to change your fleshly weaknesses will take you only so far. It is only through the Spirit that you mortify the deeds of the body.

God's Word Is the Standard

Jesus told us in John 15:2 that as branches connected to the true Vine, we *will* be purged in order to bear more fruit. Then in the next verse, Jesus said, **Now ye are clean through the word which I have spoken unto you** (v. 3). In other words, it is the Word of God that sets the standard for our purging. Without the Word, where would we obtain the information we need to discern between good and evil or truth and lies?

Only one foundation of truth exists in the entire universe, and that is the Word of God. Some religions will tell you, "Our system of religion is truth." But they are not. They are in deception, and they don't know it. Other religions will also try to convince you that they have the truth and their tenets contain sound wisdom for living, but they do not have eternal truth.

Only the Word can be trusted as the standard for truth. It didn't come from this world. It came from God Himself.

The second Person of the Godhead is called the mighty Logos, or the Word, who came to earth incarnate as the man Jesus Christ. The mighty Logos was chosen by the Godhead to cross and close the gap between humanity and God. One way He closed that gap was by providing information about the Godhead. He said, "If you have seen Me, you have seen the Father" (John 14:9).

The ancient philosophers sought something to bridge the gap between God and man. Socrates, Plato, and other famous philosophers tried to plunge their minds into infinity, asking, "What is out there? Who is the original Thinker? Who is the unmoved Mover?" But they had no answers. They only knew something had to be out there.

Then John brought the revelation those Greek philosophers sought all those years. He said, "Do you want to know who in this universe is the unmoved Mover? I'll tell you.

"Before anything had a beginning, there was the Logos. The Logos was with God. The Logos was God. And the Logos stood face to face, coequal with God. All things were made by the Logos. Nothing in creation was made without Him [John 1:1-3]. Sure, I can tell you who the unmoved Mover is. He is the mighty Logos, the Word. He is the One who has closed the gap between man and God."

So if you are trying to be purged by any other standard than the Logos, you are wasting your time. One of the most deceptive things you can get involved with is a religion peddling a bill of goods that isn't a mandate from God's Word. You can spend years trying to follow a set of man-made rules that do nothing to change you from the inside out. There is only one true purging process, and Jesus spelled it out: **Now ye are clean THROUGH THE WORD which I have spoken unto you** (John 15:3).

Breaking the Cycle of Defeat

So it is through the Spirit and according to God's Word that we mortify the deeds of the body — those fears, faults, and bad habits with which the flesh attempts to keep us in a never-ending cycle of defeat. That is the only way we can take the limits off our lives.

I have found that one of the primary roles of the Holy Spirit's leadership in our lives is to lead us out of those leftover patterns of the flesh nature's dominance. Those "leftovers" can sabotage everything God is attempting to do in our lives for the good.

One day I asked my brother (who was a detective in Memphis at the time), "Do you really want to know what has kept you from becoming a multi-millionaire?" He was wise enough to answer correctly. His job had nothing to do with it. His problem was his own limited pattern of thinking that had dominated him all of his life and had kept him imprisoned within its narrow confines.

In Mark 9:23, Jesus said that all things are possible to him who believes. Therefore, the only thing that stands between us and any kind of miracle is the fleshly pattern or system of thought that has captivated us in the realm of the soul. That unscriptural pattern is something faith can't give substance to. It is hope that has been programmed wrong — hope that has gone amiss. It is full of fear and torment instead of faith.

The Holy Spirit will replace that mess for the kind of hope that faith can give substance to. But we must yield to His leadership when He begins to root out those destructive patterns; otherwise, we will just remain in that same invisible prison until the day we die.

You see, it's no accident that right after Paul talks about mortifying the deeds of the flesh in Romans 8:13, he says this in verse 14: **For as many as are led by the Spirit of God, they are the sons of God.** Verse 13 and 14 are one continuous thought. The term "son of

God" refers to the mature believer who has been nurtured by the Holy Spirit to the point that he can now walk by his new nature rather than by the dictates of the flesh.

Therefore, Paul is describing in verse 14 a state of spiritual maturity where carnal patterns and systems of thought no longer dominate you because you are now walking after your new nature instead of according to the flesh.

Many times believers who are still immature and carnal themselves want the Holy Spirit to give them insight into other people's messed-up lives or to tell them what car to buy. But about the only thing the Holy Spirit can do with a believer in this spiritual condition is to lead him out of his own mess.

You may say, "Well, I want God to lead me into this ministry or this job promotion." But the first order of business is for God to lead you out of anything that keeps you in a perpetual cycle of defeat.

That's what Romans 8:13,14 is talking about: As many as will allow their reborn human spirit to be nurtured and taught by the Holy Spirit, they are the mature sons of God. For it is through the spirit — through the new nature within them — that they mortify the deeds of the flesh. The Holy Spirit will lead them out of patterns and systems of thought that enslave.

Paul described this condition of enslavement in Romans 7:7-24. He said, "What a wretched man I am. There is a bent toward sin loosed in my members, and the more I try to serve God, the more it wars against my mind. There is nothing in me to 'rebottle' it. Even though God gave me the Law and I try to keep it, this lust for sin persistently wages war inside of me. I can't seem to stop it."

This hopeless spiritual condition is the reason why the whole world became guilty before God and subject to His judgment. The world needed a Savior. So Romans 8 tells us how the Savior came to lead us out of our enslavement to the flesh into a walk of the Spirit.

Tearing Down Strongholds in the Soul

All you have to do is look at the root word of "mortify," which means *death*, to know you're in for a battle in the purging process. Paul describes this battle in Second Corinthians 10:

> **(For the weapons of our warfare are not carnal, but mighty through God to the pulling down of strong holds).**
>
> **— 2 Corinthians 10:4**

So Paul says that our weapons for this battle we're engaged in are not carnal. In other words, we don't wage this internal war with natural means. Instead, our weapons are mighty through God to the pulling down of invisible strongholds, or fortresses, that are erected in our lives.

Some believers think that the word "strongholds" in verse 4 is talking about some kind of invisible fortress that the devil builds at one end of a town to keep the townspeople from getting saved. These believers think their job is to tear down these evil fortresses of the enemy.

No, Paul is referring to a battle on the personal level. How do I know that? Because in verse 5 he says this:

> **Casting down imaginations, and every high thing that exalteth itself against the knowledge of God, and bringing into captivity every thought to the obedience of Christ.**

Who possesses the thoughts that are brought into captivity? Paul didn't change the subject between verse 4 and 5. If you are the possessor of the thought, you are the possessor of the fortress.

The strongholds Paul is talking about are imaginations and high things that exalt themselves against the knowledge of God. They are carnal strongholds in the realm of the soul. Paul is telling us to bring into captivity every disobedient thought, because the devil will cut us to pieces with the soulish strongholds that are not cast down. Some of those strongholds hinder us so greatly that if they aren't broken, we will die in our defeated condition, never to fulfill our godly desires or divine call.

A stronghold can consist of a certain set of imaginations that makes a person so infuriated, he separates himself from the truth through strife and unforgiveness. A stronghold can also be an elaborate system of religious thought that enslaves the hearts and minds of an entire nation. But whether it is a stronghold in the soul of an individual or of a nation, it all starts with an uncaptivated thought that exalts itself against the knowledge of Christ.

I'm so glad God has given us weapons that are mighty through God to tear down these fortresses!

They are not a part of the natural realm; they are given in the realm of His Spirit.

The most important weapon that God gave us was the third Person of the Godhead to live inside of us. Then the Holy Spirit also equipped us with another vital weapon — a supernatural language.

That language is a gift that edifies and builds us up above a carnal realm where our natural senses dominate. And as we employ this gift by praying in tongues, the Holy Spirit begins the process of purging us of every "high thing" that exalts itself against God's plan for our lives.

Where does this purging process take place? Well, everything that shows up on the outside is generally a picture of what is working on the inside of us. Therefore, mortification occurs in the realm of our character.

The Holy Spirit begins a work of discerning the thoughts and intents of our hearts, rooting out systems of thought and soulish strongholds that cause us to fail. As we keep praying in tongues for personal edification, He tears down any strongholds of the soul that have not been constructed by God's Word.

At the same time, the Holy Spirit constructs a superstructure in our spirit man by imparting revelation knowledge of God's Word. For what purpose? To mature us, to edify us, and to build our lives higher and higher into God.

The Word of God is a two-edged sword that divides asunder soul and spirit (Heb. 4:12). It is the only qualified agent to deliver such a distinct blow between spirit and soul. And in this purging process that encompasses all the realms of the soul and spirit, it is the only standard I trust as I endeavor to understand the Holy Spirit's work inside of me.

It doesn't matter how many devils come to clamor against my soul. I'm going to brace myself against the attack and still choose only the Word for my standard. That two-edged sword has penetrated my spirit, and I refuse to believe anything or anyone that is not in line with what the Word has declared.

The Last Forty Percent

If you're going to make it through the purging process, that's the kind of determination you have to develop to withstand the enemy's attacks. Why? Because mortification isn't a pleasant experience, and your flesh will want to give up. And three months of praying in tongues and edifying yourself to a certain place in God isn't going to make your purging process any more pleasant!

But that's okay. If there is one thing I don't want in my life, it is dead limbs. I'm willing to go through whatever unpleasantness the Holy Ghost deems necessary in order to rid myself of everything that sabotages God's perfect will for my life.

The dead limbs that the Holy Spirit is working on now in my life is the last forty percent. I'm on my way to a hundredfold walk.

You see, it's not so difficult to walk in thirtyfold or sixtyfold of God's will for you. But that last forty percent is a challenge. It deals with how you do or don't operate in the love of God.

When that last forty percent is purged, you respond differently when people insult you, slander you, slap your cheek, or sue you. Instead of retaliating with insult for insult, you extend nothing but the mercy of God. You esteem your testimony as your most valuable possession, and you are determined not to hurt a human being even at the cost of your own head.

The dead limbs of the last forty percent are hard to get to. A good deal of edification must take place first in your spirit before the Holy Ghost will even focus in on those hard-to-reach limbs and begin to purge them. In fact, during the first six months you pray consistently in tongues, the Holy Spirit is strengthening your spirit to get you willing to even discuss cutting those dead limbs off!

Remember, Jesus said that you are clean through the Word He has spoken (John 15:3). As the Holy Spirit girds up your spirit with revelation of the Word, you'll be able to cut off those hideous dead limbs that clutter and hinder your life.

One thing is for sure: You *won't* get rid of the last forty percent just by sitting in a pew once a week, listening to a thirty-minute sermon that you don't even plan to apply. So if you've been thinking that you don't need to pray much in tongues for personal edification, think again! You have a divine purpose to fulfill, and you don't need a lot of dead limbs in your way!

The Dead Limb of Complacency

The worst thing you need to be purged from is complacency and indifference. In its extreme, it's the type of attitude that says, "Let the town go to hell. Why should I spend my time praying for them?"

There are pastors in a state of complacency who don't want to meet under the same roof with the other preachers in town. Sure, these pastors want to see everyone in town get saved. They aren't that wicked. But they just want to be the ones to do it. Their attitude is, "If an evangelistic outreach doesn't come through me and my church, I'm not going to help make it a success."

That is called indifference or complacency. It's quite a chore for the Holy Ghost to cut that dead limb off! It's a part of that last forty percent.

The Holy Ghost has to cut the dead limb of indifference out of our lives before we will ever pursue revival above any selfish desire. Until we are purged of complacency, we'll always be focused on "*my* lifestyle" and "*my* comfort" more than other people's salvation.

Personally, the devil has often tried to use complacency as a means to keep me from entering in to the best God has for me. The enemy will whisper in my mind, "Why don't you just settle back and be comfortable? You have a good anointing. You have good meetings. Don't hundreds get filled with the Holy Spirit in a matter of weeks? Aren't you in the camp meeting circuit? Why don't you just settle down and stay where you're at? It's a good place to be."

Every time I have tried to break out of my comfort zone, I've encountered a major attack of the enemy. My flesh says, "Well, why don't I stay where I'm at spiritually? Why subject myself to more battering by the devil? Why can't I just get comfortable and live like other preachers? They seem to be content and happy."

My flesh will try to talk me into being complacent. But, you see, the hunger that is on the inside of my spirit has always been stronger than the voice of my flesh. I can only walk after the flesh so long before it becomes unbearable. I get absolutely unhappy, and I stay that way until I shake off my complacency and start to fervently pursue God again.

The Holy Spirit wants to mature us through revelation of God's Word so that we look at that dead limb of complacency in our lives and say, "I'm disgusted with that. Holy Spirit, please cut it off." He's even happy if we look at that limb and honestly admit, "God, I just don't want that limb cut off." At that point, we only need to do one thing: keep on praying in tongues. Eventually we *will* want to get rid of that dead, ugly limb. That's the edification process at work.

My Own Purging Process

By the time the Lord was finished cutting dead limbs off my life, I was nothing but a stump! He cut off all those dead limbs such as wrong believing, lusts of the flesh, love of money, and self-exaltation. And I like the fruitful limbs that have grown back in place of what was pruned away!

Lying was one of those dead limbs that the Holy Spirit targeted in my life. It took me a long time to become willing to even admit the fact that I lied at all. In my case, lying usually came in the form of misleading someone. (Of course, you've never done that!)

Here's an example: Your child answers the phone. You ask, "Who is it?"

"Mary."

"Tell her I'm gone." Then you slip out the door and close it.

Your child tells Mary, "My dad is gone. I mean, he isn't here."

Technically, you *aren't* there. You may rationalize and say, "I didn't really lie." Well, then, why are you explaining yourself?

Or a person might lie because he doesn't want to appear to be what he really is. For instance, he may be lazy. Perhaps he didn't do what he said he would do. So he tries to cover it up by bending the truth: "Uh, I kind of got busy." You didn't get too busy, you lying outfit! You could have gotten it done!

Here's another example: A friend calls you and says, "Hey, are you going to the meeting tonight?"

You say, "Uh, I was really looking forward to going, you know, but something came up." Then you call another friend and say, "Invite me to dinner so I have an excuse. I don't want to go to that meeting!"

Why did you lie? "Well, I didn't want to hurt my friend's feelings." You don't have to hurt anyone's feelings. Just say, "No, I don't think I'm going tonight." But, for God's sake, represent the truth!

Let me tell you what makes that kind of "white lie" so dangerous. In Ephesians 6:11, Paul said this:

Put on the WHOLE armour of God, that ye may be able to stand against the wiles of the devil.

Notice that the first piece of armor is the "loins girt about with *truth*" (v. 14).

So after you've told your child to lie for you or after you have misled someone by bending the truth, the devil comes along with an attack. You say, "I bind you!"

The devil replies, "Ah, shut up! You can't resist me without your spiritual armor on! So before you think about binding me, quit lying!"

So the Holy Spirit wanted to purge the dead limb of lying or misleading people out of my life for good. The biggest lie I ever told my wife before we were married was that I did not lie! I also told her I hadn't caroused and done certain wrong things that I had actually done.

I told Rosalie, "Even before I was born again, I was a hard worker, morning till night — not like these immature guys you see nowadays." You see, I wanted my wife to see me as her "knight in shining armor."

After Rosalie and I were married, we were fellowshipping with some other believers one night, and the men began to talk about the lifestyle of sin they had been delivered from. Rosalie said, "Oh, Dave never did that." But the fact was that I *had* done it; it was one of the things I had lied to her about before we were married.

From then on, it seemed as if every time my wife talked to someone, she unknowingly built on my lie.

She took my lie and spread it everywhere because I still hadn't told her the truth.

I would hear her say, "Well, my husband never did that," and I'd think, *I did do it. I lied to her in the past. I'm not lying anymore, but that is a lie she keeps building on. I'm going to have to tell her — but I don't want to!*

But later I started fasting and praying in tongues for extended lengths of time, and the Holy Spirit's bright light began to shine on those spiritual roadblocks that lay hidden in darkness inside of me. I can remember becoming more and more convicted about the lie I had told Rosalie. I finally prayed myself to the place where I told God, "Okay, Lord. I'll tell her I lied."

Then I found some excuse not to tell her that day. So the Lord woke me up in the nighttime and said, "I thought you said you were going to tell her." I sat straight up in bed, my eyes as big as sewer lids. I couldn't get back to sleep until I made another deal with God.

"Okay, I'll tell her, Lord."

"All right — when?"

"Tomorrow." With that, I was able to go back to sleep. But the next day, I found some excuse to say, "I'll tell her later."

So the Lord woke me up again the next night. He just wasn't going to let me get away with that lie! I had only two options — to quit praying in tongues or to quit lying. The praying kept my conscience alive. But my refusal to deal with the lying kept me tormented.

(A lot of Christians find themselves in that position. But most of them fall out of prayer because they don't want to deal with the problem.)

So after days of this struggle, I was sitting in my office, feeling all beaten up. My secretary came in and said, "You look tired."

"Yes, I have really been through it."

"What have you been doing?"

"I have been run through a spiritual wringer — but I'm going to make it. I'm in the process of establishing my foundation on pureness of spirit."

The night I finally decided to tell Rosalie the truth, I took her out to a fast-food hamburger restaurant. (That was my ignorant idea of buying her a nice meal to soften the blow!) Then I cautiously introduced the subject.

"Do you remember when you told those people that I had never had days of carousing like the other men had? Well, the truth is, I was just an old sinner." Then I proceeded to tell my wife the whole truth. Rosalie just kept saying, "Oh, my gosh!" as I related what my life was like before I was saved.

You may ask, "What about now? Do you ever lie to your wife anymore?" Well, after going through that ordeal between me and the Holy Ghost, do you think I'd start lying again? No, I let Him purge that dead limb out of me. Now Rosalie and I trust each other completely.

So the edification process awakened my conscience and built me up to the place where I was willing to deal with my sin. My inner man had been strengthened with might to put that fleshly work to death.

As a result of that purging process in my life, I have taken this stance for truth: Because of God's immutability, it is impossible for Him to lie. Therefore, if there is one standard that I am going to raise higher than any standard, it is the total absence of deceit and lying and the handling of the truth in all pureness of spirit. I refuse to harbor for a minute a lie or misrepresentation of the truth on the inside of me.

The Holy Spirit waits patiently for you to yield your authority to Him, for He has a work inside of you to do. He will strengthen your inner man, your reborn human spirit, with sufficient might to put to death the deeds of the flesh and to purge every dead limb out of your life one by one. As you do, the Holy Spirit has the liberty to increase His work of revealing divine mysteries to your spirit. So be assured — whether it's mortification or revelation, your prayers in the Spirit are being answered!

Oh, I'll come from a place within
   where you think that you have no strength.
And I'll say to you, "Get up and try again."
For even though you may be cast down
   from time to time,
   know this, My child —
   you are not forsaken.

Get up again and again and again,
   and My strength will be with you continually
   to begin again and again and again.
In a time when you think you will fall,
   you will not fall; you will stand.
For I will come from a place within
   and give you strength,
   says the Spirit of Grace,
   that you never knew you had.

Chapter 11

Overcoming Impasses In Prayer

God has filled me with compassion for people who start out all "bright-eyed and bushy-tailed" in their commitment to pray in the Spirit, but then reach an impasse and stop praying before they enter into the glory on the other side.

An *impasse* is a spiritual plateau or dry place that generally occurs just before God is ready to move you to a higher place in His Spirit. I want to help you understand the nature of an impasse because there is so much waiting for you in the realm of God if you will press on in prayer.

You will have to push past many impasses if you plan to persevere in prayer, the first usually being the temptation to fall out of prayer. The devil will try everything he can think of to get you out of prayer.

But if the enemy doesn't succeed in that, he still won't totally give up. Instead, he will come from a new angle. He will try to deceive you any way he can to keep you from going higher in God.

But just keep praying. Eventually you will come to the place where you are so hungry for God that you won't have to make yourself pray; it will be your heart's desire. You'll want to do whatever is necessary to draw closer to Him.

I know about impasses from personal experience. Day after day during my first year of ministry, I spent a certain amount of time praying in tongues. I was too stubborn to quit, even though there were times when every cell in my body screamed in resistance.

I have to admit it was hard for me to understand why something that was supposed to be so edifying was so hard to stick with. But since then I have come to understand why so many people who start out praying in tongues with such fervency sometimes become discouraged and give up.

Legalism and Condemnation Don't Come From God

The first reason, as we already discussed, is that people often look for spectacular changes in their outward circumstances and miss the miraculous work of the Holy Spirit taking place on the inside. Another reason is that many people view prayer as something they have to do to avoid condemnation rather than as a blessed time of fellowship with the Father that brings eternal changes.

You see, the human creature is prone to legalism. There is nothing the devil likes more than to impose a set of legalistic rules on a person. Then when that person has a hard time keeping those rules, his confidence that God will move in his life is greatly shaken.

Let me give you a classic example. When a person finally commits to an early morning hour of prayer, he looks like a militant marching off to war. He has that look in his eyes that says, "By golly, don't anyone try to stop me!" But all he has to do is miss one or two early morning sessions of prayer, and the devil is right there to tell him, "That's it — you blew it!"

That's what happened to me during that first year of praying in tongues. The first impasse I encountered was falling out of prayer. My fleshly nature would flare up, and I'd stop praying for a time. Then the devil would bring condemnation because I hadn't reported like a rigid soldier every day at a certain hour.

Why is the devil able to put us under that kind of condemnation? Because in the back of our mind, we are often convinced that it is our physical effort of filling a certain cubicle of space in a certain location for a certain hour that pleases God.

But God doesn't keep score based on the number of days you spent praying in tongues last month. He is interested in how much change has taken place in your life.

Now, please don't get me wrong; discipline and determination are essential ingredients in the godly life. But you'll miss it if you base your relationship with God on whether or not you prayed yesterday.

God doesn't slap you down with condemnation and take away your anointing because you missed two days of prayer. He's delighted in whatever fellowship you want to give Him. He wants to enter into new places of change together with you, increasing the anointing on your life at every new level.

I have learned that God fellowships with us according to the changes that take place in our lives through prayer. The more change, the more fellowship we can have with Him. He isn't interested in legalism that causes us to report to an hour of prayer. You see, prayer was never meant to be a chore, but a precious time of transformation and fellowship.

Fall in Love With Prayer

So in order for you and me to enjoy all the wonderful blessings that God has prepared for us, we must *fall in love with prayer*. But we can't do that until we understand that God isn't disgusted with us for all the well-meaning times we have started to pray and failed to finish.

When I was a new Christian, knowing that I should pray wasn't enough. Listening to preachers tell me that prayer was my obligation wasn't enough. Feeling ashamed and condemned at my lack of prayer wasn't enough. Only understanding the nature of God and falling in love with prayer became enough to make me pursue praying in tongues for personal edification.

So let me help you understand what will get you past that point where so many people fail in prayer to a place in your spiritual walk where God can unrestrainedly pour out His blessings on you. I want you to fall in love with prayer — not because it is your legalistic duty, not because you will live under condemnation if you don't, but because it is the path that leads to sharing special times of fellowship with your Heavenly Father that will change your life forever.

What Causes an Impasse?

We can become so disappointed when we give ourselves faithfully to a season of prayer, and then it appears as though God has done nothing to answer that prayer. But the truth is, God is incapable of letting us down! The breakdown occurs when we don't understand how God answers the mysteries we pray in tongues. So we stop praying before He can manifest His power in our external circumstances.

At one time or another, many of my friends fell into that trap. They would get all excited after hearing a message on praying in the Holy Ghost and building themselves up on their most holy faith. Then they would jump headfirst into hours of praying every day.

But after a few months of this kind of praying, they would hit an impasse. Instead of God working miracles in the circumstances that surrounded them — getting them out of debt, healing their bodies, and so forth — it seemed as if the opposite would take place. Many of them entered into a crisis mode, and their emotions went wild. Some of them had emotional fits of despair. Others displayed a rather weird side to their personality.

Consequently, many of these same people went on to give praying in tongues a bad name. Still others began to downplay the importance of tongues by preaching against it.

You see, when the edification process begins to throw a light on the fleshly deeds that are hidden in darkness, it illuminates not only those things that you want to get rid of, but the things you *don't*. The Holy Spirit will pull these spiritual roadblocks out of the darkness and put them on display where you can see more clearly what you're dealing with. It's during these times that your emotions can sometimes go wild.

As the light of edification burns brighter and brighter, the Holy Spirit begins to uncover some of the most difficult roadblocks to deal with, such as unforgiveness and selfishness.

At this point, some people stop praying, because every time they report to the prayer closet, the negative emotions become stronger, flooding over them with a vengeance that leaves them feeling troubled. The devil will use those emotions and everything else in his power to pull them out of prayer, throwing fiery darts of unbelief, defeat, and deception at their minds as thick and fast as he can.

Instead of feeling better as they pray, these people feel worse. So the next day when it's time for prayer, antagonistic feelings begin to rise. Their emotions lead a revolt against praying in tongues, and they rationalize, "If praying in tongues is so important, why do I feel the way I do? What good is it doing me, anyway? I'm not any worse than anyone else."

Many times what we are really hoping for is some magical formula that will activate God into changing everything around us. God forbid that we need any changing ourselves! We want God to use us just the way we are.

Coming Through on the Other Side

But a person can make it through this type of impasse if he will persist in faith and prayer. The emotions of unforgiveness, selfishness, and so forth, will become so strong that they are impossible to ignore. When the person finally recognizes how ugly these fleshly works are, the power of the Holy Spirit will give him the inner strength to deal with them. True repentance can follow, which leads to mortification, victory, and freedom.

I almost fell into the same trap my friends did when I hit an impasse in the first year of full-time ministry. But I had just become an avid "faith man," so my attitude about everything could be summed up in one sentence: "If the Word says it, I believe it!" I was determined not to be moved by what I saw, heard, or felt, but only by what the Word said. And if the Word said that when I pray in an unknown tongue, I edify myself — bless God, that was what I was going to do!

As I came through that impasse to the other side, I noticed some of the old fears and uncertainties that used to control my life were gone. For instance, the fear of lack had been crucified. It no longer tormented me with thoughts like, *I'm full time in the ministry now. I have three little kids and nowhere to preach. My goodness, where is the money going to come from?*

Through praying in tongues, that fear died. I got past the impasse and entered into a place of peace. I knew that I knew inside of my spirit that God would be the Supplier of all my needs.

Faith To Receive, Faith To Mortify

Now, don't kid yourself — it takes faith to persevere through the impasse and die to your flesh. The same faith that causes you to be exalted in this life with what the world esteems as success is to be exercised to die to the world and the flesh so God can use you.

After I got ahold of the message of faith, the first thing I used it for was the appropriation of material blessings. Until then, I had always lived on the poverty line, and I wanted a new car and a new house. So in one year, God gave me two new cars and a motor home, all paid for.

God didn't mind doing that for me. He knew that although I was mainly concerned with my own creature comforts at that time, one day I would be concerned for the rebirth of a city. And the day came when I took the same faith I had used to appropriate blessings and refocused it on my own life to achieve complete mortification.

I use this as an illustration: When one of my sons was about eight years old, he came to me and said, "Daddy, would you buy me a BB gun?" Well, did I pick up that little boy by the lapel of his shirt and commence to slap his face, all the while yelling, "Listen to me, you little flesh creature! When are you going to become an asset instead of a liability in this family?"

No, I did not. I bought him the BB gun. (Then I had to teach him how to hit the tree and *not* the neighbor's plate-glass window with it!)

Well, God didn't pick me up and start slapping me because I asked for a new car either. He gave it to me gladly, because He had faith that one day I would use the same faith to first mortify my flesh and then save cities for the Kingdom. Jesus Himself said, "Seek first the Kingdom, and I will add all these (material) things to you" (Matt. 6:33). (And by the way, it took a whole lot more faith for me to die to my flesh than it did to believe for a new car!)

The Woman Who Inherited Millions But Lost Her Testimony

As difficult as it may be to persevere in prayer through the impasse so God can complete the purging process, I can guarantee you — it is worth it all.

You see, the Holy Spirit is the One whom God sent to illuminate and strengthen your reborn human spirit to put to death the deeds of the flesh that hinder your walk with Him. But even if you don't allow the Holy Spirit to expose the things hidden in darkness, sooner or later they will still be revealed.

For example, someone once told me the story of a Pentecostal woman who always sat on the front pew of the church. She praised God and shouted with the best of them. This woman's husband was a multi-millionaire heathen. When she went to church, he would lock her out; sometimes he even beat her. But no matter what her husband did, she would come to church every time the doors were open. She was a faithful woman.

One day her husband died, and she inherited his entire fortune. However, it wasn't very long after her husband's death that this woman's cars became longer and her church attendance became shorter! Pretty soon she went from sitting at the front of the church, to the middle, and then to the back. Finally, she only came to special meetings. By that time, the only power she fell out under was the weight of the gold strapped to her wrists!

Someone said, "It would have been better if that woman had never inherited the money at all." Wrong. All the money did was expose to the light something that already existed in her, hidden in darkness.

You see, it isn't money that is evil — it's the love of money. If this woman hadn't inherited the money, something else would have brought out that trait in her down the line.

This is why Jesus said, "These are they who are sown among thorns" (Mark 4:18). The thorn seeds existed in the field before the Word was sown. When the Word seed landed on the ground, the cares of this life and the deceitfulness of riches (thorn seeds already resident within the ground) sprang up, wrapped themselves around God's prosperity, and proceeded to suck those seedling plants into a selfish lifestyle and thus to neutralize the Word (v. 19).

You see, you don't climb into a grimy cellar, turn the light on, and say, "My, my, look at all the dirt this light brought!" No, the dirt was already there. The light just exposed it.

In the case of that woman, the potential to run after money was already there. All the money did was expose the problem.

Exposing the fleshly work for the purpose of purging is supposed to be the job of the Holy Ghost. Jesus said, "If you bear fruit, I will purge you. I will trim you back. I will cut the dead limbs off" (John 15:2). He was telling us, "I will clear the thorn seeds out of your field. When the Word seed comes up and you start prospering the Kingdom, I will keep the thorn seeds far enough away from your plant that they cannot choke you."

I would much rather have the Holy Spirit expose my weakness than to have a million dollars expose it. I would much rather lend myself to the transforming power of the Holy Spirit to be purged by the Word.

You ask me, "Would you like to have a million dollars?" I'm not a liar. Yes, I would. "Do you want the million dollars to choke the life of God out of you?" Absolutely not. That's why I continually yield myself to the purging process of the Holy Ghost.

Prosperity in Perspective

Prosperity is a relevant and important subject to our lives. God wants to prosper us. When we are little baby Christians, God slaps us on the bottom, changes our diaper, and gives us toys. But we need to let the Holy Spirit grow us up and take us higher in God through the Word that pulls down soulish strongholds and sets us free.

As you mature in the Lord, your faith will adjust to the fact that the more you use everything you possess for the Kingdom, the more God is free to increase you in material wealth.

Because I live my life laboring for the world to come, God is able to put money in my hands now. And He doesn't mind that I "water my ditch" as it comes through my hands. I can buy my child a fishing pole. I can buy my wife a dress. He doesn't mind, because my focus is on laying up treasures in Heaven.

God will purge you until you have that same focus through mortification. And in the end after you have persevered in prayer and yielded to His purging process, you will be rich both in souls and in material goods.

You see, a lot of people want to be rich, but they want their wealth to grow up among thorn patches. They don't understand that real prosperity is based on God's purging process.

A person can confess God's promises regarding prosperity until he turns blue, but if he is someone who causes strife and hates people, then God will not speak to him in the secret place of his heart about good business deals. Why? Because He knows that person won't be able to use the money for His glory.

So does God care if you wear a gold ring? Not as long as you also use your faith to add souls to His Kingdom.

The Parable of Sister Goiter

God doesn't want you to be poor, and God doesn't want you to be sick. In fact, no condemning sentence of any damnable thing from which Jesus has set you free can be carried out in your life if you walk after the Spirit.

Why? Because the Holy Spirit lives inside of you to help you mortify the deeds of the flesh. In fact, He will help you mortify *everything* in your life from which Jesus has already set you free.

The Holy Spirit has been sent to help you in your weakness, so He steps in with a supernatural language to pray for you. And as you learn how to plow through every impasse and endure in prayer, He helps you leave behind poverty and sickness and every fleshly bondage.

Let me share a parable I made up to help people see how the Holy Spirit can help them win the victory through praying in tongues. This parable represents everyone who has ever tried to receive their healing (or any other miracle promised in God's Word) but could not. I've wrapped up a conglomeration of different people's failures and included them all in one woman named Sister Goiter. If Sister Goiter can get healed, you certainly should be able to get healed too!

I'm sitting in my office. I receive a telephone call.

"Hello, is this Brother Roberson?" a woman asks.

I answer, "Yes, it is."

"I heard that God uses you in healing."

"Yes, Ma'am."

"Can I come over for prayer?" she asks.

I reply, "Sure, come on over."

Soon there is a knock on my door. "Come in!" I call. The door opens, and I see a woman standing in my doorway. Oh, no! She has a four-pound goiter or growth under her chin. Four pounds! It almost looks as if she has two heads.

The woman walks into the room. "Brother Roberson," she says, "My name is Sister Goiter. Before you pray for me, I just want you to know I've been prayed for by the best. I've just come to see what you can do for me."

I answer, "Sister Goiter, come over here and sit down. May I teach you a little bit?" She nods. I open to Mark 11:24 and say, "Now, look here, Sister Goiter.

This verse says, 'What things soever you desire when you pray, believe that you receive, and then you will have it!' Do you understand what that says?"

"Yes, I do."

Then I ask, "Sister Goiter, what did you come for? This verse says, 'What things soever you desire.' So what is your desire?"

"Well, my desire is to be healed of this goiter."

"Okay," I say, "then look at what this verse says next: The moment we pray, you must believe that you *are* healed, and then you *will be* healed — whether it's now, next week, or next year. But you must believe the moment we pray that you are healed — and you will be!

"So, Sister Goiter," I ask, "when are you going to believe you are healed?"

She responds, "Well, when it's gone, stupid."

"But Sister Goiter, it says here that you must believe it's gone when you pray, and then you will have it. You may not see your answer manifested until next month or next year, but you must believe you receive it the moment we pray. Now, Sister Goiter, when are you going to believe that goiter is gone?"

"Do you want me to lie and say it's gone when it isn't?" she asks.

"No, Sister Goiter! Look at this verse again: 'What thing soever you desire.' What is it you desire?"

"To be healed of my goiter, Pastor," she replies.

"Well, then, the Bible says you must believe the moment you pray. Start thanking God that you were healed two thousand years ago through the death and resurrection of Jesus. Start thanking God that He's heard you, and then you will be healed."

She asks, "You mean, I'm supposed to believe that I'm healed before I see it?"

"Yes, Sister Goiter. Faith is the substance of things hoped for and the evidence you need for the thing you don't see [Heb. 11:1]. Sister Goiter, you're not lying when you say you are healed. You're confessing what His Word says about your problem. So do you see it?"

She responds cautiously, "I think I see it."

"Good, then you are ready for prayer. Goiter, you must die from the root in the Name of Jesus! Now!"

The power of God touches Sister Goiter, and she falls under the Holy Spirit's power. About a half hour later, she gets up off the floor. I ask her if she believes that she is healed. She responds with a simple, "Yes, I do."

I say, "But the goiter is still on your neck."

"I don't care, I'm agreeing with what the Word says. Therefore, I believe that I'm healed, and I will have what I say."

"Sister Goiter," I ask, "what if somebody says, 'Hey! That goiter is still there!' What will you tell them?"

"I will tell them that I'm not denying the fact that the goiter is in my body. But according to the Word of God, I'm denying its right to stay there. Therefore, I am healed because I believe the prayer we prayed, and I receive my healing. I am healed in Jesus' Name, and I praise God for it!"

I say, "Go home, woman, you're healed."

Three months later, I come into my church. Sister Goiter is standing in the back aisle. I notice her goiter doesn't weigh four pounds anymore — it weighs five! I remember Jesus' words in Mark 4:15 when He said Satan comes immediately to steal the Word.

So I walk over to her and say, "How are you doing, Sister Goiter?"

"I'm complete in Him," she says glumly. The doubtful tone of her voice tells me she is still looking at her circumstances instead of the Word.

"Praise the Lord!" I say, looking for an exit. "Excuse me, I have to go preach."

Three more months go by, and I get a phone call from Sister Goiter. She asks to come and talk to me.

"Can I ask you something, Brother Roberson?" she says as she sits down in front of my desk. "Does this stuff really work for you?"

"Oh, yes!" I reply.

"Then why doesn't it work for me? I've done everything you told me to do."

"Sister Goiter, have you been confessing the Word?"

"Yes, I have."

"Have you been thanking God that you're healed?"

"Yes, and the goiter has gotten bigger."

"Well, Sister Goiter, I have learned something else from the Word. Would you do one more thing that I tell you?"

"Well, I might as well. What you've already told me to do isn't working."

"Sister Goiter, will you get up one hour earlier in the morning and pray for an hour in the Holy Ghost before you go to work?"

You see, on the inside of Sister Goiter is the Holy Spirit. He knows exactly why she is not getting healed, and He wants to pray for her so badly, He can hardly stand it. I don't know her problem, but the Holy Spirit does. He was sent to help her weaknesses.

She asks, "You mean, you pray in the Holy Ghost just anytime you want to? My denomination teaches me that I can't do that."

"Sister Goiter, that's a lie. You really can."

"The only time I pray in the Holy Ghost is when I am in a service, and the power of God is moving real strong. I cry a little bit, and pretty soon the tongues come."

I ask, "The only time you can pray in tongues is when you're crying and emotional?"

"Yes, it is."

"Well, just wait here, Sister Goiter, I'm going to go get a baseball bat. I'm going to beat you with it so you'll cry, and then you can pray in the Holy Ghost!"

"You know what I mean."

"Sister Goiter," I explain, "you can pray in tongues for personal edification anytime you want to. God gave that gift to you to help your weaknesses. So tomorrow morning, you get up and pray this way: 'Father, I know You don't want this goiter to stay on me, but it's brought me to a standstill. I don't know how to stop it. I need the help of the Holy Spirit!' Then just start praying in tongues — just because you want to!"

"Well, I guess I'll try it," she says hesitantly.

Three months go by. One day I see her in the back of the church. "Sister Goiter," I ask her, "can you tell any difference in your condition from praying in tongues?"

"As a matter of fact, I can."

"What do you feel?"

"Well, I feel like I have a tired chin, a dry throat, and a tired tongue!"

"Excuse me, Sister Goiter, I have to go preach."

Five months go by. I come walking in the back of the church. There stands Sister Goiter.

"Brother Roberson, come over here!" she says. "Is there anything about praying in the Holy Ghost that causes peace and rest?"

"Oh, yes, Sister Goiter," I reply. "In Isaiah 28:11 and 12. God said through the prophet Isaiah, 'This is the rest; this is the refreshing, for with stammering lips and another tongue will I speak to this people.'"

"Wait a minute. You mean to say that praying in tongues causes the weary to rest?"

"Oh, yeah. When the cares of this life wear you out, this is the rest and the refreshing, for with stammering lips and another tongue will He cause the weary to rest as you build a superstructure of God on your most holy faith, praying in the Holy Ghost."

"Brother Roberson, I have a confession to make."

"Please make it, Sister Goiter."

"I used to be so full of fear. I was afraid that one day my husband would get up and pull the covers back, and instead of seeing me with a five-pound goiter under my chin, he would see only this massive goiter that had completely enveloped me, with little arms and legs sticking out of it. Then he would pull the covers back over me in disgust.

"I lived under that fear — but that fear is gone! And Brother Roberson!"

"Yes, Sister Goiter?"

"I'm really beginning to believe that I'm healed. Oh, and Brother Roberson."

"Yes?"

"Is praying in tongues addictive?"

"Why do you ask?" I question.

"Because now I'm also praying an hour at night."

"Keep it up, Sister Goiter. I'll see you later."

One more month goes by. It has now been more than a year since I met Sister Goiter. I come walking in the back of the church, and again, Sister Goiter calls me over to her.

"Brother Roberson, have you ever seen Mark 11:23 and 24?"

"Sister Goiter," I say, "a year ago I taught you in detail what it said!"

"I remember you reading it to me, Brother Roberson, but why didn't you tell me what it meant?"

"But I did, Sister Goiter!"

"No, I don't think you did."

"Yes, I did!"

"Let me tell you something, Brother Roberson. I'm healed! You want to know why I'm healed? Because I believe I'm healed. The Holy Spirit showed me I'm healed! Do you believe I'm healed?"

"Yes, Sister Goiter! Yes!"

So what happened to Sister Goiter? Her goiter disappeared in a week. She had learned by experience the benefits of edifying herself through praying in tongues! As she persevered in prayer through the "tired chin, dry throat, tired tongue" impasse, the Holy Spirit helped her in her weakness to leave disease behind and to build herself up on her most holy faith, praying in the Holy Ghost!

Three Levels of Sanctification

Now let's discuss in a little more detail the purging process that we have to carry through to completion if we're going to walk in the fullness of God's plan for our lives.

In His wisdom, God overcame Satan and our flesh nature by taking the understanding of our prayer language away from our intellects so the Holy Spirit could pray for us about fleshly areas of our lives that we don't necessarily want to get rid of. As the Holy Spirit prays for us, He purges us on three levels: spirit, soul, and body. That's what the Bible is talking about in Second Corinthians 7:1:

> **Having therefore these promises, dearly beloved, let us CLEANSE OURSELVES FROM ALL FILTHINESS OF THE FLESH AND SPIRIT, perfecting holiness in the fear of God.**

When you start to pray in tongues, that sanctification process starts immediately, beginning with *filthiness of the flesh*. This refers to any habitually destructive thing that is detrimental to the body, such as drinking, smoking, chewing tobacco, etc. The Holy Spirit will help you get rid of all those bad habits for you. Then, if you will keep praying, He will bring revelation knowledge that will aid in the sanctifying of your soul.

Filthiness of the soul includes such things as hatred, strife, selfish ambition, envy, self-exaltation, manipulation, lying, and unforgiveness. You won't be in your prayer closet long before it will become impossible to keep praying in tongues without dealing with these sinful strongholds of the soul. Either you will stop praying, or you'll allow your new nature to go ahead and purge those dead limbs out of your life.

If you make it through the impasse that the sanctification process can trigger in the realm of your soulish emotions, the Holy Spirit will move on to help you get free from *filthiness of spirit*. This refers to incorrect belief or doctrine that keeps you from being fully equipped with the power of God to fulfill your call.

All three of these areas of sanctification overlap one another, but the strongest purging takes place in this area of incorrect beliefs. As God answers the mysteries that you are praying out in the Holy Spirit's supernatural language, all of a sudden an awareness of spiritual things begins to flood into your understanding. Wrong believing, or filthiness of spirit, begins to fall away.

The more of the mind of Christ you pray before the Father, the more revelation knowledge the Holy Spirit reveals to your spirit and the more roots of false doctrine He destroys. He will not leave you stuck in the mire of some wrong belief that has neutralized God's power in your life.

When I first prayed to the place where I began to be purged from filthiness of spirit, I would go to meetings where I'd know on the inside that the minister was operating in the flesh.

People in the meeting would be shouting with excitement and emotions, not knowing the difference between the Spirit and the flesh. Before I was purged by the Holy Spirit, I hadn't known the difference either. But now I was being protected by the Holy Spirit, who had purged me of deception and wrong believing.

The Enemy's Strategy:
To Get You Out of Prayer!

One thing I can guarantee you: Just keep praying in the Holy Ghost, and you'll meet the ugly side of your character. And the first thing the devil will attempt to do is to get you out of prayer so your purging will stop.

Satan is in an all-out war to strip us of the benefits of praying in tongues. It saddens me to see the many casualties of that war. In many churches, groups of people have started out praying with every good intention of bringing revival to their city. But then so many things go wrong that prayer quickly becomes the last thing on their agenda.

Most Christians fall out of prayer long before enough mortification has taken place to eliminate those things in their lives that cause unrest and turmoil. They don't keep praying long enough to receive the strength to put to death with finality every deed of the flesh that hinders their walk with God.

When these believers fail to persevere through the impasse, they interrupt the Holy Spirit's commission to purge everything out of them that can distract them from the path of their divine call. They are left vulnerable to the enemy's attempts to lead them into carnality and secondary vocations outside of God's perfect will.

You see, the devil doesn't mind if you go to church. He doesn't care if you join a singles or a couples group, help in a program, or fellowship with other believers. He just doesn't want you pulling the spiritual wrestling match over into an arena such as tongues that isn't governed by the emotionalism of the soulish realm. The moment you do that, he begins to lose control, and you become unmanageable.

Remember what Ephesians 6:11 and 12 says:

Put on the whole armour of God, that ye may be able to stand against THE WILES OF THE DEVIL.

For we wrestle not against flesh and blood, but against principalities, against powers, against the rulers of the darkness of this world, against spiritual wickedness in high places.

The word "wiles" in verse 11 denotes *inroads* of the enemy into your life attained through deceit. And one of the main methods the devil uses to gain entry into your life is through the stronghold of emotionalism.

The devil will attempt to bring torment, worry, and fear into your life. He loves to fill you so full of cares that you sink into a full-blown case of depression.

So when you hit an impasse in prayer and your nerves seem to be strung out to the breaking point, remember this: It is only the wiles of the enemy. He doesn't want you to fight him through the help of the Holy Spirit. He wants you to stop praying in tongues.

So keep on praying. Some of the most productive seasons of prayer are those in which the devil pulls every emotional trick he can think of to make you stop praying, but you continue to persevere.

Mr. Self, the King Cockroach — The Last One To Go

We've seen that it's not always easy to endure through this sanctification process. As the Holy Spirit searches the inmost reaches of your heart, He'll pull some things out of the darkness for purging that you won't want to deal with. Those are the times when your emotions can go wild, causing you to hit an impasse in prayer.

It reminds me of an experience I once had while staying in a cheap motel. (When I first entered the full-time ministry, you should have seen some of the motels that churches put me in. The bathroom was down the hall, and the telephone was down the street!)

When I first came into the dark motel room, I felt for a light switch on the wall. But there wasn't one — only dirt streaks on the wall where everyone else had also looked for it.

So I walked across the floor, looking for the ceiling light's pull cord. As I walked, I heard this strange "crunch, crunch" sound. I reached the light cord and pulled. All of a sudden, all these little creatures of the night started to run in every direction. It was a bunch of cockroaches, all scurrying for the cover of darkness (except for the trail of dead ones I had stepped on!).

I've thought about that horde of cockroaches and their frantic desire for darkness. It reminds me of the deeds of the flesh in our lives that shrink from being exposed by the light of the Word and the Spirit. And for the sake of teaching, I'm going to extend that true story now into a parable.

After watching the cockroaches hurry to find cover, I looked around the room. There on the counter, where week-old food still gathered mold, sat a rat. This rat was big! He had an entire kitty-cat tail hanging out of his mouth!

But what caught my interest was the little collar and chain leash that was around the rat's neck. My eyes followed the little chain to its other end, and there stood a cockroach holding the chain with one of his six legs. You should have seen this cockroach! He was *huge*! Not only that, but he was wearing a "Superbug" outfit with a big "S" on his chest!

I looked at this cockroach, and he looked at me. Then he said, "Watch this." He jerked on the chain and said to the rat, "Roll over." That rat just meekly obeyed and rolled over!

"I'm bad, I'm *real* bad!" the cockroach boasted.

I said, "Yeah, well, I've heard about you, Mr. Cockroach, and I'm ready for you. I have a can of spiritual Raid!"

"Oh, yeah?" the cockroach said, "Well, I've lived in the penthouse of your life for a long time, and if you think I'm afraid of your praying in tongues, I'm going to show you right now how bad I can whip you! I'm King Cockroach, and I've kept the ceiling on your life all these years. It has gone no further in God, and it isn't going any further now!"

"Oh, yeah?" I challenged.

"I'm the love of money," King Cockroach continued. "I'm the lust of other things. I'm the flesh that keeps you from getting out of bed to pray. I am the one that trades programs for prayer so that your ministry will never be anything. And you think you can whip me, boy?"

"Yes, I do! I've heard about you, but I have my Raid bug spray!"

So King Cockroach put on his boxing gloves, and we went at it. Spray — "You missed me!" Spray, spray — "Missed again!"

Then I sprayed him right in the face. The force of the spray blasted his hair back. But he just licked his lips and said, "Boy, that's good stuff! I'm a highbred cockroach, and I have a date tonight, so give me another shot!"

What is this parable talking about? Well, when you start edifying yourself through praying in tongues, the Holy Spirit causes the lit candle of your reborn human spirit to burn brighter and brighter. The more you pray, the more the Holy Spirit is going to illuminate those things hidden in darkness.

Every time you move from one realm to a higher realm in God, the "cockroaches" — the deeds of the flesh that have hindered you in your walk with God — are going to scream and run for the cover of darkness. Then one by one they will die as your reborn human spirit purges them by the power it has received through edification from the Holy Spirit.

Finally, you'll make it to the penthouse of your life. That's where ole King Cockroach, Mr. Self himself, sets up his residence. He's the last one to go, and, boy, can he put up a fight!

After long seasons of praying in tongues, I finally reached the penthouse of my life. Mr. Self, the King Cockroach, put on his boxing gloves and started to fight my emotions. It was tough!

Why is Mr. Self the last one to go? Because you're either going to fall out of prayer, or you're going to give up the thing you love more than God — and "self" is the thing your flesh loves most!

So one of two things will happen: You'll stop praying, or you'll kill the King Cockroach, because you can't coexist with both of them. Your emotions will tell you, "Don't turn loose of Self," but as you keep praying in tongues, your edified spirit will tell you that you must.

Your emotions can become so strong in this internal battle that you feel as if you'd like to do anything else but pray. That's the impasse you have to push through. When you make it to that point, just stay in prayer; you're about to put King Cockroach to death. And when you do, your life and your ministry will rise to a new level of anointing!

This Is the Refreshing

Are you weary from a long, inner battle? Have imaginations and high things exalted themselves against the knowledge of God in your life? Have uncaptivated thoughts taken their toll until you feel mentally exhausted? Is it a struggle just to drag yourself to church, much less take a step further and begin to daily worship Him in private? Do your emotions say, "I'm worn out. I have sat in church most of my life, but I'm approaching the point where I don't care anymore"?

Well, Isaiah 28:11,12 says speaking in other tongues is the rest and the refreshing that causes the weary to rest.

For with stammering lips and another tongue will he speak to this people.

To whom he said, This is the rest wherewith ye may cause the weary to rest; and this is the refreshing: yet they would not hear.

Praying in tongues is a priceless gift that God has given us so we can feel rested and refreshed right in the middle of a very imperfect world!

Jesus said, "Why don't you take My yoke upon you and learn of Me?" (Matt. 11:29). What is that yoke that He's talking about? Well, remember — Jesus is meek and gentle. The yoke He asks you to take upon yourself is not trudging through life with the great burden of the Gospel on your shoulders. The yoke He asks you to take is *the responsibility to learn of Him.*

When people used oxen for plowing their fields, they always broke in a young ox by yoking him up with an old, experienced ox. If that young ox didn't want to turn at the end of the row, the old ox would turn him anyway. If the young ox didn't want to plow, the old ox would drag him along. If the young one wanted to quit at three o'clock instead of four o'clock, the old one would push him to go further.

That's what Jesus will do for us when we're yoked up to Him. So just buckle that yoke around your neck, and remember: It's a double yoke, and the other end is around Jesus. If you will yoke yourself to Him and determine to learn of Him, you will find that His ways are gentle, peaceful, and powerful.

Jesus said, "My yoke is to learn of Me" — and one way to do that is through the rest and refreshing of praying in tongues!

Stay in There!

Now, of course, the choice is yours. You don't have to pray in tongues at all. God loves you, accepts you, and will do all He can for you at whatever level of Christianity you may be.

But if you want to draw closer to God — if you want to put to death the fears, uncertainties, bad habits, pressures, and cares that stand between you and a closer walk with God — then praying in tongues is a precious gift to take advantage of. It is a spiritual key that will bring you rest and refreshing, unlock divine mysteries, and build you up higher in God.

So as you launch yourself into a season of praying in tongues, just remember that whenever you hit any kind of impasse, the best thing you can do is *stay in there*. Even when your emotions start to fight you, even when you feel antagonistic toward prayer and some mysterious force is resisting every little effort to pray — *stay in there!*

You are approaching a critical point. You are about to experience a spiritual "nuclear meltdown" — only the things targeted to melt down are your fears, worries, torments, pressures, lusts for wrong things, bondage to poverty, anger, and strife.

Then when you have come through the impasse and you're standing on the other side, get ready to enjoy a breakthrough in that area you've been believing for. You've persevered in prayer, and now you're ripe for a miracle!

As you yield yourself to My Spirit,
    then My Presence will work in you,
    illuminating you and searching
    the inward parts of your belly
    that you might understand what My will is.
I will lead you beside the streams of water.
I will sink your root system deep
    that you might manifest the kind of fruit
    that is born of My Spirit.

So hear what the Spirit would say,
    because in that day many shall cry.
But you shall be established on the rock
    of doing My sayings.
You will be one whom I can move through.

Chapter 12

Purged To Stand in the Gap

I'll tell you another good reason why it's so important not to give up on prayer when you reach an impasse. You'll never be able to stand in the gap for others the way God intends if you remain an unpurged vessel.

Before we can enter deeply into intercession, we must experience a certain degree of mortification of the flesh nature. Intercession requires dedication, determination, and endurance. Generally, each of these attributes is contrary to the flesh.

Why Prayer Groups Often Fail

That's why so many prayer groups fail, even though they begin with the best of intentions. Most people who join a prayer group don't possess stamina, commitment, or dedication. In fact, what they usually have is a whole boatload of excitement and a ton of character flaws!

These people join a prayer group thinking that they'll spend the time pulling down great spiritual strongholds over the city as they pray in tongues. But in reality, all they are really doing in the beginning is edifying themselves, not interceding for others.

If they stick with it, this edification process will cause the character flaws that have hindered them in the past to surface. The Holy Spirit will bring them face to face with the root that has borne the bad fruit — in other words, the works of the flesh in their lives that have caused them not to be a good mama, a good daddy, a good provider, etc. Raging tempers may arise in those who seemingly never had that kind of temper before.

But the capacity for these fleshly traits was there all along; praying in tongues just caused them to surface. Now it is up to the people to continue in prayer, allowing the Holy Spirit to edify their reborn spirit until it is able to purge the very root of those traits away. If the prayer group members don't deal with these revealed faults, soon they will disband over petty arguments, false doctrines, or just plain selfishness. But if they'll keep on praying, the Holy Spirit will finally get them to the place where He can take the emphasis off their personal edification and release His power through them on behalf of others.

So the devil works on keeping believers in a state of carnality. Many churches remain in that state, always fighting each other, always in turmoil. In that state of carnality, believers are not qualified for intercession, because they don't care enough that sick children are dying. They don't care that multitudes are going to hell. They are too concerned about their own rights.

We should desire to be great intercessors. God wants to place us between hell and those who are trying to get there. But first we must desire to mortify the deeds of the flesh.

Stand Steadfast in Intercession

However, we must remember that we cannot actively pray for the salvation of souls and for revival without attracting the devil's attention. Paul warned us about an impending war in Ephesians 6. He said, "Look, we don't wrestle against flesh and blood; we aren't fighting with a sword or a spear. But the war is just as real. We wrestle against principalities, against powers, against rulers of darkness of this world, and against spiritual wickedness in heavenly places" (Eph. 6:12).

Therefore, you have to determine to stand steadfast in intercession, cooperating all the time with the Holy Spirit's mortification process that continues within. As you edify and build yourself up on your most holy faith, praying in the Holy Ghost, you will attain a place in the Spirit where God can literally pour the deep intercessional groanings through you. That's when incredible, mega-amounts of Holy Ghost power begin to be released.

The amount of spiritual activity that goes into operation when God's power is delivered to a person to genuinely stand in the gap is phenomenal. This kind of power authorizes a host of angels to take legal action in others' and in your affairs to ward off catastrophes and change circumstances.

But this level of intercession also attracts powers and principalities to challenge your authority. These demonic powers will move in on you with the vengeance of a freight train. Their target will be any weaknesses or character flaws that they can use to stop and destroy you, such as your susceptibility to ungodly lusts or just plain procrastination.

That's the reason the months and months of edification through praying in tongues are so important. During that time, the Holy Spirit edifies your reborn human spirit to put to death any forces of the flesh giving the devil authority and power to hinder and control your life. He builds your spirit to such a place of spiritual maturity that the enemy can't stop you.

Once you have reached that place of enduring prayer, the Holy Spirit will begin to activate incredible waves of glory — power that floods over your soul in the form of supernatural joy and hilarious laughter.

These waves of glory are enjoyed by people who have mastered the art of enduring prayer and are being used by God to rescue others from physical disaster or eternal hell. The supernatural joy and laughter is a report from the realm of the Spirit that faith has obtained the answer; something has changed, and it will soon be manifested in the natural realm.

Groaning Within
Our Righteous Spirits

So how can we be confident of final victory in this spiritual quest from selfish carnality, to enduring in prayer through the purging process, to becoming a prepared vessel that the Holy Spirit can use in intercession? I found an answer to that question in my studies and meditation of two different passages of Scripture: Second Corinthians 5 and Romans 8.

The key to our ultimate victory is summed up in one simple statement in Second Corinthians 5:5: God has given to us *the earnest of the Spirit.* Let's look at the entire passage in context:

> **For we know that if our earthly house of this tabernacle were dissolved, we have a building of God, an house not made with hands, eternal in the heavens.**
>
> **For in this** [earthly tabernacle] **we groan, earnestly desiring to be clothed upon with our house which is from heaven** [our glorified bodies]:
>
> **If so be that being clothed we shall not be found naked.**
>
> **For we that are in this tabernacle do groan, being burdened; not for that we would be unclothed** [we don't just want to die], **but clothed upon, that mortality might be swallowed up of life.**
>
> **Now he that hath wrought us for the self-same thing is God, who also hath given unto us THE EARNEST OF THE SPIRIT.**
>
> — **2 Corinthians 5:1-5**

Now let's go to Romans 8:22-25 and compare the two passages. First, let's look at verse 22:

> **For we know that the whole creation** [every created thing] **groaneth and travaileth** [as a pregnant woman] **in pain together until now.**

All creation groans for its deliverance from the bondage of corruption in which it was placed at the fall of man. All of creation, right down to the last atom, came under a curse at that time. Now creation, pregnant with a new heaven and a new earth, groans in travail like a pregnant woman waiting to give birth.

Then in verse 23, Paul switched the emphasis from creation to you and me:

And not only they, but ourselves also, which have the firstfruits of the Spirit, even we ourselves groan within ourselves, waiting for the adoption, to wit, the redemption of our body.

Everything in creation that is imperfect is in a form of intercessional groaning, waiting to be delivered from corruption. That includes believers who have "the first fruits of the Spirit."

Notice Paul said that we *have* the first fruits, and we *wait for* the second fruits — the redemption of our bodies. What are the first fruits Paul is talking about?

Jesus died and arose from the dead, and those of us who are born again have become the first fruits — the first harvest — of His resurrection. When we bowed our knee to the Lord Jesus Christ and were born again, adoption papers were served on us, and we became His first fruits.

When I was born again, my spirit man was instantly seated in heavenly places with Christ Jesus.

Even when we were dead in sins, hath quickened us together with Christ, (by grace ye are saved;)

And hath raised us up together, and made us sit together in heavenly places in Christ Jesus.

— Ephesians 2:5,6

My spirit has taken on the express image of Jesus Christ. It has been born of Him and consequently has become the righteousness of God in Christ: **For he**

hath made him to be sin for us, who knew no sin; that we might be made the righteousness of God in him (2 Cor. 5:21). Therefore, on the inside of me, I have these righteous feelings. Something in me is so holy that it constantly wars with my flesh.

We who have the first fruits of the Spirit — in other words, we who are born again and have received the earnest or baptism of the Holy Spirit — are groaning. We groan within our righteous spirits, waiting for the entire adoption process to be culminated or completed at the redemption of our bodies — the second fruits.

The reason you are groaning on the inside of your ~~righteous spirit is that you are imprisoned in your~~ fleshly body. You live in there. Your flesh has death working in it, inherited from the first Adam. It is not only capable of sin; it *will* sin if you let it. That's why Paul says in Galatians 5:16:

This I say then, Walk in the Spirit, and ye shall not fulfil the lust of the flesh.

You are totally capable of walking in the flesh. Even more than that, your body is imprisoned in a world of warring and strife — a place where children are starving to death and men kill each other, where sin and perversion run rampant. Your righteous spirit groans within your body, because you're in an imperfect world that has all this damnable sin, and you are still capable of practicing it yourself.

In fact, Paul said that all creation is travailing like a pregnant woman, sold to the bondage of slavery, crying and groaning to be delivered out of that bondage. I am in the middle of all this mess, and the righteousness that has been implanted within me makes me groan for a new heaven, a new earth, and a new, glorified body.

Saved by Hope

This is starting to sound like the passage in Second Corinthians 5, isn't it? Remember what verse 4 says:

For WE THAT ARE IN THIS TABERNACLE DO GROAN, BEING BURDENED: not for that we would be unclothed, but clothed upon, that mortality might be swallowed up of life.

What are we groaning for? We are waiting for our adoption process to be made complete. When? At the redemption of our bodies. In other words, when we are clothed with our glorified body, a house from Heaven not made with hands.

When Jesus returns, our bodies will be changed in the twinkling of an eye from corruptible to incorruptible as we receive our resurrected bodies (1 Cor. 15:52). That time is coming. But in the meantime, while we are still imprisoned in our bodies, we need Someone to help us. That's why God gave us the Holy Spirit — to empower us during this time of waiting to have victory over the dominance of the flesh.

Then in Second Corinthians 5:5, Paul goes on to say this:

Now he that hath wrought [or saved] us for the selfsame thing is God, who also hath given unto us the earnest of the Spirit.

So God has wrought, or saved, us for the culmination of His great plan. Actually, Paul is saying the same thing but in a slightly different way to both the Romans and the Corinthians. In Romans 8:24 and 25, he said we are *saved by hope.*

> For we are SAVED BY HOPE: but hope that is seen is not hope: for what a man seeth, why doth he yet hope for?
>
> But if we hope for that we see not, then do we with patience wait for it.

We are saved by the hope of what? We who have the first fruits of the Spirit are waiting for the redemption process to be made complete at the resurrection and glorification of our physical bodies. We don't see it yet, so "we do with patience wait for it."

We don't have any choice but to wait. We can believe God for Jesus' return until we turn blue and seven shades of white and green, but Jesus is still going to come back when God says it's time for Him to come back!

The Earnest of Our Inheritance

Notice what else Paul says in Second Corinthians 5:5, as he encompasses the entire ministry of the Holy Spirit in our lives in this one simple statement: *God gave us the earnest of the Spirit.*

To find out more detail about the Holy Spirit's ministry as the earnest of our inheritance, we have to go back to Romans 8. Paul says in essence, "It doesn't matter if you're imprisoned in a body that is capable of sin. Sure, you're still trapped here in hope of a glorified body. But you don't have to wait alone — you have the earnest of the Spirit. And this is how the Holy Spirit carries out that ministry."

If you're at all familiar with the real-estate business, you know that "earnest money" is a token of your sincerity to make the purchase. It is money against the promised possession.

Well, when you were born again, God said, "I'm going to give you a little bit of Heaven to go to Heaven with, because when this purchase is finished, I want you, the promised possession, to come home to be with Me." So God put His "earnest money" — the Holy Ghost — down on you against the promised possession. In other words, God sent the Holy Ghost as the earnest of our inheritance to guarantee us three things:

1. **The Holy Spirit is God's guarantee of the power to fulfill your ministry here on earth.** He offers Himself in edification through the supernatural language of tongues to pray the plan of God into your life. He is your only true promise of power and of divine direction and leadership to fulfill your ministry. His is the only earnest that will see you through. No other path holds that guarantee.

2. **He is your guarantee of a glorified body.**

3. **He is the power to finally deliver the purchased possession — you — to God as He brings you on home to Heaven.**

So the earnest of the Spirit guarantees to help you fulfill your ministry, to deliver you to your glorified body, and to bring you home to Heaven. That is God's guarantee to you: If you follow Him, He will never lose

His earnest money against the promised possession. Never.

As you use that basic diversity of tongues called tongues for personal edification, you begin to instigate the earnest of the Spirit. At that level, the Holy Spirit starts to deal with all of your problems, no matter how bad they are. If you keep yielding to His work in you, He will deliver you out of all of them.

The 'Ministry of the Earnest'

Paul describes how the Holy Spirit carries out His "ministry of the earnest" in Romans 8:26:

> Likewise the Spirit also helpeth our infirmities: for we know not what we should pray for as we ought: but the Spirit itself maketh intercession for us with groanings which cannot be uttered.

We know from our earlier discussion that the word "infirmities" refers to our inability to produce results because of the limitations imposed on us by the flesh. That's why we who have the first fruits of the Spirit groan out of our righteous spirits — we desire that these limitations be removed. And the Holy Spirit in like manner helps our infirmities.

I appreciate the Holy Spirit's help, because I found out long ago that I'm not too smart when it comes to producing results in spiritual matters. For example, when I look at a crippled, deformed child in a wheelchair and come face to face with my inability through unbelief to produce results, my righteous spirit groans inside of me.

If I knew how to pray as I ought, that child in the wheelchair would rise up whole and normal and walk. So the Holy Spirit has to help my inability to produce that result.

You see, we all have a call and a place in God's plan, even that severely handicapped child in the wheelchair. What glad tidings should we be preaching to that child? "Little believer, you don't have to be that way anymore, because that wasn't in God's plan. You have a divine call just like I do. And unless the Church can help set you free of that condition, you will never fulfill that call as God intended."

If that isn't our message, then what good *is* the Gospel? Is it only for good-looking people who have money in their pockets and drive a Lexus? Do we think that a little deformed child is any less called by God than ourselves?

The preacher's message should be "Captive, you don't have to be captive anymore. Blind, you don't have to be blind anymore. Poor, you don't have to be poor anymore. Prisoner, you don't have to be locked up in your own body anymore."

If that isn't the preacher's message, did he stop where it was comfortable enough to live the good life, forgetting the desperate needs lying just outside his comfort zone? Doesn't he care about prayer? Is he so caught up in the cares of this world that he thinks he can excuse himself? No excuse will hold water on that day when he stands before Jesus expecting a big, fat reward, and Jesus asks him, "Why didn't you endure in prayer?"

This is a realm of which few of us have any understanding at all. When faced with something like a wheelchair case, we may say, "Well, I'm just going to pray and believe God." But if we really believed God when we prayed for that person, why didn't the person get healed? No one knows — not even the person in the wheelchair. But I'll tell you who does know — the Holy Spirit. And as the earnest of our inheritance, He is sent to help us in our inability to produce results!

What does this have to do with intercession? Well, it wasn't until I had been praying hour after hour in tongues for about two years that I began to experience the deep intercessional groanings of the Spirit coming from deep within my spirit as He willed.

I wondered why I hurt inside, so God spoke to my spirit: "Do you like the plan the devil has for the world?"

I answered, "No, I don't! In fact, I hurt inside."

He said, "Yes, you are groaning out of your righteous spirit for the culmination of all things and for the redemption of your body. You are groaning to see this whole horrible mess come to an end."

I said, "Yes, Sir, you're right!"

I began to experience hurt that came from deep inside of me every time I walked away from someone in a wheelchair who didn't get healed. I would know beyond a shadow of a doubt that Jesus had borne that person's sicknesses and pains, yet I'd feel the limitations imposed on me by the flesh. Or I would hurt inside when I saw entire civilizations starving to death in plain view of the world.

I would want to do something about that person's crippled condition or the sad plight of those desperately poor nations — but I couldn't in my own strength! However, the Holy Spirit could as He moved on my spirit with tongues of deep, intercessional groanings, activated severally as He willed.

The Holy Spirit Helps Our Infirmities

My experience was right in line with Romans 8:26, which says the Spirit *also* helps our infirmities. That means He helps in conjunction with someone who is already helping.

This throws us back to verse 23, where Paul says that *we* are groaning out of our righteous human spirit. So when Paul says in verse 26, "*Likewise* the Spirit *also* helps us...," he is saying, "In the same manner that you are groaning out of your human spirit, He will also help you."

This is how it works. A mountain comprised of fleshly works stands between you and God's plan for your life. The Holy Spirit will focus in on that mountain "with groanings that cannot be uttered" (Rom. 8:26). You have entered a mild form of intercession, but it is for yourself that you stand in the gap.

These groanings are not just referring to speech so profound that you can't utter it. It's also talking about reaching a place in the Spirit where you begin to hate whatever stands between you and God's plan so badly that you enter into a state of groaning or grieving.

Your heart cries out, *I wish this was out of my life! Lord, I hate this!* At this point, you have given the Holy

Spirit the faith He needs to come alongside and move the mountain out of the way.

If you persevere in prayer and refuse to let the mountain defeat you, at some point you will experience a "meltdown," where the Holy Ghost removes the mountain and you come out on the other side victorious. Why? Because you cannot continue to report to prayer and still retain your problem. You will either have to quit edifying yourself and yield to those works of the flesh or allow the Holy Spirit to purge them out of your life.

The Holy Spirit will pull out the problem at the right time, when you're ready and can survive the purging. Your part is to just keep praying.

Don't stop. Push through the impasse. The Holy Spirit will illuminate this purging process for you, and when it's all over, you'll be able to see and understand that massive mountain that was removed from your life. You will thank God that you are one step closer to mighty intercession.

Praying in Tongues vs. Deep Intercessional Groanings

The combination of the two passages we've been looking at in Second Corinthians 5 and Romans 8 settled for me the age-old issue of the difference between praying in tongues for personal edification and the deep intercessional groans of the Spirit — that diversity of tongues that is operated by God as He wills.

The truth is, even if you start out praying in tongues with a cold, indifferent, stony heart, only two ingredients are necessary to bring you to the place where the Holy Spirit can move through you in deep intercessional groanings: your knowledge that your indifference is wrong, and your decision to pray in the Holy Ghost by your own will as often as possible.

As you continue to pray in tongues, the Holy Spirit will edify you and charge you up into the love of God until compassion gets hold of you — until at times, as you walk away from yet another person still bound to his wheelchair, you feel as if you can't even live unless you see results. This is the kind of groaning that says, "I can't stand this anymore. It hurts too badly. I will put aside all of my selfishness and strife and all of our differences. I'll do whatever I need to do to serve the purposes of the Holy Spirit."

Putting our differences aside is a major part of what delivers us into true intercession. Dead religion consists of "I have my rights! Vindicate me!" That's where most of the church world lives, and that's why most Christians seldom visit the realm of miracles. Therefore, the Gospel of glad tidings doesn't reach that little deformed child bound to a wheelchair. He doesn't get a chance at his reward because the Church failed him.

But when we get to that place where we groan out of our righteous spirits over this world's pain, sin, and misery, we don't want to fight with anyone anymore. We just want to pray. So why don't we put all of our differences aside and start praying!

It is the groaning of our righteous spirits that the Holy Spirit picks up on. If He examines me and sees that my new nature is crying for help in groanings —

hurting but not knowing how to pray as I ought — He says, "Excuse Me, but I have been sent to help your infirmities. I want to add My groanings to your cries for help, for that will translate to pure power for you to rise above the inabilities of the flesh.

"You have come to a standstill. In your own strength, you can't pull this off. You don't have the power. You don't know how to do it, but I do!"

So the Holy Spirit adds His anointing of power — His intercession, His groanings — to blend together in unison as one with the groanings of your spirit. At that point, He empowers you to rise above the problem and do something about it.

In Galatians 4:19, Paul made a revealing statement that provides insight into the distinct difference between tongues for personal edification and deep intercessional groanings:

My little children, of whom I TRAVAIL IN BIRTH again until Christ be formed in you.

How many women pick the day to give birth to their child? How many choose the day their baby will be born without man-made intervention? How many stop the process and say, "I think I'll wait two days"? Not too many, I would imagine. Women can start the child-bearing process as they will, but they cannot end it according to their own will.

In the same manner, at your own will you can start the process that will lead to intercession and travail by praying in the Spirit and edifying yourself. But even after you have reached that place of sensitivity in which you groan out of your righteous spirit because of the imperfections of this world, the deep intercessional groanings of the Holy Spirit only come upon you as He wills.

Steps to Intercession

Intercession is born in us when the needs of others move our spirit so strongly that we finally give the Holy Spirit something to add His power to. That is when faith in its purest form flows from our spirit.

Let me tell you the steps that lead to true intercession after you begin the edification process by praying in tongues at your own will.

The Holy Spirit will first build you up to that place of sensitivity we've been talking about. You will start to look at your husband or wife or lost family member and say, "Oh, God, above everything else, I would that he [or she] be saved." At this point, the desires of your heart begin to change in the edification process. You are taking the first steps toward intercession.

Although you may *think* you are directing the Holy Spirit's prayer, you are not. You have your list of prayer requests: Joe needs a car; Susie needs this; Jan needs that. All of those things are almost irrelevant to God.

So you sit there with your big list and say, "Okay, I claim all these things." When you say, "I claim it," God hears it. Then you say, "Now I'm going to pray in the Spirit about it." At this point, the desires of your heart begin to direct your prayers rather than your mentality.

What did God say? He said that He would grant the desires of your heart if you delighted yourself in Him (Ps. 37:4). That means that if you delight yourself in the Lord in prayer, the desires you have will come from Him, and these are the desires He can fulfill.

As you pray in the Spirit, the Holy Spirit will begin to plant a little seed. That is the conception of a miracle. It is the birth plan for your backslidden spouse or your child on dope or a lost relative. He plants that seed directed by the desires of your heart. As you pray in tongues, God will begin to form that little "baby" by the authority of your spirit.

Several months go by. You keep praying, and that miracle growing on the inside of you begins to "show" as you carry it to fruition.

Soon you don't care if anyone around you is praying or not. You get up early. You pray at all times of the day and night. You walk around and crave spiritual things that you never used to care much about.

The months go by as you continue to pray. Suddenly, by an act of God's will and not your own, it is time for birth, and you begin to groan. The labor pains are getting closer and closer. It is only a matter of time before that "baby" is birthed in the spiritual realm.

After long hours of edifying myself through praying in tongues, God began to slip me over into intercession to birth things in the Spirit.

For example, I remember a time when the symptom of partial deafness temporarily manifested in my body while I was interceding. That night a woman who was totally deaf came to my service, and God opened her ears! She could hear music and the voices of her husband and son for the first time in her life. Why? Because God was able to bring me to a place in the Spirit where I stood in the gap for this woman's healing.

So is it worth the hours and days and months that it takes to build that superstructure in your spirit by praying in tongues so that one day the Holy Ghost can begin to use you in mighty intercession? Oh, yes, my friend, it's worth every minute.

It is a high honor to stand between Satan and the people he is trying to kill, steal from, and destroy. And nothing can compare to knowing that those you're praying for may have known hell as their eternal destination — except that you paid the price to be purged so you could stand in the gap and set the captives free!

For in these last days, many shall scurry
   to and fro.
Fear will encompass the earth.
Men's hearts shall fail
   for looking upon those things
   that are coming upon the world.
But run not here and run not there,
   for your answer is within.

Look up, saith the Spirit of Grace,
   your redemption draweth nigh.
Establish your feet on the foundational rock
   of doing My sayings.
Be ye strengthened with all power and might
   in the inner man,
     for it is the inner strength
     that will accomplish My purpose
     in My people.
Through that inner strength will I empower
you
   in these last days to stand.

Chapter 13

Prayer and Fasting:
The Power Twins

Let's say you've just committed yourself to a season of praying in the Holy Ghost. You're hungry to know God more intimately and to walk in His plan for your life, so you're ready and willing to yield to the Holy Spirit's purging process and to push through any impasses you might encounter.

But what about those areas in your life in which you have been defeated time and time again? What about those deeds of the flesh that have wedged themselves so tightly into the nooks and crannies of your life — the ones that taunt you into believing that you will never be any better than you are now and that you will never accomplish anything more than what you've already accomplished? Is there anything that can help set you free in these areas once and for all?

I have good news for you — Jesus has given us an important key for just such a purpose! It isn't a very popular key; yet when a person employs it, that key will shut down the flesh nature with the same vengeance that God used to slam the door on Noah's ark against an entire world that had gone the way of the flesh. That key is *fasting*.

You see, if you ever learn to shut your flesh down, *you will shut Satan down*, because the only power he has is through the seduction and manipulation of the flesh nature, which includes the mental and emotional realm as well as the physical body.

My First Experience With Fasting

God introduced me to fasting during a time when I had reached an impasse in my prayer life. I had gotten so hungry for God from just praying in tongues that I was looking around for ways to get closer to Him. During this time, my heart cry was "Help me produce something for the Kingdom in the next month or two, Father. I have to see something tangible!"

I found out right away that an impasse was overcome more quickly when I fasted. Not only that, but the workings of my flesh surfaced much more quickly as well! I learned that fasting accompanied with prayer *multiplied* what was already in me.

The first time I went on a fast, I had amazing results. As soon as I came off the fast, everything in my world went wrong!

I came off this long fast, which I refer to as a "seeking time," and almost had to stagger into meetings. I had weak knees, and it wasn't from a lack of food! I could hardly stand up to preach. It seemed as if God's anointing had lifted from me. When I laid hands on people to pray for them, they wouldn't have fallen under the power of God even if lightning had hit them!

On top of that, we were in debt for an entire month's budget. I tucked myself away to fast and pray — and I came out of that time only to be more in debt than before! I told God, "The least You could do is to supernaturally arrange for the bills to be paid while I'm locked away with You!"

I was getting a little short-tempered about the situation. Anger was building up on the inside because I wanted to know why.

Then I began to see clearly. I came to realize that during the fast, certain areas of my flesh nature that hadn't been put to death in the past had come to the surface. When these fleshly works began to surface, the anointing *felt* less, but in reality was greater than ever before.

This is what Paul meant when he said in essence, "For I would rather glory in my infirmities (or weaknesses as a man) because when I am stripped of my dependency on my flesh, it places my dependency on the Holy Spirit" (2 Cor. 12:9,10). When we feel weakest in our own natural strength, we are usually the strongest, because unmortified areas of our flesh are in the process of dying.

Fasting and prayer in combination help cause those fleshly works to come to light in our lives more quickly. Tests and trials will also bring them to light, but I would rather not wait for the trials. Fasting and prayer allow the Holy Spirit to reveal those things hidden in darkness and to deal with them before the trials come. This in turn causes our character to be strengthened.

What Jesus Taught About Fasting

In Matthew 17, we find an account that reveals what Jesus taught His disciples about fasting.

Jesus climbed up what we call the Mount of Transfiguration with James, Peter, and John. There Jesus had a visitation of God. Afterwards, He charged the three disciples who were with Him to tell no man what they had seen; then they came back down the mountain.

Meanwhile, the other disciples were trying to cast a devil out of a man's son at the foot of the mountain. The disciples had cast devils out before this with no problem, but now they had run into one that just wouldn't come out of the person. While they were making their unsuccessful attempts, a crowd had collected around them.

The disciples were probably feeling frustrated, flustered, and embarrassed. This is the situation that Jesus, James, Peter, and John walked into when they came down off the mountain.

> **And when they were come to the multitude, there came to him [Jesus] a certain man, kneeling down to him, and saying,**
>
> **Lord, have mercy on my son: for he is lunatic, and sore vexed: for ofttimes he falleth into the fire, and oft into the water.**
>
> **And I brought him to thy disciples, and they could not cure him.**
>
> **Then Jesus answered and said, O faithless and perverse generation, how long shall I be with you? how long shall I suffer you? bring him hither to me.**
>
> **And Jesus rebuked the devil; and he departed out of him: and the child was cured from that very hour.**

Then came the disciples to Jesus apart, and said, Why could not we cast him out?

And Jesus said unto them, Because of your unbelief: for verily I say unto you, If ye have faith as a grain of mustard seed, ye shall say unto this mountain, Remove hence to yonder place; and it shall remove; and nothing shall be impossible unto you.

HOWBEIT THIS KIND GOETH NOT OUT BUT BY PRAYER AND FASTING.

— Matthew 17:14-21

So this man came to Jesus and said, "Lord Jesus, please have mercy on my son. He's crazy — out of his mind — and often a spirit throws him into the fire. I brought him to Your disciples, but they couldn't cast this devil out."

Notice how Jesus answered the disciples: "You faithless and perverse generation, how long shall I suffer you?" In other words, "How long am I going to have to do this for you?" Jesus wouldn't have said that if He hadn't expected His disciples to cast that devil out.

Jesus rebuked the devil, and it departed out of the boy. Then the disciples did the same thing I would have done. They came to Jesus privately and said, "Why couldn't *we* cast that devil out?" (I definitely wouldn't have yelled that question over the heads of the crowd, because Jesus would have probably yelled the answer back to me: "Because of your unbelief!")

Notice again Jesus' answer to them in verse 20:

And Jesus said unto them, BECAUSE OF YOUR UNBELIEF: for verily I say unto you, If ye have faith as a grain of mustard seed, ye shall say unto this mountain, Remove hence to yonder place; and it shall remove; and NOTHING SHALL BE IMPOSSIBLE UNTO YOU.

Jesus said the reason that devil wouldn't come out of the boy was the disciples' unbelief. He went on to say that if they ever learned to deal with that unbelief, they would be able to say to a mountain, "Be removed!" and it would obey them. Finally, Jesus said something absolutely incredible: "*Nothing* shall be impossible to you."

So Jesus was saying that if I ever learn to deal with that particular kind of unbelief, I have a promise from Him that absolutely nothing will be impossible to me. When I realized that truth, I wanted to know what kind of unbelief Jesus was talking about here so I could isolate it and deal with it!

A Subtle Kind of Unbelief

So I began a search to find out what kind of unbelief Jesus was referring to. I discovered that it's a subtle kind of unbelief a person may not even know he has until his life is over. If the disciples knew why they couldn't cast the devil out, why would they have bothered to ask Jesus? They didn't know, so they asked Him.

This subtle unbelief puts a ceiling on your life that defies you to pull yourself out of the mess your life is in or to accomplish the thing God wants you to accomplish. As long as that ceiling is there, one year will be like the next, until one day you'll realize five years have passed, and your anointing hasn't changed; in fact, *nothing* has changed. You're just the same now as you were five years ago.

Why? Because you keep operating under an invisible ceiling that hangs over your life, and you don't even know it's there. And even if you did know, you couldn't break through that ceiling in your own strength.

Let me explain a little more with this hypothetical situation. Suppose five little crippled, deformed children in wheelchairs are brought to my meeting, their arms and legs twisted and their heads leaning over to one side. I come in, and as I begin to preach, I see these five little children.

Now, I can't blame the fact that the children aren't healed on *their* faith. They aren't required to have any. I also can't say it isn't God's will to heal them, because even though the disciples couldn't cast that devil out, Jesus revealed His will when *He* cast it out.

So I walk over and lay hands on the children. I reach down on the inside of me and pull out every ounce of faith I have. I milk every cell, every fiber of my being for faith to pour out on these kids — but still they don't get healed.

Suddenly Jesus in His glorified body walks in the room. I say, "Jesus, I'd like to ask You a question."

Jesus says, "Hold on just a minute, Brother Roberson." Then He walks over and heals every one of those children, just like that! He comes back to me and asks, "Do you have a question?"

"Yes, I do. Why didn't You heal those kids when I prayed for them?"

Now, do you think Jesus is going to tell me anything different than He told His disciples? No, He looks at me and says the same thing: "They didn't come out of their wheelchairs healed because of your unbelief, Mr. Roberson."

I protest, "Jesus, that's impossible! If there was any way to have more faith, I would have had it. I turned my being inside out; I pulled on every fiber within me. How can You say they didn't get healed because of my unbelief?"

"Because there's a subtle kind of unbelief in you that you don't know about, Brother Roberson."

But this one thing I have discovered about Jesus, my Teacher. He never outlines a problem like this without going on to give me an answer before the teaching is over. It's not enough to outline a problem; I need an answer. There must be some way I can deal with that kind of subtle unbelief on purpose so that absolutely nothing is impossible unto me.

Fasting Helps Move Mountains

In my search, somehow I knew my answer lay in what Jesus told His disciples in Matthew 17. I found that answer in verse 21: **Howbeit this kind goeth not out but by prayer and fasting.**

Jesus analyzed the whole situation in one word: "howbeit." "Howbeit" is an analytical word meaning *nevertheless* or *however this particular situation may*

302

be. Jesus was in effect saying that even though mountains can be moved with faith the size of a tiny mustard seed, we will encounter some situations that require prayer and fasting to overcome.

Jesus was talking about a lifestyle of prayer and fasting here. Most deliverance preachers in the old days taught about and encouraged that kind of lifestyle. Today we don't teach or emphasize its importance nearly as much. The result? Although we live in a time of Church history when teaching the Word has risen to the forefront, many are unequipped to do the Word, which includes casting out demons and moving mountains of all kinds.

Often we associate fasting only with deliverance from demonic influence because of Jesus' statement here that a certain kind of demon can be cast out only by prayer and fasting. But Jesus also told His disciples that the reason this devil wouldn't come out was their own unbelief (v. 20).

So Jesus didn't just associate fasting with demonic deliverance; He also associated it with moving your mountain. He said, "If you had faith as a grain of mustard seed, you could speak to the mountain and it would be removed, and absolutely nothing would be impossible to you."

Right after saying that, Jesus made the statement about prayer and fasting. This indicates to me that these two things have something to do with bringing me from a place of unbelief — where my mountains refuse to move, where everything is impossible to me — to a place where nothing is impossible to me.

Therefore, my fasting doesn't move God; He isn't the One stuck underneath an invisible ceiling. My fasting also doesn't move the devil; he isn't the one with my problem. Somehow fasting deals with *my unbelief.*

But my question to God for so many years was this: "What in the world does fasting have to do with unbelief?" Of all the places to find that answer, I found it back in Romans 8:

> **And if Christ be in you, the body is dead because of sin; but the Spirit is life because of righteousness.**
>
> **— Romans 8:10**

If Christ lives in you, you qualify for the rest of this verse, namely, that your spirit is *life.* It has entered into the *zoe,* seated-in-heavenly-places-with-Christ, God-kind of life.

But notice, the same verse that says my spirit is life also declares my body to be dead. Well, I know my body isn't physically dead because I'm still wearing it. So what kind of "dead" is Paul referring to? To understand this passage in Romans 8, we must refer back to something Paul said in Romans 6:6:

> **Knowing this, that our old man is crucified with him, that the BODY OF SIN might be destroyed, that henceforth we should not serve sin.**

What is this "body of sin"? It is no less than the old nature inherited from the first man Adam before we were born again. This is the "sin nature," the unregenerated spirit within us all before our spirit passes from death to life in the new birth. It was that sin nature that used to energize the lusts of the flesh, such as self-exaltation and the love of money.

So if Christ be in you, then positionally God has declared the sin nature, the "body of sin," to be dead and your reborn human spirit alive unto Him.

We understand positional truth pertaining to our spirit. For instance, we know that Jesus was made to be sin for us and that we were made the righteousness of God in Christ (2 Cor. 5:21). We are now seated in heavenly places with Christ Jesus (Eph. 2:6). We are above and not beneath (Deut. 28:13).

However, we may know very little about positional truth pertaining to our flesh. The essence of that truth is this: The moment we were born again, God declared the "body of sin" — the sin nature or the "old man" — to be dead. Positionally, the flesh has lost its "power source" to commit sin. It lost its right to dominate and rule over us any longer.

So when you pray in the Holy Ghost, worship God, and confess His Word, you are enforcing the positional truth that your spirit is seated in heavenly places with Christ Jesus. The more you pray in the Holy Ghost, the more you execute that position of grace. On the other hand, when you fast, you are enforcing the positional truth that the "body of sin" was crucified with Christ and your flesh no longer has the power to rule over the operation of your spirit.

Thus, when you begin to fast and pray, you execute two positional truths in the realm of the Spirit. That's why prayer and fasting are the power twins.

Breaking Down the Ceiling of Flesh

Sometimes it's not only that subtle kind of unbelief, but the flesh that constructs a ceiling over our lives. The devil will erect some kind of stronghold in our flesh realm, such as smoking, drinking, anger, gossip, or lust. Then he uses that stronghold to control us. Every time we attempt to receive from God or to accomplish something for Him, he turns up the pressure in those areas so that we feel hopeless and out of control.

So what do we often do? We pray superficial prayers; we go to church; we try to minister; we implement programs; we substitute many things for the power of God that is absent because of the ceiling of flesh over our lives. But our lives stay the same all the time, never increasing. We may instigate more programs, but the power never changes. Our lives keep bouncing off that ceiling of flesh.

Then one day, we decide to fast and pray. We begin by praying in the Holy Ghost and worshiping God. Then as our spirit begins to be built up, we start to fast. As we add fasting to our prayer lives, we slam the door on Satan's accessibility to the control center on our lives.

Pretty soon the ceiling of the flesh over our lives begins to drop down. It isn't long before the operation of the flesh is at the same level as the operation of the Spirit in our lives, so we continue to fast and pray.

Finally, the operation of the flesh drops below the operation of the Spirit; its power is broken. When that happens, answered prayer is the automatic result, and the things we've been believing for begin to come to pass. We start seeing answers to prayers that have been lying dormant for years — even prayers that we forgot but God didn't.

At this point, if the devil comes to inspect that computer-like program he implanted in our soul to destroy us, he will find it *gone* — and God's program in its place! Why? Because through fasting, we have enforced the positional truth that our "old man" was crucified with Christ. The flesh is rendered powerless to force us into sin. We have released the operation of the Spirit.

Fasting Doesn't Move God

Personally, I thank God for fasting, because many times I have come to a place where I didn't know how to go on in God. I didn't know how to break the last barriers of flesh down. In those situations, I found fasting to be a tool, a means to an end. It was the "super-charger" I needed, combined with praying in the Holy Ghost, to push me over into victory.

But we make a mistake if we think that we move God with our fasting. How can we move Someone who has so expressed His willingness to move on our behalf? Romans 8:32 makes it crystal clear:

He that spared not his own Son, but delivered him up for us all, how shall he not with him also freely give us all things?

Our fasting doesn't move God; it moves *us* to a place where we can receive *from* God. Fasting destroys the hold that the flesh has had on our lives so that, instead of operating out of the flesh, we can continually operate out of the Spirit!

You see, God isn't the One holding the power back. If He had His way, every one of us would be operating in raising-the-dead type of power tomorrow!

Fasting Helps Preserve the 'Old Wineskin'

Let's take this a step further. In Matthew 9:14 and 15, the disciples of John the Baptist asked Jesus a question about fasting. It took me a long time to understand Jesus' answer.

> **Then came to him [Jesus] the disciples of John, saying, Why do we and the Pharisees fast oft, but thy disciples fast not?**
>
> **And Jesus said unto them, Can the children of the bridechamber mourn, as long as the bridegroom is with them? but the days will come, when the bridegroom shall be taken from them, and then shall they fast.**

The day that Jesus is talking about is the change from the Old to the New Covenant; it's *our* day.

Then all of a sudden, for no apparent reason, Jesus goes on to say this:

> **No man putteth a piece of new cloth unto an old garment, for that which is put in to fill it up taketh from the garment, and the rent is made worse.**
>
> **Neither do men put new wine into old bottles: else the bottles break, and the wine runneth out, and the bottles perish: but they put new wine into new bottles, and both are preserved.**
>
> **— Matthew 9:16,17**

Let's catch what Jesus is saying here. The disciples of John came to Jesus and said, "The Pharisees fast often, and so do we. But we have noticed, Jesus, that these men who follow You don't fast at all."

Then Jesus answers, "No, they don't have to fast while I'm with them. I'm the Bridegroom." In other words, at that time the disciples were between two covenants, the Old Testament and the New Testament. And before Jesus sent the seventy disciples out, He literally put His anointing on them.

The disciples cast devils out and raised the dead. When they came back and talked to Jesus about what they had done, they were more shocked that demons had to come out than the demons were! Luke 10:17 says, **And the seventy returned again with joy, saying, Lord, even the devils are subject unto us through thy name**. But, you see, it was Jesus' anointing they were walking under.

So in essence Jesus says, "No, while I'm with you, you don't have to fast, because I put My anointing on you. But the day will come when I'm taken away, and there will be a change of covenants. On that day you *will* fast. And would you like to know why you will fast in that day?"

The disciples say, "Yes! That's the question we're asking You."

Jesus says, "I'll tell exactly why you'll fast in that day — because you don't put new wine in old bottles and new patches on old garments."

So as I meditated on Jesus' answer to the disciples of John, I thought, *That was His answer to why we are*

*going to fast under the New Covenant? They asked Him
a question about fasting. What kind of answer is it to
say, "You don't put new wine in old bottles"?* (I don't
think I understood half of what Jesus said in the early
days of my ministry!)

I finally came to understand what Jesus was saying. The moment you were born again, your spirit was
seated in heavenly places with Christ Jesus. But,
unfortunately, He had to leave you in the old garment
or old wineskin — this earthly body. One day a trumpet will sound, and this earthly body is going to be
transformed from corruptible to incorruptible.

**In a moment, in the twinkling of an eye, at
the last trump: for the trumpet shall sound,
and the dead shall be raised incorruptible, and
we shall be changed.**

— 1 Corinthians 15:52

Can you imagine our bodies being glorified in the
time it takes a person to blink?

At that moment, I won't own a body anymore that
was given to me from the loins of the first man Adam.
Instead, I will be a manifested son of God, born of Jesus
Christ, comprised of spirit, soul, and glorified body.

The rapture is the next great event in the timetable
of God's Church. But meanwhile, as generations of
saints can testify before us, we are still wearing an old
garment or old wineskin that is dying day by day and
is capable of sin.

When I belonged to that ultra-Holiness church, people would tell me that it was the devil who was tempt-
ing me to sin, and I understood that. But I *didn't*

understand what it was in me that wanted to agree with the devil!

I wanted Galatians 5:16 to read this way: "This I say then, walk in the Spirit, and all the warrings and lusts of the flesh will go away." But it doesn't say that. It says, **This I say then, Walk in the Spirit, and ye shall not fulfil the lust of the flesh.**

That's why Jesus said, "When I'm taken away from you, there will be a change of covenants. Your spirit is going to be seated with Me. But, unfortunately, I'll have to leave you in the old wineskin. That's okay, though, because fasting is going to have the same effect on your old wineskin as if you went out and bought a new one. Fasting will preserve your old wineskin so the new wine, My power, can operate through it until I give you a new wineskin — a glorified body."

It's a sad thing when a preacher's old wineskin bursts in full view of the entire world, spilling out the new wine because the vessel that carried it wasn't strong enough to maintain it. That situation brings a reproach on the Gospel. Perhaps if that preacher had known a little more about fasting, his old wineskin might have been better preserved against sin.

So fasting has the same effect on your old wineskin as if you had gone out and bought a new wineskin. Fasting preserves the old wineskin against sin. It helps mortify the deeds of the flesh while the new wine operates within the old wineskin.

The Forty-Day Fast of Jesus

We can learn much about the purpose of fasting by looking at the forty-day fast Jesus went on when He faced Satan in the wilderness and defeated him.

Then was Jesus led up of the Spirit into the wilderness to be tempted of the devil.

And when he had fasted forty days and forty nights, he was afterward an hungred.

And when the tempter came to him, he said, If thou be the Son of God, command that these stones be made bread.

But he answered and said, It is written, Man shall not live by bread alone, but by every word that proceedeth out of the mouth of God.

Then the devil taketh him up into the holy city, and setteth him on a pinnacle of the temple,

And saith unto him, If thou be the Son of God, cast thyself down: for it is written, He shall give His angels charge concerning thee: and in their hands they shall bear thee up, lest at any time thou dash thy foot against a stone.

Jesus said unto him, It is written again, Thou shalt not tempt the Lord thy God.

Again, the devil taketh him up into an exceeding high mountain, and sheweth him all the kingdoms of the world, and the glory of them;

And saith unto him, All these things will I give thee, if thou wilt fall down and worship me.

> **Then saith Jesus unto him, Get thee hence, Satan: for it is written, Thou shalt worship the Lord thy God, and him only shalt thou serve.**
>
> **Then the devil leaveth him, and, behold, angels came and ministered unto him.**
>
> — Matthew 4:1-11

As I read this passage of Scripture, I wondered, *What was the reason for Jesus' forty-day fast, and why did Satan challenge Him at the end of it?*

When discussing this with others, the answer I often heard went something like this: "The fasting reduced Jesus to the weakest state of vulnerability. In that weakened state, Jesus showed the supremacy of His power over the devil by not giving in to temptation."

But, in reality, the opposite is true. Jesus fasted forty days in preparation for facing the devil. Why? Because He knew that fasting shuts the flesh down and *strengthens* us, not weakens us, against the devil.

Why was Jesus led by the Spirit into the wilderness to be tempted by the devil? Because He as our Substitute was being tempted in our place. Then after He overcame the devil, He could turn around and give us the perfect standing that He had obtained from defeating Satan in the temptations of the flesh. That's why Jesus could later say in Luke 10:19:

> **Behold, I give unto you power to tread on serpents and scorpions, and over all the power of the enemy: and NOTHING shall by any means hurt you.**

So then fasting has the same effect on our flesh as it had on Jesus' flesh: It braces us against the temptations of the devil and helps us mortify or shut down the flesh by enforcing the perfect standing Jesus has already given us.

In order to understand how perfect and powerful this standing is that Jesus has given us over the flesh, we must learn what Jesus had to withstand to obtain it. You see, nothing can be declared perfect unless it cannot be improved upon. This means that the standing Jesus has given to us over the flesh and the devil could only be declared perfect if it had withstood Satan's most diabolical testings and schemes.

Jesus had to be subjected to the worst that Satan had — the worst torments, fears, pressures, and cares, the worst temptations of lust and riches. This was the entire reason Jesus was led into the wilderness. He was on a mission from God as our Substitute to obtain for us as part of our redemption a perfect standing over the flesh.

Now we can enter into God's Presence, armed with the standing of grace He has given us — not because of what we have done but because of what Jesus has done.

> **For we have not an high priest which cannot be touched with the feeling of our infirmities; but was in all points tempted like as we are, yet without sin.**
>
> **Let us therefore come boldly unto the throne of grace, that we may obtain mercy, and find grace to help in time of need.**
>
> **— Hebrews 4:15,16**

There before the throne of God, we can find mercy to help in our times of need — our temptations, testings, and trials.

In order for Jesus to deliver this kind of standing to us, He had to face Satan on three levels: spirit, soul, and body. This confrontation had to be carried out not in Jesus' deity, but in His humanity. That's why Jesus said, "*Man* (referring to His humanity) shall not live by bread alone, but by every word that proceeds out of the mouth of God" (Matt. 4:4).

The pressures, the torments, the loneliness, and the fear that Satan attempted to put on Jesus are indescribable. They can only be described as similar to the horrors one may see in the lower level of an insane asylum where people reside whose spirits have been completely taken over by demons. The demonic opposition Jesus faced was the type that spawns such deranged drives for power and wealth as Adolph Hitler and the Nazis possessed, where one culture tries to completely annihilate another in the quest for dominance or world power.

You see, Jesus had to face the worst Satan had. He couldn't just win a victory over some low-level, expendable, second-rate demon that simply afflicts or torments. He couldn't even deal with just a ruler of the darkness or a principality. Jesus had to face *Satan himself*! And in doing so, Jesus defeated Satan on all three levels: spirit, soul, and body!

Number one, Jesus defeated Satan on the level of the *body*. Satan challenged Him to meet the needs of His physical body — but on Satan's terms:

And when the tempter came to him, he said, If thou be the Son of God, command that these stones be made bread.

— Matthew 4:3

Satan attempted to pressure Jesus with the worst torment of the physical body: the threat that the basic necessities to sustain life will not be met. The attempt failed.

Number two, Jesus defeated Satan on the level of the *soul* when Satan tried to tempt Him to commit suicide.

Satan took Jesus up to a high pinnacle of the temple in the Holy City and began to pressure Him in the emotional realm of the soul to commit suicide by jumping off the pinnacle:

And saith unto him, If thou be the Son of God, cast thyself down: for it is written, He shall give his angels charge concerning thee: and in their hands they shall bear thee up, lest at any time thou dash thy foot against a stone.

— Matthew 4:6

Jesus knew that God had given the angels charge concerning Him, but He wasn't about to tempt God by jumping off the temple just because the devil told him to.

You see, suicide is the last step into a state of hopelessness after a long battle with torments and fears. In that hopeless state, the person says to life, "You have no real answers." In that sense, it is the worst torment of the soul, and Jesus defeated Satan in that very arena.

Satan may try to badger us in the soulish realm of our emotions, but today we have access to a perfect standing against soulish torment. That standing was given to us by Jesus, the Prince of Peace, and will sustain us no matter what Satan tries to do.

Number three, Jesus defeated Satan on the level of the *spirit* when Satan tried to tempt Jesus to worship him.

It's interesting to note that when Satan tested Jesus in the physical realm, he used food, and when he tested Him in the emotional realm of the soul, he used suicide. But when Satan tested Jesus in the realm of the human spirit, he used power and money by offering Him the glory of the kingdoms of the world.

This shows us that Satan has a strategy to conquer a man's spirituality. The devil knows that men will switch their allegiance more quickly from worshiping God to worshiping him because of power and riches than anything else he has to offer.

Satan offered to make Jesus the wealthiest, most powerful Man in the world. All Jesus had to do was turn Himself over spiritually to Satan and worship him.

But, thank God, Jesus withstood Satan. Then he turned around and gave us the standing He had attained through His victory on all three levels. Somehow fasting had helped prepare Jesus for that time of temptation so that He could, as our Substitute, give us His standing. Now when we fast, we execute Jesus' standing over the flesh as we yield to God and withstand the devil.

Ways To Fast

We just looked at a forty-day fast that Jesus went on to prepare to confront the devil's temptations. But there are several ways to fast. The one I have found to be the most practical and effective for the person carrying on in today's busy society is the common three-day fast. This can be done in one of two ways.

If you can't get away somewhere and just pray because of your schedule, I recommend that you go on a juice fast using mild juices such as grape or apple juice. During that time, pray as much as you can. But if you *can* get away, I suggest you go on a total consecrated fast of just water (filtered or distilled, available at most supermarkets).

If you aren't familiar with fasting and want to go on more than a three-day fast, I recommend a series of shorter periods of fasting. For example, you could fast three days a week for three weeks straight. For that time period, stick to fresh vegetables, fruits, and salads, staying away from heavy meats and breads. Then when your time of fasting is over, you can go back to those foods if you desire.

Eventually you may want to go on a more extended fast, especially if you are dealing with some kind of stronghold in your flesh realm (mind, emotions, or body) that you want to shut down or mortify for good.

The Fast God Chooses

To understand the kind of fast God chooses, let's take this subject one step further and go to Isaiah 58.

Is not this the fast that I have chosen? to loose the bands of wickedness, to undo the heavy burdens, and to let the oppressed go free, and that ye break every yoke?

Is it not to deal thy bread to the hungry, and that thou bring the poor that are cast out to thy house? when thou seest the naked, that thou cover him; and that thou HIDE NOT THYSELF FROM THINE OWN FLESH?

— Isaiah 58:6,7

That last phrase of this passage of Scripture was the part I got stuck on. I thought, *Lord, what do You mean when You say the fast You have chosen is that I hide not myself from my own flesh?* I wondered if God was talking about the same thing Jesus spoke of in Matthew 6:17,18:

But thou, when thou fastest, anoint thine head, and wash thy face;

That thou appear not unto men to fast, but unto thy Father which is in secret: and thy Father, which seeth in secret, shall reward thee openly.

Or was God making the same point in Isaiah 58:7 as Paul made in First Corinthians 7:5 when he addressed husbands and wives?

Defraud ye not one the other, except it be with consent for a time, that ye may give yourselves to fasting and prayer; and come together again, that Satan tempt you not for your incontinency.

Jesus taught about a fast in which we are to wash our faces and go about our daily business, not appear-

319

ing unto men that we are fasting. Then Paul taught about a fast in which we could lock ourselves away on the "mountain," so to speak, giving ourselves completely to fasting and prayer. Both types of fast are taught in the Bible.

But I still wondered what the Lord meant when He said I am not to hide myself from my own flesh. It took me about three years of study and meditation to understand what He was talking about.

The day you decide to fast is the day you decide to quit hiding from your own flesh — from whatever it is in you that just doesn't care about the lost, the poor, the naked, or those who are cast out of God's house. It's the day you decide to quit hiding from whatever ceiling is in your life stopping you from operating in God's power. The day you decide to fast is the day you decide to quit running from yourself.

Jesus said, "That demon didn't come out because of your unbelief." He also said, "That kind only comes out by prayer and fasting." And what does fasting have to do with your unbelief? It executes the position of the flesh that God has declared: It has no right to dominate you. It has no right to rule over you.

When you live a lifestyle of fasting and prayer, there is no operation of the flesh that the devil can lay hold of to destroy your life with. This is what Jesus meant when He said, "The prince of this world comes, and he has nothing in me" (John 14:30).

Why is that? Because fasting and praying in the Holy Ghost destroys those fleshly works and releases God's power in you. And the moment the operation of the flesh drops below the level of the operation of the

Spirit, you receive a new anointing in your life and ministry.

Prepare for Satan's Tactics

As we pray and fast, hiding not from our flesh, we set captives free. Let's look at Isaiah 58:6 again:

> **Is not this the fast that I have chosen? to loose the bands of wickedness, to undo the heavy burdens, and to let the oppressed go free, and that ye break every yoke?**

Often the first captive that needs to be set free is ourselves. As the flesh is dealt a death blow through fasting, we rise in freedom to walk more fully in the Spirit. Once we grow to a place of greater spiritual maturity, we begin to set others free.

Remember, it is at this point that we will draw the devil's attention. He doesn't want anyone to be free, and we have become a major threat to his kingdom of darkness!

You may ask, "Aren't you inviting trouble?" No, I'm not inviting trouble; I'm anticipating the strategies of Satan. The Bible tells us that when the Word is planted in any way, shape, or form, the devil comes to steal it so that it will not produce fruit (Luke 8:11-15).

If we aren't spiritually aware of the devil's tactics, we will have a rude awakening. We will be caught unprepared, and the devil will have a better opportunity to steal from us or from those we love.

We aren't in Heaven yet. We are living on a planet that has had war declared on it. The devil was thrown out of Heaven, and now he is active here on the earth. He cannot cause trouble in Heaven, so he does his best to cause trouble here.

As long as the devil is active here on earth, the storms will continue to beat down upon our homes. But just as surely as Jesus revealed that the storms would come, He also guaranteed that if our house is built on the rock of hearing *and* doing His sayings, the devil can do *nothing* to tear that house down (Matt. 7:24-27). The enemy isn't powerful enough. He doesn't have the equipment to force our house off the Rock of Jesus Christ.

The more that we get a revelation of the entire plan of God, the more victory we are going to have here on earth. The more quickly we come to a place of esteeming the glories of Heaven as a greater prize than the temporary short-sighted goals of this earthly existence, the more power we will have operating in our lives for the victories in the battles here on this earth.

The Missing Ingredient: Supernatural Peace

I didn't understand how all of this worked until several years ago when I fasted and prayed during an extended seeking time. I was looking for the change in my life that would make the difference. I wanted something I could put my hands on. I was waiting for the angels to appear or the heavens to open.

Those things didn't happen, but when I came out of the seeking time, I was left with something I never had before. I entered into a degree of peace I never knew existed. God put me on the Rock to stay!

You may ask, "Didn't you always walk in peace?" If you had asked me that before the fast, I would have answered, "Oh, yes!" because I didn't have anything to compare it with. But this new peace was different. It was unshakable!

This peace felt so good and so strange at the same time. When things seemed to go wrong, I found out that I could enjoy waiting with patience for God's plan to materialize! I could take my responsibility in a situation without taking the care or burden of it.

So through prayer and fasting, God had caused me to enter into a peace that was a tangible force keeping me in a position to receive His power. He spoke to my spirit about this peace, saying, "This is what you've been looking for. It is the missing ingredient."

You see, conditions on this earth aren't going to get better. Jesus told us in Matthew 24 what the last days would be like: wars and rumors of wars, earthquakes, sorrows, persecutions, false prophets, and the love of many waxing cold. The storms of life are getting more violent. As time goes on, they will rage more and more severely.

Fasting and prayer empty us of our fleshly nature and allow God to fill us with His character. As the flesh loses ground, the peace of God can begin to rule in our lives (Col. 3:15). We climb from one level of peace to another. Our faith becomes greater and greater.

All of this is waiting for you and me. We are capable of so much more than merely overcoming the crises of life. Each of us is meant to be a force on this earth for God — and prayer combined with fasting are the power twins that help us attain that goal!

For in the quietness of My Spirit,
    My voice is known,
    and My ways, My principles, and My precepts
    are shown.
So fly away with Me, saith the Spirit of Grace,
    for I and no man will exalt you
    and give you your rightful place in Myself.
For peace will be the fruit,
    saith the Spirit of Grace,
    the peaceable fruit,
    when you give me that rightful place.

Chapter 14

How To Effectively Pray in Tongues

There seems to be a need in the Church for some down-to-earth, practical teaching on the "how-to" of praying in tongues. So let me give you some basic guidelines to help you effectively "build yourself up on your most holy faith, praying in the Holy Ghost."

It Isn't How Loud Or How Soft You Pray

People come to me all the time and ask, "How do *you* pray in tongues, Brother Roberson?"

I just simply answer, "I pray like this," and then I demonstrate, praying quietly under my breath.

"But don't you pray out loud?"

"No, not usually," I reply. "God isn't hard of hearing." (Of course, if I do pray louder, He isn't nervous either!)

Then someone asked me, "Well, what about warring tongues?"

I asked, "How do you do that?" The person demonstrated, almost screaming in tongues.

"Why do you yell like that when you're talking to God?" I asked.

"Well, I thought I was talking to the devil."

"No, no, First Corinthians 14:2 says you're talking to *God*. Now, you can pray that loud if you want to. But I'll tell you what, it won't be long before your tonsils will be playing Bach's Fifth Cantata! You're going to blow those tonsils out!"

So there is the group that says, "You aren't getting anywhere with God praying in tongues unless you pray in a warring tongue." They scream and shout in tongues, thinking they're addressing the devil.

But the issue isn't whether you shout or whisper when you pray in tongues. You aren't producing any more for the Kingdom of God by yelling in tongues than you are by praying in tongues under your breath, because it's the Holy Spirit who supplies the language. You didn't create it; *He* created it. And if the Holy Spirit is the Originator of the language, it is always full of power.

(The same is true with worship: It isn't how loud or how quiet you worship; it's how much of your entire being you pour into every statement of adoration. You can't truly worship the Lord while your mind is wandering off down the street analyzing some problem.)

When I first began traveling in the ministry, I used to walk back and forth in my motel room, praying in the Holy Ghost. I was still very ignorant about prayer, so I would pray in tongues just as loud as I could. I thought that increased volume made my praying more powerful. I hadn't learned yet that God isn't deaf and that He can hear my prayer anywhere and in any tone of voice.

Later I came to realize that the moment the Holy Spirit's supernatural language comes out of my mouth, it is released to God. It doesn't make any difference if I am whispering or shouting; the words that come out of my spirit in tongues still mean the same because I'm talking to God.

Is Fervency in Prayer a Requirement?

You may ask, "What if I don't pray real fervently when I pray in the Holy Ghost? After all, doesn't James 5:16 say, ...**The effectual FERVENT prayer of a righteous man availeth much?**

Yes, it does say that, but James is talking about the prayer of faith in that verse. The prayer of faith occurs when you line up your sights on some "mountain" in your life and say, "Mountain, move!" That kind of fervent prayer avails much when you have enough strength in your character to stand your ground against hell or any other opposition until that mountain moves.

But if you don't have enough strength of character yet to do that, praying in the Holy Ghost will help bring you to a place where you *can* hold your ground until you receive your answer.

So whether or not you're praying fervently in tongues doesn't really matter. It just depends on what God is doing in your spirit.

For example, sometimes the Holy Spirit gets quite forceful in my spirit as I pray in tongues, and I feel like I'm fighting something. But when that forceful unction lifts, I let it lift. I trust the Holy Ghost to lead me; He knows what I'm praying about. But I don't stop praying. I just go back to praying quietly under my breath.

Pray to a State of Peace

At the church I pastor in Tulsa, Oklahoma, we meet together regularly to pray as a corporate body. At these prayer meetings, I often have everyone sit down and "glue" themselves to the chair. They are to do nothing but sit there and pray in tongues.

Over the years, some people have had a hard time doing that because their flesh was still "on the go." They couldn't even sit and pray in the Holy Ghost for two hours without moving. It was obvious that they weren't well acquainted with themselves or with the Holy Ghost.

Sometimes in prayer I enter into such a state of peace that I just lie on the floor for two or three hours. Everything is so quiet, I don't even want to move. At those times, the Holy Spirit begins to teach me things from His Word, and the truths He reveals seem so crystal clear. What a wonderful place in the Spirit that is!

But most Christians don't know anything about the place of utter peace that can be reached through praying in tongues. They have never stayed still long enough in prayer to get acquainted with it.

"Do you have something against walking while you pray in tongues, Brother Roberson?" No, I have nothing against walking and praying. But there comes a time for learning discipline in prayer and for getting acquainted with the Holy Ghost. These can often best be accomplished by keeping your body as still as possible while your spirit prays out the mysteries of Christ in tongues.

Edification Doesn't Spell Feelings

A lot of times, people look for feelings when they pray in tongues. That's why I pin people to a chair during corporate prayer — to help them get beyond looking for feelings.

"Do you ever feel anything when you pray in tongues, Brother Roberson?" Oh, yes, don't get me wrong. I welcome the emotions when they come. Once in a while something will build and build and build in my spirit until it is finally delivered to my soul, and then my emotions go, "Wow!" But I don't judge whether I'm receiving anything based on what I feel. I just keep praying in tongues, believing the Word that says I am edifying myself.

You see, tongues originate in your spirit by the power of the Holy Spirit. Emotions are added when the tongues pass through your soul. That's why whether you shout or whisper in tongues doesn't make a lick of difference to the outcome of your prayer if you're the one who added the emotions.

In my early days of praying in the Holy Ghost, I thought that maybe I wasn't praying effectively if I didn't feel a tingling in my fingers or rise to a certain state of emotional "high." Then I went through a period of time when every time I prayed in tongues, an emotional war would wage on the inside of me. I almost quit praying because I thought Heaven had been closed against me. I was judging whether or not I was getting through to Heaven on the emotions I was or was not experiencing in prayer.

Now I know that edification doesn't spell feelings. Praying in the Holy Ghost is a step deeper than our emotions. Emotions belong to our soulish realm, but power and edification belong to the spiritual realm.

The Holy Ghost even leaves our intellect out of praying in tongues. That's a big blow to our carnal pride! We may pray three hours in the Holy Ghost without God ever letting us in on what we were praying about!

For example, one time I had a vision of Old Mexico, and I prayed and prayed in the Spirit, trying to find out when that vision would come to pass. I badgered God about it, asking Him why He wouldn't show me more of the coming revival I had seen in the vision. "Please show me what meeting it was that I saw," I prayed. "Show me what I have to do."

Finally, the Lord interrupted me one morning in prayer and said, "If I tell you in English what I have planned for you, you will just mess it up!" He was right, because later when I found out what it would cost to fulfill what He wanted me to do in Mexico, I needed a lot of extra edification just to handle it!

So praying in tongues is deeper than your emotional realm. It comes from your spirit — the foundation upon which your life rests, the part of you that the Holy Ghost was sent to nourish, teach, and edify.

That may not mean you'll always enjoy wonderful emotions. But edification is the necessary process by which you are transformed to the Word you have heard — the Word that sets the standard in your life.

The Role of Worship

So edification doesn't necessarily include my emotions. If I want feelings, I worship, because that is designed to bring the godly emotions I need for fortification to my soulish realm.

You can't do anything better in the midst of a trial than to worship. Worship sustains you, stabilizing your emotions to go through the trial victoriously.

(However, you don't want to just be sustained through a problem; you want to go further in God and *be set free* from it. That is the job of the Holy Ghost, and that is where praying in tongues comes in, because all permanent change comes from within.)

That's why James said you are to count it all joy when you fall into temptations, testings, and trials. Rejoice in the midst of your afflictions, your infirmities, your perplexities. Just count it all joy. As you turn all of your attention to God, releasing your emotions in admiration and worship of your Father, that joy will stabilize your soulish realm, which is the part of you the devil likes to operate against.

Personal Breakthroughs Through Worship

A prominent evangelist and close friend of mine was once caught up into Heaven to visit with Jesus.

While there, Jesus told him, "My people do not worship Me enough."

Often the only time we spend time in praise and worship is at church. If this is true, a change needs to be made.

The greatest experiences with God I've ever had in my life, besides seeing Him heal a blind or deaf person, took place while I was worshiping Him privately with only a few other people present.

For example, I mentioned earlier that soon after I had been baptized in the Holy Spirit at church and had spoken "with stammering lips," I had a spiritual experience while worshiping God in my own home.

At that time I was going through an intense spiritual battle. I could just feel the fleshly carnal nature trying to creep back and overpower me.

As Rosalie prayed with me, I walked back and forth, back and forth in my living room, fervently praising and worshiping God. I didn't want to give in to the flesh, but it seemed as if I was almost powerless.

I really didn't know how to pray at that time. I hadn't been saved very long, and the year after I was born again, I had been in and out of church. When I was "out," I could be found in some not-too-nice places.

So I walked back and forth, resisting the temptations of the flesh as I prayed and praised God the best I knew how. I didn't know what to do except lift my hands to God and say "Hallelujah" and "Praise God" over and over.

Suddenly a warm sensation came over me, beginning in my uplifted hands. The sensation flowed down through my arms and shoulders into my chest and seemed to reach up into my mind.

As this sensation flowed into my legs, I fell over backwards. My breath was knocked out of me, but I hardly noticed. Instead, I immediately began to effortlessly speak another language. For hours I continued to yield to the Holy Spirit, and that supernatural language increased until it had become a full, fluent prayer language.

This strong anointing of the Holy Spirit, which began at about midnight, was on me until four o'clock in the morning. It was a life-changing experience for my hungry heart.

The second time I experienced a powerful move of the Holy Spirit, I was once again worshiping God. At this time, I was thinning trees in Oregon, working to provide for my family.

I was on a campaign to get my boss and a fellow employee nicknamed "Fort" saved. Fort was a skinny young man who was burnt out on dope and a habitual liar. I testified to him and the boss night and day.

Later when my boss didn't have enough money to pay me anymore, I quit and continued to work for free just so I could continue witnessing to these two men. Because I wasn't being paid, my boss couldn't tell me where to fell trees. This worked to my advantage, because I could choose to work by Fort's side.

Anytime Fort would turn off his saw for a break, in my zeal I would begin to preach. You should have seen how quickly he turned his saw back on again!

Well, I finally talked Fort into getting born again. He received Jesus in a logger tent about a quarter mile from the Lake of the Woods outside of Klamath Falls.

As Fort sat there in the tent, I and another Christian logger walked around with uplifted hands, worshiping the Lord and trying to "pray Fort through" to salvation. (At this time, I didn't believe someone was truly saved unless he "felt" something.) Every few minutes, I would lay hands on Fort and pray in the Holy Ghost.

Then all of a sudden in the early hours of the morning, the Presence of God entered that tent. To this day, I can't tell you if it was an angel or the Holy Ghost.

I fell over backwards onto a cot and began laughing hilariously in the Holy Ghost. I became so drunk in the Spirit that I couldn't rise off the cot. In the midst of all this, Fort was saved and filled with the Holy Ghost.

All three of us laughed and giggled in the Holy Ghost and prayed in tongues and rejoiced until dawn. Everyone within hearing range must have thought we were crazy.

The next day my boss was angry at me for what had gone on in that tent the night before. But I didn't have to answer to him because I was working for free. Then to my surprise, the boss came to me that night and said, "Something is wrong with me."

I said, "I know what it is. We need to pray through."

My boss replied, "Okay, but can we go to the other side of the lake where there aren't any people?"

"Sure, we can," I answered. So the other Christian logger and I took the boss to the other side of the lake and prayed him through to the Kingdom as well!

Soon afterward, Fort disappeared. When he reappeared a few days later to pick up his paycheck, he was drunk and back on drugs. He didn't come back again.

Then a few years later, after I had entered full-time ministry, I held a meeting in Klamath Falls. I was sitting in the back room after the service when a plump, clean-cut young man walked in.

"Hi, do you remember me?" he asked.

"No, I don't," I said.

"I used to work with you in the woods. My name is So-and-so." That didn't mean anything to me. Then he said, "You called me Fort."

"The only Fort I knew was a habitual liar and a dopehead!"

The young man just laughed and said, "That was me!"

I looked at him in amazement. "That was you? Well, what are you doing at this meeting?"

"Oh, haven't you heard? I'm one of the cooperating pastors sponsoring this meeting!" I just about fainted! That all-night Holy Ghost revival we had experienced in the logger tent years earlier had produced good fruit for God's Kingdom after all! And it all came about as two believers worshiped God.

How To Spend Three Hours
With the Lord

From time to time I have been asked what I consider to be the most powerful way for a person to spend three or four hours in the Presence of God if that's all the time he has to do so in a given week. After many years of praying and waiting on God, my answer boils down to these three basic things:

1. **Worship and praise** (which supplies the sustaining power needed for the duration of our trials, trading our weaknesses for Christ's strength)

2. **Confession of God's Word** (speaking to the "mountains" in our lives that need to be removed — sickness or pain, finances or torment, worry or fear, etc.)

3. **Praying in tongues** (the supernatural language that not only edifies but supplies revelation knowledge)

You see, it isn't the general messages that you hear a minister preach for an hour each week that will change your life. The anointed teacher or pastor can only supply some of the information required for needed change.

But the real change comes when in the privacy of your own home, you apply the Word to the problems you are facing. Your life is transformed in direct proportion to the private time you spend praying in the Spirit and in confession of the Word and worship.

Now, it's important to understand that the guidelines I'm about to give you for spending time with God are just that — guidelines. They are not a set formula that you must follow to the letter in order to enjoy fellowship with the Father.

Just follow the leading of the Holy Spirit as you develop these three areas in your walk with God. As you do, you will enjoy a new dimension of answered prayer and a strong, continual awareness of God's Presence.

The First Hour: Worship

The first hour I would enter God's Presence in worship, praise, and thanksgiving. I'd say, "Here I am, Father. I don't have any needs to present, because all of my needs were met at the Cross two thousand years ago. I'm just here to fellowship with You because You're my Father and I'm your child. I'm going to ascend on Your holy hill and see how high I can go praising and worshiping You." My goal is to develop a relationship with God based on fellowship instead of need.

Too many times believers enter into God's Presence only when they are instructed to do so in church or when they need something. But one of the highest forms of worship is to enter into His Presence in our private lives to praise and worship Him as our Heavenly Father simply because our name is written in the Lamb's Book of Life.

God is exceedingly glad that we are His children and that He is our Father. And as a Father who enjoys His children, He wants to spend time with us fellowshiping around His throne. He likes it when we lift up holy hands and tell Him just how much we love Him in pure fellowship.

So how do we enter the Presence of God? Well, the Holy Spirit was sent to glorify Jesus (John 16:14). His entire ministry is to bring you into Jesus' Presence. Then Jesus in turn brings you into the Presence of the Father. And the same principles Jesus taught His disciples about entering into the Father's Presence applies to entering the Presence of Jesus.

Jesus said, "When you pray, say, ...**Our Father which art in Heaven, Hallowed be thy name** (Matt. 6:9). That word "hallowed" means to sanctify His Name in our lives, raising it high above everything else. It means to enter His Presence with reverent worship.

Hypothetically speaking, we are always in God's Presence. We have Jesus' Name. We can petition God at any moment of the day.

But when we have time to enter the Presence of God with protocol, then let me tell you right now, there is a way that pleases Him.

First of all, there is a way to offer myself to God in private worship. The first part of me I should offer up before Him is my soul — my intellect, my will, and my emotions.

I may not feel like offering up my soul to God. No one may be leading me to do so. A band doesn't follow me around, creating an atmosphere for worship. I don't always have a cassette or a compact disc available to play worship music for me. But when I enter into God's

Presence offering my soul, I almost always end up worshiping Him in spirit.

Secondly, when I come before Him, I am to show Him respect. An ambassador will show honor to an earthly king by bowing before him and offering him gifts. How much more should I show respect as I enter the Presence of the King of Kings with the offering of my soul?

Sometimes we forget whose Presence we are entering into. Yes, Jesus is our best Friend. Yes, He is our Confidant. But when we approach Him with a petition or with worship, He is our High Priest, and He deserves our highest honor and respect.

For that very reason, it is highly important that we do not let our soul wander off down the street to solve some problem when it is supposed to be worshiping the King of Kings. If we want our soul to be blessed by the King, then we must keep our soul in the Presence of the King. To do otherwise would be highly disrespectful, to say the least.

The Second Hour:
Confession of God's Word

Then I would spend my second hour with the Lord reconciling the problem I'm currently facing to the Cross. How? By replacing with the words of my mouth the image of the problem that the devil sends my way with the image that is in the Word. That is my inheritance and my right as a believer.

As I entered the second hour, I'd say, "Father, I thank You that devils are subject to me. I thank You that disease, which is caused directly or indirectly by devils, is subject to me in Your Name. I thank You that I have been delivered from poverty and that it is also subject to me in Your Name. I thank You for all these things, Father.

"Now if You will excuse me, Father, the devil is invading my territory. So I'm going to use the faith and the Word You have given me to meet that invasion head-on with the power of confession.

"You said that if I do not doubt Your Word with my heart and if I confess it with my mouth, the same incredible power that wrought the most phenomenal miracle of all, the rebirth, will also operate to remove my mountain."

So I would spend the next hour hurling the confession of God's Word directly at my problem. I'd talk to that mountain in my life the same way Jesus talked to the fig tree in Mark 11:14.

For example, if I was dealing with financial lack, I'd confess something like this over and over: "Poverty, you have been reconciled to the Cross. Jesus Himself has borne my poverty by an act of grace. Though He was rich, for my sake He became poor that I through His poverty might be made rich [2 Cor. 8:9].

"Do you hear me, poverty? I have a covenant with God. You cannot stay in my life. You are cursed. You are leaving my life!

"And, prosperity, I call you in from the north, the south, the east, and the west! Finances, I command you to increase! I am enforcing my rights as a believer by a gift God has given me — the confession of faith in His

Word!" For that entire second hour, that's how I would talk to that mountain of poverty, cursing it and commanding it to move out of my life.

I've had the time of my life just picking on the devil, doing exactly what I've just described. I don't think anything makes him more upset!

Now, someone may say, "I can understand worshiping God for an hour, but isn't confessing the same thing over and over to your problem a form of begging?" No, it isn't. You are begging God when you ask Him again and again for something He has already provided, such as healing or deliverance from an addiction that has kept you in bondage.

Confessing the Word of God is using the faith God has already put in your heart to enforce what He has already said about your problem. Once we have prayed the prayer of faith over the problem, we are not to talk to God about the problem — we are to talk to the *problem* about *God*!

The Third Hour: Praying in Tongues

Finally, as I entered the third hour I'd say, "Well, Father, I have reconciled that problem to the Cross. I have aggressively wielded the sword of the Spirit, the Word of God, this last hour and have changed a few things in the Spirit. I thank You that I have received my answer.

"But now will You excuse me, Father? I need a little edification, a little strengthening of my spirit man, a little praying out of the mysteries of Christ."

Then I'd spend that third hour praying in tongues. I'd just lie down, sit down, or walk back and forth, building myself up on my most holy faith as I prayed in the Holy Ghost.

When you do that, many times you will start feeling so edified that you won't want to quit! You'll say, "I think I will tag another hour of praying in tongues onto this one!"

You see, I have found something I can do during that third hour on purpose, just because I want to, that carries a promise from God to edify the part of me in which I'm not supposed to doubt — my heart.

What am I saying as I pray? Most of the time I don't know because my understanding is unfruitful. But I do know that my spirit is communicating divine secrets and mysteries before the Father and that I am building myself up on my most holy faith in my inner man, or my heart.

So if I had only one three-hour time period that I could spend with the Lord during a week, that would be the way I would spend it. If for some reason I only had one hour that I could spend in prayer that week, I would break it into three segments of twenty minutes apiece for worship, confession, and praying in tongues. All three kinds of prayer are designed to benefit you and to make you receptive to the finished work of the Cross.

The Benefits of Meditation on the Word

Meditation on God's Word is one of the most important guidelines I could give you for unlocking divine mysteries through praying in the Holy Ghost. For more than a quarter of a century, I have endeavored to pray in tongues just as much as possible in my own walk with the Lord, and I have reaped rich rewards. And some of the greatest benefits I've experienced have come from meditating on the Word as I pray.

What is meditation? Meditation is the process of assimilating God's Word into your soul and spirit. As you meditate on the Word of God, the Holy Spirit takes God's counsel in the form of the Word and reconstructs it in your spirit in such a way that it becomes *your* insight, wisdom, and counsel.

Meditation can take you from simply acknowledging that God's Word is true to having the Word engrafted into your spirit. In other words, the Word not only becomes a part of you, but as it becomes implanted in your heart, *you* become a part of *it*!

Meditation on the Word
And Praying in Tongues

I gave you some practical guidelines about what to do if you only have three hours to spend with the Lord. But that doesn't negate the fact that the more you pray in tongues, the more clear and definite the divine channel becomes through which God communicates with you. It is to your eternal benefit that you pray *much* in the Holy Ghost, building yourself up on your most holy faith.

As you pray in tongues, the Teacher of your new nature uses the supernatural language He brought all the way from Heaven to begin an illumination process inside of you. Within that language resides not only the mysteries of God's plan for your life, but the understanding of all Scripture.

Therefore, the Holy Spirit lives in hope of the day that you'll give yourself over to the meditation of God's Word. When you do, you make His ministry of illumination so much simpler.

I consider it to be a blessing that my mind is unfruitful while I spend three or four hours praying in tongues. Why? Because I've learned to employ my mind with God's Word while my spirit is praying. It has become automatic for me: When I sit down to pray in tongues, I pick up my Bible and start reading.

My favorite practice is to take a book like Galatians, Ephesians, or Philippians and just read that book over and over again while I pray in tongues for hours. Often I sit in a chair or lie on the floor and pray an hour or two. Then I set my open Bible in a convenient place and start walking around the room praying.

I pray for a while, my spirit listening in case the Holy Spirit says something through that channel of communication. Then I go back to the Bible and read the entire book through again, still praying in tongues.

I'm glad that my mind and my spirit can receive from God at the same time. The Holy Spirit takes all the accumulated knowledge that I've deposited into my mind through reading something in the Bible over and over, and He uses it for the day-and-night meditation process. This is where much of the revelation knowledge I receive originates.

Meditating on the Word
In the Early Church

Meditating on the Word while praying isn't something new or unique to me. Think back to the early apostles. In Acts 2, the apostles were filled with the Holy Spirit on the Day of Pentecost. Then in Acts 6, they faced a problem regarding the fair administration of food among the believers.

The apostles said, "Look, it isn't right that we are distracted from the Word of God to serve tables. Let's appoint some men who are highly esteemed among you for this job so that we may give ourselves continually to the Word of God and to prayer" (Acts 6:2-4).

Now, what part of the Word did the apostles give themselves to? All of the Old Testament promises. Remember, that's all the Word they had at that time. They couldn't open a Bible and have the entire foundation of the Church laid out before them on their lap like you can!

So the apostles gave themselves continually to all the Old Testament promises while at the same time giving themselves to prayer. What kind of prayer would the apostles be talking about? Well, what experience was freshest in their minds? They had just received the promise of the Father — the baptism in the Holy Ghost with the evidence of speaking in tongues. So they were praying in that new language the Holy Spirit had given them!

The apostles prayed in tongues continually while meditating on the promises of the Old Covenant. This practice helped establish the foundation of the Church, because God was able to bring forth the mysteries of Christ.

We can also see the principle of meditating on the Word while praying in the Spirit in the life of the Apostle Paul. Remember, except for Jesus, Paul received more revelation knowledge than any other man since Moses.

We already know one of his keys to receiving that revelation knowledge: After he was filled with the Holy Ghost, he made the statement that he prayed in tongues more than anyone (1 Cor. 14:18). But meditation on God's Word was another important key.

You see, Paul said he was a Pharisee, a "Hebrew of Hebrews" (Phil. 3:5). That means he began to memorize the Old Testament scriptures for seven hours a day beginning at the age of three.

I believe that all of the Old Testament scripture stored inside Paul, combined with his praying in tongues "more than ye all," were crucial in enabling Paul to receive so much revelation knowledge for the foundation of the Church. That revelation knowledge brought the Old Covenant together with the New Covenant.

As far as I can ascertain, Paul was the only apostle who thoroughly understood the relationship between the Law and our covenant with God through Jesus Christ — the law of the Spirit of life: **For the law of the Spirit of life in Christ Jesus hath made me free from the law of sin and death** (Rom. 8:2). Today that understanding seems commonplace, but in Paul's day, it was unheard of. And two keys that enabled Paul to receive such a depth of revelation knowledge was praying in tongues and meditating on the Old Testament scriptures.

Confession:
The Highest Form of Meditation

God created you and me with a capacity not only to believe, but to conform to whatever it is that we are believing and continually subjecting ourselves to. Unfortunately, this ability can operate in us for the bad as well as for the good.

That's why God gave Joshua this instruction when Joshua was about to lead the children of Israel into the Promised Land:

> **This book of the law SHALL NOT DEPART OUT OF THY MOUTH; but thou shalt MEDI-TATE THEREIN DAY AND NIGHT, that thou mayest observe to do according to all that is written therein: for then thou shalt make thy way prosperous, and then thou shalt have good success.**
>
> **— Joshua 1:8**

What an incredible set of instructions! First of all, God said, "Don't let the Word of God depart out of your mouth." That means there should never be a time when the Word in your mouth is replaced by anything else. When you let the Word depart from your mouth, you set yourself in agreement with the circumstances that are arrayed against you.

But if you continue to confess the Word, you are operating in the covenant between you and God against the adverse circumstance. And as you continually

349

subject yourself to the Word by confessing it over and over, you are applying one of the highest forms of meditation.

Circumstances are no respecters of persons. They will come at you day and night. But when you stand face to face with those situations that seem impossible to overcome and keep confessing God's promises over and over, you *are* meditating day and night. Through meditation, you are giving the Word of God the opportunity to transform you and your thinking so you can actually become that victorious person you are meant to be.

You *will* eventually conform to what you continually subject yourself to. That's why God told Joshua to let not the Word depart from his mouth and to meditate day and night; He wanted Joshua to continually be subjected to the Word.

Paint a Picture of Your Answer

Due to our busy schedules, most of us cannot read, study, or memorize the Word day and night. But we *can* meditate on the Word day and night. Reading, studying, and memorizing can only assist meditation; they do not replace it.

You can actually take a journey into a whole new set of circumstances in your spirit and mind as you meditate day and night on what God has said about you and your problem. Soon you won't be conforming to the problem anymore. Instead, your faith, your thoughts, and your attitude will leave the problem behind to embark on a journey into God where every promise is yea and Amen (2 Cor. 1:20).

You can find a place in God where your mouth has described the victory so many times that it has painted a picture on the inside of your spirit. That picture of victory becomes so powerful, it replaces anything and everything that spells defeat.

So whenever you face a problem or are about to charge ahead to conquer something for the Kingdom of God, start hearing and reading scriptures that address your particular problem. Keep on doing that until there is a huge reservoir of the Word on the inside of you.

Then meditate on those scriptures day and night, saying them over and over. Roll them over and over in your mind until the picture the Word paints in your heart becomes stronger than the picture the obstacle paints in your mind.

Pull the Word up out of your spirit and roll it over and over in your mind while you are driving, cleaning house, or working on your job. Whenever you can, describe your victory out loud. Use your words to paint pictures of your victory. Then God will do for you what He promised Joshua: "For then you will make your way prosperous, and then you will have good success."

The Role of Meditation
In Overcoming My Failure

I can attest to the truth of this vital principle from my own personal experience. For example, I will never forget the first time I tried to preach. It was a Wednesday night service in a small Holiness church in

Oregon. Besides my wife Rosalie, there were only three or four people present.

I was sure I could do it. Many times those same four people had sat with my wife and me in coffee shops, talking about Jesus. I would get so carried away preaching and pounding on the table that I'd almost spill our coffee!

But now as I stood up in church in front of those same four people to deliver the Word in an official capacity, something happened! I guess it was the fear of being put in a position where I felt as if I had to produce.

Even in high school, I'd choose to take a lower grade in English rather than to give an oral report. The blood would drain out of my face; I'd turn white and get dizzy just at the thought of doing it.

Yet here I was, standing behind a pulpit with an entire page full of notes and everyone looking at me. Rosalie said I turned white as I stood there, trying to gather my courage to begin. Then the door suddenly opened, and three more people came in and sat down. That did it! They were perfect strangers!

I almost passed out as I leaned forward, gripping the pulpit for support. I can still remember watching my knuckles turn white as I stared down at them. I was afraid to look at the people.

Finally, I pulled myself together enough to read my text — but then my mind went completely blank! Earlier that day I had thought of a hundred things to say, but my mental "slate" had been wiped clean by panic.

So, as an emergency measure, I picked up my notes and began to read. But the situation only grew worse. By the time I had finished reading my notes, I had absolutely nothing left to say. I was paralyzed with fear!

I looked sheepishly toward my pastor for help, so she walked up to the pulpit to rescue me. I hurt so bad inside I wanted to cry. It was a long walk back to my chair. I sat down just in time to hear the pastor apologize to the people, saying, "I'm sorry, folks. He told me he was called to preach..."

The entire ordeal had lasted about seven minutes. That night I buried my face in my pillow and cried until some of the hurt was gone. It was a long time before I stood behind a pulpit to preach again — almost two years!

It seemed as though that night had confirmed everything I had already known. I just didn't have what it took to be a preacher. My grandpa's words rang in my ears: "You're never going to amount to anything!"

After being devastated by my first attempt at preaching, I knew there was a mountain of bad programming and poor images to overcome. But, glory to God, in the months that followed, something happened to break that deadly pattern. I learned about the importance of meditating on God's Word!

Two years later, I summoned the courage to make my second attempt at preaching. But something was very different this time.

Even though I hadn't physically stood before a crowd for any reason for those two years, through meditation I had stood before crowds and preached hundreds of times. I would close my eyes and see myself preaching. I could even hear myself preach the message over and over again in my spirit. I was painting a picture of victory on the inside of me.

You see, I meditated on verses that described the image of truth that I needed to conform to — verses such as **I can do all things through Christ which strengtheneth me** (Phil. 4:13) and **...greater is He that is in you, than he that is in the world** (1 John 4:4). I kept meditating on those verses until they actually changed the way I saw myself!

It was incredible. When the moment came, it was as though I had preached hundreds of times. I was amazed at how easy it was to conform to the image that had been created in my spirit through meditation.

That's what makes meditation so powerful: It replaces the problem with the Word and the fear of failure with faith in every area of your life.

Assimilating the Word Into the Soul

Your soul was created to assimilate. For example, if you moved to a country where people spoke a language you didn't know, you would begin to assimilate that language just by being in constant contact with its use. Your entire soul would kick in to cause you to learn that language automatically. You wouldn't have to deliberately sit down with a tape that told you to say

"Thank you" or "How are you" in that language over and over until you finally memorized it.

In the same way, you can approach God's Word in such a manner that your soul — your intellect, will, and emotions — automatically assimilates it and then begins the process of transforming you according to its truth.

For example, some men in my church who are called to helps asked me what books of the Bible they should meditate on in order to excel in their particular calling. As businessmen, one of their main concerns was that they could learn to possess money without money possessing *them*.

So I told them, "Take the Book of Proverbs and read it fifty times. Read it deliberately and precisely, acknowledging what is in each verse. You may not understand what the verse means, but at least understand what it says.

"If you run across a word you don't know, look it up in a dictionary so that the next time you see it, you'll know what it means. But don't do any studies or cross referencing. Just read the Book of Proverbs fifty times."

Why did I instruct those men to do that? Because by the time they read Proverbs at least fifty times, they would have assimilated the entire book into their soul!

Perhaps there are three verses — one in chapter 2, one in chapter 5, and one in chapter 9 — that will give them understanding of a verse in chapter 14. But it won't come together for them until they've read the book fifty times and assimilated it into their soul.

You see, when you read a book of the Bible over and over, you set yourself up for day-and-night meditation. You are feeding your spirit the raw material that the Holy Ghost needs to illuminate the entire book for you! Eventually the central theme will be born in you. Then all satellite verses will be pulled in, along with the understanding of how they relate to each other.

Understanding how verses relate to one another in a passage of Scripture is an important part of the meditation process. One of the first things the Lord taught me regarding meditation was never to take a verse out of context.

If there is a verse I'm trying to understand, the Holy Spirit alerts me to find where the subject of the verse begins and ends and then to read over that passage many times. In this way, I assist Him in my meditations.

The assimilation process will happen automatically, even when you go to sleep. For instance, suppose you read First John one hundred times. (By the way, that's a good beginning assignment for offering your soul for meditation. Anything in you that doesn't love people will go to war against that book!) Then suppose that soon afterward, someone wronged you in some way, and you made a mountain of unforgiveness out of a molehill of offense.

The mind of God that you assimilated from First John will help you sort out what is and what is not important while you sleep. It will magnify the truth you assimilated regarding God's love and level that mountain of unforgiveness.

That's what I mean by day-*and*-night meditation. The assimilation process will happen automatically, just as it does when learning a new language in a country where everyone speaks that language but you.

Your soul was designed to transform you to whatever you subject it to the most. If it's a new language that everyone is speaking but you, you will automatically begin to learn it. And if you're giving yourself to praying in the Holy Ghost and to the Word — reading it, speaking it, rolling it over and over in your mind — then your spirit man will automatically begin to be illuminated by the revelation knowledge of God's truth!

These guidelines I've given you for praying in the Spirit are by no means exhaustive. They are just signposts pointing the way to a more effective prayer life. Remember, your key to unlock divine mysteries is praying in tongues, your destination is God's perfect will for your life, and your Helper throughout the journey is the Holy Spirit living within!

Continue seeking My face
    so you can go from death to death
    [of the fleshly nature]
    and from glory to glory.
You will see wonderful, wonderful things
    take place.
Not only will you be in the planting,
    but you will also be in the harvest.
For I have spoken, and it shall be so.
So I give you the keys, and I call.
Come. Come. Come.
Come, saith the Spirit of Grace.

Chapter 15

The Divine Progression To Agape Love

I consider it the utmost honor to spend an hour in God's Presence with the third Person of the Godhead as He creates a supernatural language on the inside of my spirit. Why? Because with every syllable I speak in that language, the Holy Spirit is working a miraculous transformation within me.

You see, years ago I thought tongues for personal edification had to do strictly with speaking mysteries and divine secrets and building myself up with revelation knowledge. Only later did I find out that it has just as much to do with purging me so I can learn to walk in agape love — the kind of love that seeks not its own and denies itself on behalf of others.

Agape vs. Phileo Love

I have no higher goal in life than to learn how to walk in this God-kind of love, so I want to know more about it. I know a lot about "phileo" love, but I want to know about agape.

I have yoked myself to Jesus, whom John revealed when he said, "God is love" (1 John 4:16). Jesus doesn't just love us; He *is* Love. He is incapable of anything else but love. That's why we haven't understood Him the way we should — because we haven't understood agape love.

We usually don't have trouble with phileo love. Phileo can be a strong love, but it has its own interests at stake, as well as those of the one loved. It's more of a conditional love that says, "I can love you if somehow you bring me pleasure" or "I will love you, but I want something back from you."

So most of us know how to love people with phileo love. But we haven't done very well at walking in agape. Agape is a self-denying love. Its total focus is the interests and welfare of the beloved.

Phileo love may send me to war because I love my country. I may even give my body to be burned for the hope of a better life for my children. I will sacrifice my life on that altar.

But if agape love goes to war, it is with higher motives. I may still sacrifice my life so my children can live free from threat of harm. But at the same time I have the enemy soldier on my heart. My prayer is that the war would cease and that my enemy would be born again.

Most marriages are based on phileo, not agape. The spouses love each other for what they can receive from each other. If marriages were always based on God's selfless, agape kind of love, there would be no more divorces.

Agape Love Is Merciful

Agape love says, "Be merciful just as your Heavenly Father is merciful" (Luke 6:36). How merciful is our Heavenly Father? Well, you and I were lost and headed for hell. We had nothing to bargain with. We had absolutely no right to approach God. We were not capable of bridging the gap on our own.

But God had mercy on you and me. We didn't deserve and couldn't earn His mercy; we had no way to approach an infallible God. But *He* approached *us* in His mercy. He crossed that void with Jesus' blood.

So how do you obey Jesus' command to be merciful even as the Father is merciful? Jesus provided the guidelines in Luke 6:27-38.

When someone sues you for your coat, you give him the cloak you are wearing. When he slaps you on the cheek, you turn the other cheek. When he takes away your goods, you give him more than he asked for. When he despitefully uses you, you pray for him and forgive him. When he hates you, you keep walking in love.

Why? Because you are having mercy on him. You are bridging the gap with the blood of Jesus when the person doesn't deserve it. *That is agape!*

The result of walking in this agape kind of love is revealed in Luke 6:38:

> **Give, and it shall be given unto you; good measure, pressed down, and shaken together, and running over, shall men give into your bosom. For with the same measure that ye mete withal it shall be measured to you again.**

Jesus was saying this: "If you will be children of the Most High, who is merciful even to the evil and the unthankful, and give agape love to others, then My Father will restore whatever you may have lost — pressed down, shaken together, and running over. While the thief is taking your money out the back door because you extended mercy, My Father will march in the front door with agape and restore to overflowing all that you lost!" That's why agape cannot fail (1 Cor. 13:8)!

However, walking in agape love is easier said than done. For most of us, if someone came against us with a lawsuit, our first reaction would be, "Oh yeah? Well, go ahead and sue me — but you'll know that you have been to court, buddy!"

So how do we ever attain that place of agape where we are merciful just as the Father is merciful? The Scriptures teach us that praying in tongues is a major key to help purge us as we journey through a progression of steps toward the agape kind of love.

Feeding the Seed of Agape Through Prayer

Even though God has planted the nature and force of agape love in your spirit, it may be so repressed and so dominated by your soulish emotions that you hardly know it exists inside of you. But when you pray in tongues, you bypass the operation of the physical soul and throw a lifeline to your spirit.

Soon the edification process starts feeding that seed of agape in your heart, causing it to germinate and grow. The force of love in your spirit grows bigger and bigger until one day, it dominates the emotions of the soul instead of the other way around. This is called taking off the old man and putting on the new.

> **That ye put off concerning the former conversation the old man, which is corrupt according to the deceitful lusts;**

And be renewed in the spirit of your mind;

And that ye put on the new man, which after God is created in righteousness and true holiness.

Eph. 4:22-24

Perfect Love Casts Out Fear

As you clothe yourself with your new man by giving yourself to the Word and to prayer, the Holy Spirit through your spirit edifies, purges, and develops your character until everything you say, think, or do is governed by agape. Let's look at First John 4:17,18 to learn more about this powerful force.

Herein is our love made perfect, that we may have boldness in the day of judgment: because as he is, so are we in this world.

There is no fear in love; but PERFECT LOVE CASTETH OUT FEAR: BECAUSE FEAR HATH TORMENT. He that feareth is not made perfect in love.

That word "herein" points us to the next verse, which tells us how we will know when love is being perfected in us. Herein is God's love perfected in us: Perfect love casts out fear, for fear has torment. So when we find ourselves being purged from torment and fear, then love is being perfected in us.

For instance, if you decided to sue me, how could I extend mercy to you if I had fear and torment about the outcome of the situation? But when love has been perfected in me, I know I can't lose. Oh, you may take everything I possess at the time, but Luke 6:38 says that my Father is going to restore it all back to me, pressed down, shaken together, and running over. He'll give me more than I had before!

So what is the sign that I am drawing nigh unto God and approaching agape love? It is this: Along the way, I am shedding torment and fear as I enter into rest and refreshing.

I used to think love was a feeling, but it isn't a feeling. I used to think love was an attitude that would help me survive through dealing with the unlovable. But it isn't an attitude either.

Encompassed within agape is an abiding presence of peace. As you grow close to God and His love is perfected in you, that peace begins to dominate as fear and torment lose their hold. That is the first sign that you are being purged from phileo to agape.

As a minister, I wish I could open up your heart and just put agape in you in such strength that you would forever lose all the torment and fear that has plagued your life. I understand the process by which you can attain that goal, but all I can do is teach you about it.

I can hammer it into your intellect. As much as possible, I can teach with the anointing of God straight to your spirit. But I can't make that process toward perfect love take place in your life.

However, if I can talk you into giving yourself to praying in the Holy Ghost, then *you* will cause that process to begin in your own life. You will start to edify and build yourself up in your inner man through the power of the Holy Spirit.

Then the Holy Spirit will begin the mortification process by building up your inner man to purge all those insecurities, intimidations, carnalities, and lusts that have hindered your life. This is how God's love is perfected in you. As the Holy Spirit edifies your new nature, torment and fear begin to fall off you and you draw close to agape.

Covet Earnestly Agape Love

To discover more about the role of praying in tongues in moving us toward a fuller revelation of agape love in our lives, let's take a look at First Corinthians 13, the great "love chapter" of the Bible.

First, let's look at this chapter in context to the chapters that surround it. First Corinthians 12 is a magnificent chapter dealing with the eradication of ignorance concerning the spiritual gifts, operations, and government of God. Chapter 14 is a most phenomenal explanation of spiritual forces as pertains to praying in tongues.

So Paul goes from a discussion of the government of God to an explanation of the operation of the Spirit and of tongues. Then he nestles First Corinthians 13 in between these two chapters. But first, he makes a profound statement:

But COVET EARNESTLY the best gifts: and yet shew I unto you A MORE EXCELLENT WAY.

— 1 Corinthians 12:31

Paul was saying in essence, "I want to show you a more excellent way. If you want to save yourself a lot of trouble, then you need to covet this kind of agape love with everything in you the same way you covet the best gifts."

Just how important is it to pursue agape love? Paul makes this statement in First Corinthians 13:13:

And now abideth faith, hope, charity [agape love], **these three; but THE GREATEST OF THESE IS CHARITY.**

If I had been the one to choose, I probably would have said that faith is the greatest thing, followed by hope. Hope encompasses the time you spend feeding yourself with God's Word, which causes your faith to manifest. But Paul says, "Greater than faith and greater than hope is self-denying agape." That means there is *nothing* more important in your life to covet and earnestly desire than agape love.

The word "covet" in this verse is just as strong in meaning as it is in the Ten Commandments, where it says, "Thou shalt not covet thy neighbor's wife" (Exod. 20:17). When this word is used as an emotional negative, it means a lust so powerful that it consumes a man, causing him to relentlessly pursue what he covets until it takes over his entire character.

But when "covet" is used in a godly sense, it means pursuing something God wants you to have with a heartfelt hunger until you apprehend it.

I never had a problem with coveting earnestly the best gifts. I have fasted, I have prayed — I have done everything I knew to do in order to be qualified for God to use me.

So it came as a shock to me when God spoke to my spirit, saying, "Go ahead and lust after My gifts with everything that is in you. But I'm going to show you a more excellent way to covet after the best gifts."

I said, "God, You have the audacity to say that after I have spent my life in fasting and praying and coveting after Your best and highest, You are going to show me a more excellent way?"

The answer to that was *yes*, God did have the audacity, and *yes*, He was going to show me a more excellent way!

In Paul's original epistle to the Corinthians, there was no division between chapters 12 and 13. So right after Paul's statement about coveting the best gifts and showing the Corinthians a more excellent way, he goes on to introduce the subject of love: **Though I speak with tongues of men and of angels, and have not charity...** (1 Cor. 13:1).

In other words, the most excellent way to covet earnestly the best gifts is to go after agape with that same intensity. When you do, you will be pursuing and coveting the best gifts God has for you in the most powerful manner possible.

What are the "best gifts"? Well, you are called to fill one of the eight operations of God. For you, the best gifts are those that qualify you for the office or operation you are called to fulfill.

The Purging Before the Power

With great intensity I sought God for years for the gifts that would equip me for *my* call. I would pray, "Oh, Lord, please use me in Your power. I'll fast and pray — I'll do anything I have to do so You can move through me in Your power!"

You see, since the day I was born again, God's call has raged on the inside of me. Every time I get lost in the Holy Ghost while I am in prayer, I see the Spirit of God moving in revival. I see people running to the altar to be born again and great miracles happening everywhere, such as missing limbs growing out and eyes popping into empty eye sockets.

This vision follows me; whenever I lapse into the Spirit, I see it. It is a driving force. And I have determined that I will keep yielding myself to the Holy Spirit until one day I see with my own eyes the Presence of God move in my life and ministry with magnificent glory beyond my imagination.

So for years I sought God earnestly — begging, fasting, and praying for an anointing powerful enough to cause great revival. But I can testify now that had He delivered to me what I was pressing Him for, it would have destroyed me. There were faults and character flaws that still had to be purged. If God had given me the power before the purging, my life and ministry would have eventually been destroyed.

This was actually the case for many men of God in the past. They sought God and His power with just such intensity, but then hidden weaknesses began to surface as they yielded to the deceiving strategies of the enemy.

For instance, Alexander Dowie was so greatly used in the miracle power of God at the turn of the century that he was able to form an entire city called Zion outside of Chicago with ten thousand of his followers. God's power operating through Dowie's ministry caused raging revival. But eventually Dowie began to believe that he was the Elijah to come. That deception led to the downfall of his ministry.

Learning To Hate Whatever Hinders

So instead of immediately answering my intense, fervent prayers for an anointing that would cause revival, God told me to pursue conforming myself to agape love with that same intensity and fervency. He assured me that as I pursued love, I would also be pursuing His power in a more excellent way.

So I began to pursue agape love, and I learned to hate those things that were wrong in my life with more fervency than I had ever hated them before. It was a godly anger that preceded their purging.

You see, when you get to the place where you hate with an intensity those faults you know are keeping you from a close walk with God, you will finally do something about it.

So in pursuit of the most excellent way, I made it my quest to conform to the agape kind of love. But my efforts seemed to achieve the opposite results. The more I learned about love, the more my knowledge magnified the things that were wrong in my life. It left me in a hopeless state, believing that I was the most miserable of creatures who would never be able to walk in the level of agape outlined in First Corinthians 13.

I didn't understand that the Holy Spirit was bringing to the surface for purging anything that the devil could use to destroy me in my pursuit of agape. It was all a part of the process to help me become yielded enough to God for the full equipping of the office He has called me to. I also didn't know about the progression to power outlined in this same chapter that would deliver me to the agape love I was pursuing.

Agape Isn't Learned Overnight

You see, all of us preachers love to preach on this thirteenth chapter of First Corinthians. We love to major on this agape kind of love.

Agape love doesn't behave itself unseemingly. It seeks not its own, asking no recompense or reward for services rendered. It isn't given based on the reaction of the other person. It isn't easily provoked. It thinks no evil. It rejoices not in iniquity but rejoices in the truth. It bears all things, believes all things, hopes all things, endures all things.

This love never fails; you will take it to Heaven with you. Tongues will cease. Prophecies will cease. Knowledge will vanish away. You won't need any of these. But you *will* cross that heavenly border and enter the Presence of God with agape.

Oh, yes, we preachers love to talk about agape love. We break down the word in the Greek; we paint a picture of this perfect Christian who is not easily provoked. Then the next day we counsel someone, "Oh, yes, you have your rights. Sue them!" God help us! We get so engrossed in the subject of love in First Corinthians 13 that we miss the sequence of power that delivers us there!

We think that we can preach on agape love one day, and the next day everyone who heard the message is going to be perfect and nice to each other. They won't act ugly anymore. There won't be any more criticizing, backbiting, throwing of fits, or stomping out of the room in a temper tantrum.

We tell the people, "You shouldn't do that sort of thing," and then assume that everyone will just automatically stop. Why do we assume that? It seems like most of us preachers were born yesterday!

When you start understanding all that agape love encompasses, you realize that most Christians don't walk in this kind of love on a daily basis. Most never will. That kind of love is difficult to conform to if you have even an ounce of flesh that hasn't been mortified.

So it is one thing to preach about this agape and say that once we conform to it, we will never fail. But it is another thing to understand the process by which we can conform to that kind of love.

This process is what we have missed. It is a progression through the edification of tongues that leads us to a place in the Spirit where we are finally strong enough to yield totally to agape love.

Agape Love by Willpower Alone?

We will never walk in agape love to the fullness that God intends by the strength of our own willpower.

For instance, have you ever noticed that people can only be nice for so long to a person who is getting on their nerves before their will snaps? Then they say, "Get out! Get out of my house!" They stretched their will as thin as they could stretch it — and when it broke, there went their ability to act nice!

It's easy to fantasize about agape. We can get this faraway look in our eyes and quote, "Though I give my body to be burned and give away all my goods to feed the poor, but have not love...." But there is a deadly, knock-down-drag-out fight for our lives out there in the world, where people try to destroy other people and the devil is out to destroy everyone. The prospect of walking in agape love doesn't look as nice and easy out there as it does in church while we are under the anointing.

Do you want to be just like Jesus? You may say, "Oh, yes, I want to raise the dead, be the head of a big organization, and become the best preacher in the world. Oh, yes, I want to be just like Jesus."

Okay, then, Jesus says to owe no man anything but to love him (Rom. 13:8).

What does that mean? Well, it doesn't matter how many payments I make on my debt of love to you, I can never pay that debt in full. You could slap me on the cheek, and I would turn the other cheek. You could despitefully use me, and I would pray for you. You could hate me, and I would do good for you.

Those are all descriptions of agape. No matter how many times you "do me ugly" and I in turn make another payment of love to you, agape will keep me in your debt.

Another thing about Jesus — He seeks not His own. And He says that if a man sues you for your car, you are to go fill it up with gas, polish it, and get it tuned. Then tell the man, "I am giving this to you in the Name of Jesus. I want you to know that you didn't take it from me, because the only thing that is taken from me is what God allows. And if He allows it, I sow it. I'm sowing this car to you, so I polished it, tuned it, and filled it up with gas. The devil is stealing nothing from me."

It is nice to admire someone who walks in enough agape love to do something like that. But how do *you* get to that place in your spiritual walk?

You might as well face it — you aren't going to make it to agape unless you find some way to let the Holy Ghost purge you of anything that is contrary to agape love in your life. If I were you, I would take His way!

The Progression to Agape

We have seen that in First Corinthians 12:28, the government of God begins with the office of the mighty apostle, the first operation, and ends with the diversities of tongues, the eighth and final operation of God. Then in First Corinthians 13:1-3, Paul reverses the order.

> **Though I speak with the tongues of men and of angels, and have not charity, I am become as sounding brass, or a tinkling cymbal.**

And though I have the gift of prophecy, and understand all mysteries, and all knowledge; and though I have all faith, so that I could remove mountains, and have not charity, I am nothing.

And though I bestow all my goods to feed the poor, and though I give my body to be burned, and have not charity, it profiteth me nothing.

Starting with the eighth operation of diversities of tongues, Paul builds us through six phases all the way through mountain-moving faith and ultimate giving to agape love.

So because the subject of agape love is so dominant in First Corinthians 13, we have missed the sequence or the step-by-step progression that would eventually build us up through six levels of spiritual maturity and deliver us to agape love.

At this point, you may be saying, "I'd sure like to see that reversed order you're talking about, Brother Roberson." Well, let's take the first three verses of First Corinthians 13 phrase by phrase and find out what Paul was really saying. As we do, we'll discover the divine progression to agape love.

Six Steps to Spiritual Maturity

There are six distinct levels of spiritual maturity listed in these first three verses that the Holy Spirit will work in the life of any believer who will spend time praying in the Holy Ghost.

Level One: Let's look at verse 1 again:

Though I SPEAK WITH THE TONGUES OF MEN AND OF ANGELS, and have not charity, I am become as sounding brass, or a tinkling cymbal.

When we received the baptism of the Holy Spirit and began to speak with tongues, it automatically qualified us for the first level of spiritual maturity, *the unlimited accessibility to tongues.*

The term "tongues of men" refers to the supernatural empowerment of the Holy Spirit to preach in any language on the face of the earth of which we have no previous knowledge. "Tongues of angels" is talking about the language used in Heaven. I suspect that most of the time we are speaking the language of angels when we pray in tongues to edify ourselves and to pray out the mysteries of God's plan for our lives.

This verse isn't discrediting tongues for the sake of love. In essence it is saying this: Even though I am baptized in the Holy Spirit and have the ability to speak with other tongues, it will do me no good unless I begin to employ that gift to build myself up on my most holy faith, praying in the Holy Ghost and keeping myself in the love of God (Jude 20,21).

There are multitudes of church congregations who have been baptized in the Holy Spirit and speak with tongues, yet the people are full of strife and unforgiveness. And I have personally known so-called Spirit-filled people who would destroy a person at the drop of a hat.

So a person can speak with tongues, but those tongues will not profit him unless he yields to the Holy Spirit's purging work that will deliver him to agape. It is impossible to pray in tongues for extended periods of time and not undergo change.

Level Two: Then in verse 2, it says this:

> **And though I have THE GIFT OF PROPHECY, and UNDERSTAND ALL MYSTERIES, and ALL KNOWLEDGE; and though I have ALL FAITH, SO THAT I COULD REMOVE MOUNTAINS, and have not charity, I am nothing.**

Somehow praying in tongues produces in us the second level of maturity, which is *the use of the gift of prophecy.*

As you pray out the mysteries of Christ in your spirit, God begins to answer them. Suddenly the Holy Spirit latches on to one of those mysteries, pulls it out of your spirit, and reveals it to your intellect so you can release it through prophecy.

Level Three: As we continue to pray in tongues, we will attain the third level of spiritual maturity through the *understanding of divine secrets or mysteries.*

Level Four: The revelation of these mysteries will come alive and begin to operate in our spirit, producing in us *the understanding and accumulation of knowledge,* the fourth level of spiritual maturity.

Somehow, then, as the mysteries of Christ are revealed to me — the mystery of healing, the mystery of righteousness, the mystery of love — I begin to erect pillars in my spirit. As I pray mysteries up before the Father, God answers those prayers by a supernatural imparting of divine insight. Every time the Holy Spirit causes me to understand a mystery, one more pillar of that superstructure is erected.

One pillar is erected by a revelation of righteousness, another by a revelation of peace, and still another by a revelation of agape love. Finally, the entire edifice is framed through praying mysteries in the Holy Ghost.

It is a combination of all these divine secrets revealed to my spirit that will eventually construct an entire library of knowledge, an edifice full of the revelation knowledge of Jesus on the inside of my spirit. And whenever I want to, I can reach in and pull out any volume that I need!

Level Five: So the mysteries are prayed in pillars, but the building constructed is knowledge. It is the understanding of all these mysteries filling your inner library of knowledge that produces the capacity for *mountain-moving faith* in your heart as you are transformed by the Word of God. This is the fifth level of spiritual maturity.

It is the combination of praying in the Holy Ghost and the meditation of God's Word that produces the kind of faith that moves mountains. Why? Because faith comes by hearing the Word of God, and the Holy Spirit is the One giving divine insight into the Word through the supernatural language of tongues.

At this level, Jesus said that *nothing* shall be impossible to you!

Level Six: First Corinthians 13:3 gives us the sixth level of maturity:

And though I bestow all my goods to feed the poor, and though I give my body to be burned, and have not charity, it profiteth me nothing.

Somehow our praying in tongues will help produce in us the capacity for *agape giving.*

I always wondered how a person could bestow all their goods to feed the poor and give their body to be burned, yet still not have the agape kind of love. Then the Holy Spirit revealed the answer to me.

Some Christians live off the self-exaltation that comes from putting their giving on display. They even delight in extreme sacrifices — especially the kind that puts their humility on public display to be admired by men. Some have even made the ultimate sacrifice of losing their lives for the wrong reasons.

I finally began to understand that sometimes it takes a lot more to stay and labor your entire life for the Gospel's sake than it does to die and go home to be with the Lord. Agape love would rather be a *living sacrifice* than a *dead martyr.*

I cringe inside when I think of how many times I have given into an offering because of the lust of my flesh. It wasn't the preacher's fault. I was the one who saw the Cadillac in my mind and gave him my dollar to make sure I would get it. But the Bible says that if I don't give out of agape love, it simply will profit me nothing.

However, when agape love becomes the basis for our giving, God cannot and will not let us down, for *love never fails.*

My Purging
In the Pursuit of Agape

Those six levels are the step-by-step progression God uses to help bring us to a place of spiritual maturity where agape love is a way of life. Throughout this progression, the purging work of the Holy Ghost continues.

How do I know? Because the Holy Spirit is still in the process of purging me. I have prayed and sought God for more than two decades to understand the price of revival and of walking in His power. During that time I have had wonderful visitations from God.

But I have also had times when the devil attacked me right after a divine visitation, and I found myself one-quarter of the way down before I was able to turn around and stop the attack! The Holy Ghost used those difficult times to help me get a good look at myself, and I didn't like what I saw. It was after one of these attacks of the enemy that the Holy Spirit took me to First Peter 5 to help me understand what I was going through.

Humble yourselves therefore under the mighty hand of God, that he may exalt you in due time:

Casting all your care upon him; for he careth for you.

Be sober, be vigilant; because your adversary the devil, as a roaring lion, walketh about, seeking whom he may devour.

— 1 Peter 5:6-8

What is the price of revival? The Holy Ghost took me to this passage of Scripture and said, "This is it."

You see, the devil is seeking people who are "devourable." And according to this scripture, those who fit this category are people who did not get rid of all their care by casting it on the Lord. They pamper their cares; they bathe in their worries; they let their anxieties promenade back and forth in their imaginations until an anthill is an immovable mountain. Thus, they remain vulnerable prey, easily devoured by the strategies of the enemy.

But Peter says, "Go ahead and cast all your care on God. To do so is an act of humility. It is an act of the power of the Holy Ghost."

'After That Ye Have Suffered A While'

Then Peter goes on to say in verses 9 and 10:

> **Whom resist stedfast in the faith, knowing that the same afflictions are accomplished in your brethren that are in the world.**
>
> **But the God of all grace, who hath called us unto his eternal glory by Christ Jesus, AFTER THAT YE HAVE SUFFERED A WHILE, MAKE YOU PERFECT, STABLISH, STRENGTHEN, SETTLE YOU.**

When the Holy Spirit first took me to this passage of Scripture, I thought, *What in the world do afflictions accomplish in a believer?* And for the life of me, I couldn't understand why the God of all grace would allow us to suffer for a while.

I asked the Lord, "With the devil trying to devour me and with all these afflictions and trials raging around me, why didn't You just reach down and deliver me out of it all? What did it accomplish for You to let me suffer awhile before coming in and helping me overcome the situation?"

Now I can tell you exactly what afflictions and persecutions accomplish. These trials cause your impurities to float to the surface as you progress toward a life of agape. Nothing will expose those impurities faster.

And notice, you're not unique in this uncomfortable experience. The same afflictions are being accomplished by Christians around the world. Every believer that desires to go on with God will at some point experience the purging work that takes place during a difficult test or trial.

However, it's important to understand that God doesn't send you tests and trials. He said that Satan is the one who comes to devour through cares, worries, and fears. But when the devil engages you in conflict and causes your weak places to be exposed, God expects you to use the power of His Word to weld those weak places with truth and make them strong.

Those difficult times of trial brought things to the surface that had to be purged from my life so God could establish, strengthen, and settle me. I didn't understand why God was letting me suffer through the trial at the time, but I do now. I've seen the fruit of His purging work in me!

After Purging, Peace

In the last several years, a deep peace has grown in my heart that defies description and surpasses understanding. I have found a secret place in the Holy of Holies of my spirit where I enjoy constant communion with the Prince of Peace Himself. There in that secret place, He has explained revelation knowledge to me that I wanted to understand for years.

This peace is an aggressive weapon against the enemy because nothing has made me more unmanageable for the devil. When this peace began to dominate my life, the worries, fears, and intimidation I used to operate under gave way. Those deeds of the flesh literally died beneath the power of this peace.

Established, Strengthened, Settled

Years ago if you had asked me, "Brother Roberson, what are you asking God for?" I would have said, "I just want to be used by God. I want Him to be able to anoint me to bring about great revival.

"I want the kind of revival in which fifty deaf and dumb people are brought to the service, and the power of God fills that section until they jump up yelling, 'I can hear! I can talk!' Then those who were healed infiltrate the city. Within ten days, the entire city is trying to get into the meeting, and revival is born! That's what I want."

Then if you had asked, "Do you think you can handle that kind of anointing, Brother Roberson?" I would have said, "Yes, I do. All the Lord has to do is give it to me, and I'll show you!"

But then the devil began to rage and fight me over this revival I was desiring. Through every attack, I was thankful for the supernatural peace that sustained me.

After I suffered awhile, the impurities started coming to the surface. I got a good look at a few major faults and told the Lord, "Okay, God of all grace. I see what You're trying to purge out of my life. I will get right on it."

Did God stand by and let me suffer for a while? Yes, but only because I had been asking Him to use me, and He said, "These things are keeping you from being used by Me." When I asked Him why He didn't deliver me from my struggles the first day, He said, "Because you didn't believe those things stood between Me and you the first day."

Afterward, I came to better understand why God answered my prayer for revival the way He did. He had to put to death whatever it was in my character that had given Satan a foothold through intimidation and fear.

Otherwise, right in the middle of revival at the opportune moment, the devil would have exposed those weaknesses and used them against me. But instead, God stepped in with His grace to establish, strengthen, and settle me through the purging process of praying in tongues.

I was even ready for some more purging toward agape love when it was all over. The truth is, I don't mind the purging anymore because of the degree of peace I have attained by yielding to the Holy Ghost in this process over the years.

Besides, I know God wants to exalt me above all my messy trials. It isn't His fault if I have to remain in the fire until I can see the flesh that still operates in my life.

I thank God for every one of my weaknesses that is exposed by the turmoil around me. I *want* the God of grace to step in and deal with those weaknesses. I don't want to just keep living with unpurged weaknesses, going through the same suffering and the same kind of trials year after year because I'm unaware that they even exist.

I don't want to take my place in history as one of those who failed. I want to clean myself up so God can send revival!

I'm too hungry for God to just sit in church, pay my tithes, and warm a pew with the seat of my pants every Sunday and Wednesday. I desire His highest and best too much to spend the week on the golf course and then step up to the pulpit with an intellectual discourse that tickles people's fancy.

Revival is raging in my spirit. I don't want to remain on neutral ground until the devil comes and steals what I have, making me just a nominal preacher one step away from not even preaching on prayer anymore.

If fasting and praying in tongues will cause my impurities to surface, so be it. If the progression to power includes praying in tongues to edify me up above a carnal, sense-dominated walk, then let's get on with it.

If the more excellent way to attain God's highest and best is to seek after agape, then go ahead, God of grace, purge everything out of me that keeps me from walking in love! If it takes letting me suffer until I can see the problem, I don't mind, because I want to be established, strengthened, and settled. I want to experience even greater waves of God's glory!

However, I have decided that I'm not waiting around for a test or trial to reveal my weaknesses. I found out that praying divine secrets and mysteries in the Holy Ghost causes the lit candle of my reborn human spirit to burn brighter and brighter, illuminating all my dark places that need to be purged.

If I yield to the Holy Ghost's work in me, those weaknesses will come out on their own without a difficult trial. That is called growth and edification *on purpose*, just because I want to!

Tongues Will Cease

So the goal is agape, and the means for attaining the spiritual maturity to walk in agape is tongues for personal edification. But notice what Paul says in First Corinthians 13:8:

> **Charity never faileth: but whether there be prophecies, they shall fail; whether there be tongues, they shall cease; whether there be knowledge, it shall vanish away.**

Whereas agape love is eternal, tongues will cease when we leave this earth. Love will cross the barrier of death and go on to Heaven with you. But you won't need to supernaturally speak in any of the languages of this earth once you're in Heaven. The diversities of tongues will cease. The only language you will speak there is the common tongue of Heaven. You will be able to walk up to anyone you meet and hold a conversation with them in perfect clarity.

I remember hearing a well-known minister speak of a visitation he once had from Jesus Himself. Witnesses say that he just seemed to be looking at something they couldn't see, speaking in an unknown language. He seemed to be having a conversation with someone, because he would speak in tongues for a moment and then stop to listen as if someone was answering him.

Later those in attendance at that meeting found out that the minister had had a vision in which Jesus stood there and talked to him. He would hear the unknown language Jesus spoke as English in his own mind, and then he would answer back to Jesus in tongues. The two were holding a conversation in the language of Heaven.

So the time for gaining the benefits of praying in tongues is *now*, not after you die and go to Heaven. God has given you this gift to use in this life for your own good.

But this precious gift will do you no good unless you let the Holy Spirit create His supernatural language inside of you and then speak it out of your mouth. You have to give yourself to praying in tongues so the Holy Spirit can edify you, purge you, and build you up on your most holy faith, keeping you in the agape love of God.

God Can't Pour Out His Glory On an Unpurged People

Why does God want to set us free from everything that hinders and binds us in our lives? Of course, He sets us free so that we ourselves can be blessed. But also, God wants us to serve humanity. He wants us to be free from sin so that we can bring the lost to Jesus, motivated by the agape love of God.

We have a Great Commission to fulfill: **And he [Jesus] said unto them, Go ye into all the world, and preach the gospel to every creature** (Mark 16:15).

God wants us to be full of wisdom and empty of sin so we can offer people the truth in love.

You see, God wants revival on this earth. You don't have to coax Him. He isn't sitting on His throne, saying "Oh, I rather enjoy sitting on My throne and watching people go to hell. I just don't feel like revival. I have a headache and don't feel like a big move of My Spirit."

No, God isn't like that. He is constantly searching to and fro for a people to whom He can prove Himself strong. He wants so desperately to pour out His anointing on people for the purpose of revival.

But God knows that as soon as He does, Satan is going to come in with a "mop-up operation" that puts intense pressure on those operating in God's power. And those who can't stand against the devil's attacks will wish they had never been born!

So God pours out His glory in a measure, and that glory saturates our being. But the only part that makes it to productiveness is the part that isn't eaten up by dead limbs that haven't been pruned out of our lives.

That's why it is so crucial that we continually yield ourselves to the purging work of the Holy Ghost — not just for our sake, but for the sake of a lost and dying world.

Walk in the Spirit

In this book I have outlined the ability of the Holy Spirit as He works on the inside of us to guard us against deception and to help program our spirits with that very special plan that God has set aside for us.

Sometimes I feel like a voice in the wilderness crying, "Pray, please pray!" Long and hard I've been crying out, for God has ordained me to preach on how to walk in the Spirit and how not to fulfill the warrings and lusts of the flesh. As much as possible, I have been faithful to do so.

God desires to lead you out of a walk dominated by the flesh into a walk of maturity and sonship. This is His priority, and it is your option. You have to choose to accept the leadership of the Holy Spirit. You have to choose to walk out of a life dominated by the flesh and into a life dominated by the Spirit.

As God taught me, I have taught you that one of the major keys to this walk in the Spirit is the edification that comes to a person who spends any amount of time at all praying in the Holy Ghost.

So are you going to pray in tongues a little more than you used to? A lot more? If you are, then watch out, my friend, because you're going to take your place in history! You're going to find God's compassion. You're going to find His power. You're going to find His plan.

The time is short, so don't delay in your quest to unlock the greatest mysteries of all time — the mind of God for mankind, for your generation, and for your own personal life!

Appendix

Appendix 1

Hindrances To Receiving The Baptism in the Holy Spirit

Receiving the Holy Spirit is such a simple thing. However, the devil tries to complicate matters, doing his best to build strongholds in people's lives against speaking with other tongues.

Maybe you have desired the baptism in the Holy Spirit for a long time, but something seems to hinder you from receiving this precious gift from God. I'm going to talk about some of the most common hindrances to receiving the baptism in the Holy Spirit that I have come across in my years of ministry. I also want to give you some scriptural truths and guidelines to help you overcome those hindrances.

Strongholds of the Mind

The devil will try to reach into a person's past and use negative teachings the person has heard to build mental blocks or strongholds in his mind against speaking with tongues.

A mental stronghold is a system of thoughts empowered by a person's emotions. This system has been created by a lifetime of faulty reasonings and thought patterns that block the mind from cooperating with God's truth. However, these strongholds can be pulled down by replacing them with *God's* reasonings found in His Word.

Some people may have sat under the wrong teaching that tongues are not for today. Others may have been taught that only uneducated, emotional people speak in tongues. Whatever the deception, these people need correct teaching to help them break out of the stronghold of the mind that hinders them from yielding themselves over to speaking in tongues.

Also, sometimes a spirit of denominationalism is present. Religious spirits often try to blind the minds of people so they cannot comprehend truth. They convince people to camp on their own "revelation," even if their doctrine is contrary to the Word. When these "mind-blinding" spirits are in operation, they must be bound in Jesus' Name. Only then will the person who is seeking the baptism in the Holy Spirit be set free to receive from God.

'I'M NOT GOOD ENOUGH TO RECEIVE THE HOLY SPIRIT'

One of the main strongholds in people's minds comes from the teaching that a person has to become good enough to receive the baptism in the Holy Spirit.

Some "holiness" churches teach that a person must be sanctified before he or she can be baptized in the Holy Spirit. People are taught that God will not fill them with His Spirit unless they are already free from deeds of the flesh, such as smoking, drinking, and chewing tobacco.

Consequently, people seek the sanctification experience for years and years but never seem to have the power to get rid of certain sins in their lives. And because they don't believe they are good enough to receive the baptism of the Holy Spirit until they *are* sanctified, they never get filled.

But the fact is, the opposite is true. The Bible says that it is *through the Spirit* that you mortify the deeds of the flesh (Rom. 8:13). The Holy Spirit works in your new nature to put to death everything that is displeasing to God in your life. So to deny people the infilling of the Holy Spirit — the very means God uses to accomplish the clean-up process in a person's soul and flesh — is against the Scriptures.

You see, you can never become good enough to receive the gift of the Holy Spirit on your own. That's why God literally takes out your old nature and creates a new nature in your human spirit when you are born again. It is this new, righteous nature, *not* your works, that God uses as the basis for baptizing you in the Holy Spirit. No other preparation can be made other than what has already been accomplished when you were washed in the blood of Jesus.

The Holy Spirit who has done the work of recreation is now ready to infill you — to step into that new nature you have received and help set you free from every form of sin and bondage. This is the work of sanctification Paul talked about in Second Corinthians 7:1:

> **Having therefore these promises, dearly beloved, let us cleanse ourselves from all filthiness of the flesh and spirit, perfecting holiness in the fear of God.**

To accomplish that work, the first thing the Holy Spirit wants to do when He infills you is to pray for you. So He begins to create a supernatural language of tongues on the inside of your spirit. That same language He is creating in your spirit then automatically begins to form in your mouth.

The moment you give utterance to those words and start praying in tongues, you walk into a divine classroom. Standing at the chalkboard is none other than the Master Teacher, the Holy Spirit. He has come into your life to teach, empower, edify, and sanctify you.

That's one reason God took the understanding of tongues away from us. That way we don't know when He's praying for us about the sin in our lives we don't want to deal with. As we pray in tongues, we may be thinking, *I want a Lexus*, while the Holy Spirit is actually saying in the language of tongues, "I think you should stop yelling at your spouse!"

So don't try to become good enough to receive the Holy Spirit. Let Him dwell in you in His fullness, and determine to pray much in other tongues. As you do, He will lead you in the mortification process that will make you more like Him.

'I DON'T HAVE TO SPEAK IN TONGUES TO BE FILLED WITH THE HOLY SPIRIT'

There is a line drawn in the Spirit between the actual creation of the supernatural language in a believer's spirit and the journey of this language from his spirit to his lips to be uttered. It is on this line that the devil is most successful in erecting strongholds that hinder believers from speaking in tongues even after they have been filled with the Holy Spirit.

For example, many believers wrongly believe, for one reason or another, that God wants them to have the baptism in the Holy Spirit without the experience of speaking with tongues. Although this type of situation is possible, it is not the perfect will of God. People who think that way truly do not understand the great things God wants to accomplish in their lives through this simple but precious gift of speaking with tongues.

'I'M WAITING FOR THE HOLY SPIRIT TO MAKE ME SPEAK'

Other Christians labor under the misconception that they must wait for God to move on them and cause them to speak in tongues. In reality, God is trying to get them to receive what He has already done.

You see, when we ask the Holy Spirit to fill us — *He fills us!* The entire time we are trying to get Him to give us the language of tongues, He is waiting for us to receive and give utterance to the language He has already created inside our spirits. He creates the language, but *we* are the ones who do the praying. This truth is revealed in Acts 2:4:

> And THEY were all filled with the Holy Ghost, and BEGAN TO SPEAK with other tongues, as THE SPIRIT GAVE THEM UTTERANCE.

But the devil doesn't want people to know that. He tries to make them believe that the reason they haven't spoken in tongues is God's reluctance to give them this foundational revelation gift. The enemy knows that if he can convince people that, for some reason, they are not able to receive the gift of tongues, he can discourage them from pressing on through to the actual utterance of the language itself.

Many times people in this situation become so discouraged, they stop seeking the baptism in the Holy Ghost because they are afraid of failing again. They come to the wrong conclusion that, in some way, they aren't worthy enough for God to fill them with His Spirit and give them the gift of tongues.

That's why many believers are actually filled with the Holy Spirit when they pray but have yet to speak in tongues.

The Holy Spirit created His supernatural language in these believers' spirit as soon as they asked to be filled. But the strongholds in their mind blocked them from yielding over their tongue to the utterance of that language. The Holy Spirit does as much as He can in these believers' lives, but they forfeit the great benefits that speaking in tongues provide.

How To Overcome Strongholds of the Mind

If the devil is trying to use any of these strongholds of the mind against you, I have some good news for you. There is nothing more powerful than God's Word, centered around godly worship, to pull those strongholds down!

Perhaps you have struggled to receive the baptism in the Holy Spirit. Maybe you have spoken only a few words in tongues and would like to be set free to speak fluently in the language the Holy Spirit has given you. Well, the key is to build up your faith until it is stronger than the stronghold in your mind that prevents you from receiving what you desire from the Lord.

I would suggest that you diligently study what the Word has to say on the subject of the baptism in the Holy Spirit and speaking in other tongues. Listen to teaching tapes on the subject. Read this book you hold in your hands again and again until these scriptural principles about speaking with tongues are planted deep in your heart.

Then find yourself a place of worship, put on some worship music, and spend some quality time alone with God. The fact is, one of the most powerful ways to minister to your own soul and to get yourself ready to receive from God is to worship Him. This is why Ephesians 5:18,19 says:

And be not drunk with wine, wherein is excess; but BE FILLED WITH THE SPIRIT;

Speaking to yourselves in psalms and hymns and spiritual songs, singing and making melody in your heart to the Lord.

As you worship the Lord, begin to speak the Word and praise Him for the answer: "Lord, I am a receiver. Thank You, Lord, for filling me with the Holy Spirit. Thank You for giving me the ability to speak with other tongues."

You see, your soul will transform you to whatever you subject it to the most. Jesus will become to you whatever you call Him, because faith comes by hearing and hearing by the Word (Rom. 10:17). If you call Him your Baptizer long enough, you will destroy with the Word all those strongholds in the soul that have hindered you from receiving the gift of the Holy Spirit.

Focus in on God and His faithfulness to give you the gift you desire. As you stay in that place of worship, your mind and emotions will begin to be baptized with the Presence of God, and the Holy Spirit will come upon you to fill and overflow your spirit. Continue to worship the Lord until all the debris in your mind that is keeping you from speaking with tongues is cleared away.

You may not tangibly "feel" anything at this point, but you will notice that new words are floating up from your spirit and forming in your mouth. The Holy Spirit is creating that language on the inside of you.

When that happens, just stop worshiping in English and speak out the words your tongue wants to form. Yield over to that language the Holy Spirit is creating in your spirit. Then continue to speak in tongues until those supernatural words are flowing out of you fluently, like rivers of living water.

Demonic Strongholds of the Soul

Another reason some believers are hindered from receiving the baptism in the Holy Spirit is that some kind of demonic stronghold has been carried over from their unsaved lives, and they have not yet been delivered from it.

For example, these believers may have been involved in drugs, in a cult, or in the occult. Their involvement could have been as simple as dabbling with horoscopes or "playing" with a Ouija Board. But even dabbling in these areas of darkness can open the door for demons to take up residence in people's lives.

The more heavily involved a person has been in this type of activity, the greater the possibility that a demon actually gained access to possess that person's unregenerate spirit.

Now, when people are born again, any demons present have to move out of their newly created spirits. But sometimes an evil spirit finds opportunity to merely move over and take up residency in the new believer's soul. In this case, the demon may hinder a person from receiving the baptism in the Holy Spirit and the gift of tongues, but he CANNOT stop the person from receiving.

So if you have ever had any association with a cult, drugs, the occult, and so forth, and you have had trouble receiving the baptism in the Holy Spirit, consider this possibility: A stronghold may exist in your soul because of that past association. Subconsciously you may still be leaning to some of that old influence.

If that is your situation, you can take hold of your rights according to the Word of God and confess by faith that you are free of the strongholds that are hindering your soul. Just pray this prayer by faith:

Heavenly Father,

I repent for seeking knowledge outside of You through the occult [or through drugs, a cult, etc.]. I ask You to forgive me.

I also command every evil spirit who may have gained access to my life when I opened the door through these demonic activities to leave me now in the Name of Jesus. I now shut the door to all such spirits.

I ask You, Heavenly Father, to fill those empty places with Your Holy Spirit.

Now according to Your Word in John 8:36 that says, "If the Son therefore shall make you free, ye shall be free indeed" — I am free!

In Jesus' Name, amen.

Perhaps you were once strongly involved in these activities. For instance, most cults instruct people to invite spirit guides into their lives, which constitutes idolatry. If that is the case, you may need to fast and pray to prepare yourself to receive your deliverance from that stronghold of the soul. When you sense you are ready, pray the prayer outlined above.

After you have dealt with any possible stronghold of the soul that may have been hindering you from receiving, follow my earlier suggestions. Find a place of worship, and begin to thank God by faith for setting you free, filling you with the Holy Spirit, and giving you a supernatural language of tongues.

Stay in that place of worship until you receive what you desire from God. Then as you go about your daily life, remember to continually praise the Lord for your new freedom and for the gift of the Holy Spirit you have received.

Appendix 2

Prayer of Salvation

Before you can be filled with the Holy Spirit and receive His supernatural gift of tongues, your human spirit must be born again in Christ Jesus. Without the new nature that sets you free from sin, the Holy Spirit has nothing to work with.

Do you believe that Jesus actually died for your sins and rose again to give you new life? Would you like to receive Him as your Lord and Savior right now? If so, please pray the following prayer from your heart:

Dear Lord Jesus,

Please come into my heart and forgive me of my sins. I want to receive you as my Lord and Savior. I want to be born again.

I receive you now as my Lord and Savior. I receive God as my Father.

Thank You for saving me. Amen.

Welcome to the family of God! Please write us at the address on page 409. We would like to hear about your decision for Christ and want to help you get started in living a victorious life as a child of God.

Appendix 3

Prayer To Be Filled With the Holy Spirit

If you are reading this book and have never been baptized in the Holy Spirit, it is a simple matter to receive this precious gift. All you have to do is just ask in faith for the Lord to fill you with the Holy Spirit and give you the gift of speaking in tongues.

When you do that, the Holy Spirit will come upon you, and you will sense His Presence. Immediately the Holy Spirit will move into your new nature and begin to create a language on the inside of your spirit. When He does, your tongue and mouth will begin to shape the same words He is creating inside.

Now pray this prayer from your heart:

Heavenly Father,

Your Word says that You are faithful to give the Holy Spirit to those who ask You (Luke 11:13).

So in the Name of Jesus, I ask You to please fill me with the Holy Spirit. I thank You for giving me a new language. I believe I receive it now. Amen.

After you have prayed this prayer, don't speak your native language any longer. Yield yourself to the Presence of the Holy Spirit, and begin to speak out those words that you don't understand with your mind.

It may sound a little like baby talk in the beginning. But as you continue to yield yourself to speaking the words the Holy Spirit gives you, you will begin to pull more of a flow out of your spirit. Soon you will be speaking fluently in your new, supernatural language. Continue to pray in your new language for at least fifteen minutes to establish yourself in this gift you have just received.

You have reason to rejoice! You have just entered through the doorway that will lead you into the supernatural realm of God!